WALKING THROUGH FIRE

A Life of
Nawal El Saadawi

Translated from the Arabic
by Sherif Hetata

DAVID PHILIP
South Africa

ZED BOOKS
London & New York

Walking Through Fire was first published by
Zed Books Ltd, 7, Cynthia Street, London N1 9JF, UK
and Room 400, 175 Fifth Avenue, New York 10010, USA in 2002

Distributed in the USA exclusively by Palgrave, a division of St Martin's Press,
LLC, 175 Fifth Avenue, New York, 10010, USA

Published in Southern Africa by David Philip Publishers (Pty Ltd),
208 Werdmuller Centre, Claremont 7735, South Africa

Copyright © Nawal El Saadawi 2002
Translation copyright © Sherif Hetata 2002

The right of Nawal El Saadawi to be identified as the author of this
work has been asserted by her in accordance with the Copyright,
Designs and Patents Act, 1988

Typeset in Berkeley by Kathryn Perry
Cover designed by Andrew Corbett
Printed and bound in Malaysia

All rights reserved

A catalogue record for this book is available from the British Library

US CIP has been applied for

ISBN 1 84277 076 4 hb
ISBN 1 84277 077 2 pb

Southern Africa ISBN 0 86486 515 5 pb

Contents

ONE

The Threat

It is spring. A flood of green is sweeping over Duke forest. The sky, turquoise blue, carries me back to my village. I am in North Carolina, a southern state on the East Coast of America, in a small town called Durham. People in Durham look up at the sky and say this is Carolina blue.

It is the early spring of 1993. The windows in our house look out onto a rose garden. The roses have started to bloom blood-red, snow-white, amber-yellow, orange and silver-grey. Through my open pores the scent of roses steals its way into my body, a first warm breath after the cold of winter.

Here, reality is like a dream. I open my arms, stretch my body, touch it with the tips of my fingers in search of certitude. The only certitude is my body, yet to me it seems like the body of another woman. The woman who is called Professor Dr Saadawi, three strange names which I hear being pronounced by people every day, by students sitting in attentive rows in the same way as I used to sit, more than forty years ago, in the auditorium of the medical college in Cairo University.

I get out of bed slowly, afraid of waking up from the dream, creep over to the mirror. There she is, standing tall, her shoulders slightly bent, her skin brown like the silt brought down by the Nile, her hair snow white, thick, tossing around her head, her nightgown of white cotton crumpled with a pattern of small flowers scattered over it.

I look down at her feet. They are big feet like those of her grandmother and she wears cheap rubber slippers bought from a

1

small store in her village, Kafr Tahla. As she stands there a man walks in, watches her for a moment, then says 'Sabah El Kheir,[1] Nawal', and her memory comes back as she replies 'Sabah El Kheir, Sherif'.

Sherif had travelled with her to Duke University at the beginning of January. In Egypt her name had figured on a death list drawn up by a fundamentalist movement. Her life was threatened, so the authorities placed armed guards in front of her flat, and a bodyguard accompanied her wherever she went. When the opportunity came she decided to leave the country.

She looks around in surprise. Her eyes travel over the beautiful old house, the rose garden, the maple trees. Here she is in these wonderful surroundings teaching a course on dissidence and creativity, a subject she loves. Her students make teaching a pleasure, call out to her 'Professor Saadawi' as she walks through the campus. Yet, exile means exile, and there is nothing she can do to change it.

I stand at the window, look out at the sunshine streaming down on expanses of green, on elm trees fluttering with new leaves after the bareness of winter, on tall pines singing in the wind, on triangular conifers reflecting the circles of morning light like Christmas trees, on thousands of anonymous forest trees. For me, they seem to grow wild, to multiply endlessly over expanses of American soil stretching to a horizon I cannot see. I watch their tops being touched by the sun, or turning black under a cloud. I remember the stories told to me by my grandmother and they are transformed into witches or devils, their long tresses hanging down on either side of their heads as they reach up into darkness.

Throughout my life devils have surrounded me. In my village, when I was still a child, I used to look for them. In Cairo, after I had grown up, they looked for me. Often they carried other names like 'the visitors of the dawn', men who turn up just before dawn, before the red rays of the sun begin to colour the sky, when people are still plunged deep in sleep, in that phase of sleep we call the minor death where you do not dream, or where, if you dream, the dream is not remembered. It is at this particular time of the night that the visitors of the dawn start moving, steal through the streets and up stairs, to stand behind a door and listen. Then they ring the bell. If no-one

---

[1] 'A morning of bounty to you', i.e. 'Good Morning'.

answers they knock. If no-one opens they break it down or prise it open with an instrument that does it silently.

My memoirs, written on sheets of greyish paper, keep piling up on my desk. After leaving Egypt I started to write. The threat of death seemed to give my life a new importance, made it worth writing about. I felt that the closer I moved towards death, the greater became the value of my life. Nothing can defeat death like writing. Were it not for the Old Testament, Moses and Judaism would not have lived on. Were it not for the New Testament, Jesus Christ and Christianity would have died off long ago. And were it not for the Qur'an, the prophet Muhammad and Islam would not have survived to this day.

Is that why writing was forbidden to women and slaves?

I had spent the last five years of my life away from Egypt. For four years I lived in Durham, working as a visiting professor at Duke University. Every morning I walked from my house in Sylvan Road to the campus. To reach the campus I had to cut through a small forest, slipping through the tree trunks on my rubber shoes, listening to the sound of their tread in the whispering silence, to the crackle of leaves under their soles, or the occasional song of a coloured bird hidden in the foliage, filling me with a yearning for the voice of my daughter calling out to me in the morning. When the sun's rays fell on my face I would remember the winter sun in Cairo, then look up at the sky and feel that nowhere in the world had I seen a blue as pure, as limpid as this, with not a speck of dust, or a particle of smoke. A filtered blue without impurities, a limitless sky extending to the Atlantic Ocean, without mountains, or frost, or snow, just sun and sunlight, just elms and pines and conifers, from spring through summer, to autumn, from green to a celebration of colours red, blue, violet, yellow, brown, russet and golden into the black, white and grey of winter. I look up at the sky and there, soaring above my head, is a bird, a single bird, blue and green with red legs, the likes of which I have never seen. Then once more, suddenly, the silence of the forest under the deep, motionless, endless expanses of blue, the awe of complete silence, and of nature creeping through my veins, and up there the sun, the ancient Egyptian sun god Ra'a, my eyes captivated by the power of his light, by his head creeping out behind a filmy cloud, by his hair long like that of Noot, the goddess of the sky.

Images float through my mind. I am the goddess Isis, the daughter of Noot, standing on a stage in the big hall of my primary school more than fifty years ago. I touch my dead husband Osiris with the tips of my fingers and bring him back to life. I am a young child walking on the bank of the River Nile. I look into the waters, watch the little waves shining in the dark night like silver fishes. They part, and out of the depths rises a woman. She is half-naked and sits on the bank combing her hair. She smiles at me like a mother, with tenderness, but I run away from her afraid that she will grab me and devour me in the deep waters.

How did the female goddess who was capable of restoring life to the dead become transformed into a witch who devours children? I never asked myself this question until I reached the age of twenty-five, until I had become a young physician in my village, carrying a torch in my hand as I walked through the night looking for what my grandmother used to call ogres or witches or devils.

*　*　*　*

The winds blow in from the Atlantic Ocean to strike this small town in the south of the United States. High waves sweep the deserted shores eighty miles away. Huge white birds bigger than the seagulls I have seen at home flutter their wings to keep their balance on a rocky edge. I hear them shriek, like the shriek of the hurricane blowing in from the ocean, or the howl of wolves in the village night, or the cries of genies from the river depths.

Memories come and go with the tread of my feet as I walk through the forest. They take me back home to my city, Cairo. I can see my friends. They are no longer images in my memory, or names in my diary. They move, they speak, they laugh. I have restored them to life, like my friend Raga'a on the bank of the Nile. I know he is dead, but I take his arm and walk with him across Abbas Bridge in Giza. His shoulder keeps touching my shoulder. He sways a little as he walks, as though he has one leg shorter than the other, treads on the ground more heavily with his right foot. At that time I did not like his walk, but now it seems attractive, distinguishes him from other men, gives him something special. I can recognize him from a distance, from the way he walks, his well-ironed grey suit, his shoes shining despite the dusty roads. On holidays he was always fully dressed, never sat on stone benches near the Nile, never cracked melon seeds between his teeth, or ate green fava beans from their pods.

I liked to do all these things. I liked to sit on rocks jutting out into the sea, to receive the spray of the waves on my body, to be refreshed by the feeling of wet clothes clinging to my skin, to walk in the rain, let it drop on my hair and face. But he preferred to sit on a clean seat in a smart casino and look at the sea from a distance. These small faults spoilt our friendship, were irksome to me.

Now, as I walk through the forest, I realize suddenly that he is not with me, that I am alone. He died twelve years ago in October 1981. Four days before his death he sent me a letter from Paris. It lay for months on my desk with the rest of my mail. I was away from my home in Giza living in a cell in the women's prison of Kanater north of Cairo.

I walk out of the forest onto the road leading to the department in which I teach. In a few moments I will be in class giving my first lecture. I pull my arm away from Raga'a. We part but I do not say good-bye, for he will be there in my memory for me to bring back some other time. I look up at the campus trees, their branches resplendent with the colours of spring flowers. Sherif is hastening to class ahead of me. I can see him from behind wearing a brown pullover with small yellow triangles, and brown rubber-soled shoes. He carries a leather satchel and walks fast, his shoulders slightly bent. His hair is long, flying in the air like wings with a bald patch in the middle. His body is slim and taut as he presses forwards, his obstinate head ready to break through obstacles in his way, with the determination that took him through fourteen years of prison. Throughout the fourteen years spent in the prisons of Egypt he did not change. His will remained the same, his features remained the same. Maybe his bones became slightly more pronounced, his skin tanned dark brown by the desert sun. Maybe the silent man became more silent, his slim body slimmer from years with little food, tautened by the iron bars surrounding him. It was as though for him time had not counted, had just fallen away.

We met in the spring of 1964, a spring still hovering between the remains of winter clouds and the first scents of orange blossom. Neither of us believed in the marriage institution, in a marriage contract which sounded like the lease for a rented shop. But we lived in Cairo, the capital of Egypt, a country where man and woman cannot meet without the official seal, for without this seal the devil is their bedfellow whenever they embrace. Cairo (Al-Kahira) means the triumphant. But it is my oppressed city and ever since my childhood I have carried this feeling in my heart. It is a city that I love and hate. The moment I arrive there from a journey abroad, I want to leave again. The moment I am ready to depart, have climbed into the plane, fastened the seat-belt around my waist, I feel like jumping out and running back. It is a city that accompanies me day and night wherever I go, like the vivid remains of a dream. To me, it remains the nightmare of being hunted down, besieged, imprisoned, the pulsations of love, the pain of defeat, the exhilaration of resistance, the falling down then standing up again and again and again in a struggle that has no end. Cairo offers me a chalice of life and death from which I drink, and, every time I come back, I leave again with the intention never to return.

If there is such a thing as time then it is the time I create by writing. I bring back the things I lived in that city of mine, a city drowning in the mists, a city without time or place or geographical location. At a distance it appears to have no existence except in my imagination, as though life for me is beginning here and now, with the movement of the pen between my fingers, with the movement of the air in and out of my chest, and the movement of the hands around my watch. The present moment is the only reality in my life story. It is an infinite moment which stretches from birth to death, from the past after the past is no more, to the future which does not yet exist.

I stop writing for a moment. Through my window on the branch of a tree I can see a new-born squirrel basking in the sunshine. Suddenly a huge hawk pounces on it and starts to tear the small body into pieces, to devour it from head to tail. My eyes cannot pull themselves away from the sight of the killing, my head refuses to move. The small squirrel puts up a feeble, vain resistance, but the ferocity of the hawk leaves it no breathing space and in no time everything seems over as I sit there, my hands hanging helplessly on either side of my body, staring at the distant branch, listening to the sound of soft bones being crushed between the blades of the powerful beak, as though it were my bones that were being crushed, as though it were my body throbbing with warmth and life that was being devoured by the eagle, by that city of Cairo before I had the time to touch, to taste, to know and enjoy the full flavour of my life.

Like prophets and gods I reach for life after death by writing. I do not have the courage of my friend Raga'a who died without writing anything. 'What use is writing, Nawal,' he said to me, 'if the censors delete what is most important?' Raga'a was a poet whom I met for the first time in my clinic during the year 1959. I had opened this clinic in Giza Square at the beginning of 1958. My writer friends used to gather there in the evenings after I had finished work. He had written a poem about the union between Egypt and Syria and the censors had mauled it so badly that nothing was left except fragmented, distorted remains of the original text. Four days before he died he wrote me a few lines. In his letter he said: 'I am writing to you from Paris where I have been able to settle at last. You are the only one I have continued to remember throughout this long exile. But how can I tell whether my love for you is a reality?'

* * * *

Memories keep flitting through my mind as I stand in the classroom behind the table. Sherif has started to introduce the new course which we had decided to call 'Dissidence and Creativity'. Today at this university of Duke we are beginning a new experience, that of being a husband and wife who at night sleep in the same room and who during the day teach in class together. Despite some moments of struggle between us, Sherif nevertheless is not a man bothered by his masculinity. The battle he has waged was not aimed at proving his sexual supremacy. From a very young age he had never stopped dreaming of changing the world. It was a dream that went through different phases of a struggle against capitalism for an ideal socialist system built on freedom, justice and love, the three things which brought us together more than thirty years ago.

My city Cairo stretches its body out under the morning sun, like a voluptuous belly dancer who has offered her nakedness to many eyes throughout the night, only to wake up chaste and pure with the rising sun, or like the wife of the ancient god Amoun, hiding behind a veil like the Virgin Mary as she looks down on the brown waters of the river Nile. Close to her rise the Pyramids of the Pharaohs on the sandhill of Giza, tombs of the gods who had ruled Egypt since the slave system started to prevail. They refused to step down from their throne after death. They discovered the afterworld so that they could continue to rule even after they had died, buried their belongings, their silver and gold, their sceptres and crowns, their food and even the hot dishes they liked with them. All these things were placed close to their dead bodies, together with fruit, sweets and carefully cut pieces of opium and hashish to ensure that they could continue to enjoy living in their illusions, in a world of hallucinations, indulge their lust, fornicate and make love, satisfy all their appetites until the day would come when they would be resurrected in the kingdom of everlasting bliss.

The Egyptian Pharaohs, who were the first to discover religion and to invent spirituality and monotheism, were also the lords of lust and of sensual materialism. They sold illusion to the wretched of the earth with the chants of Akhnatoun, in the Bible of Moses, Aaron, Abraham, Isaac, Jacob and Joseph, down to all the wise men and prophets who followed them. They were the princes of love and war, of medicine and mummification, of astrology, philosophy, art and architecture. Their heritage includes the pyramid of Cheops and the body of the Sphinx, the head of Nefertiti, the paintings of Cleopatra, the female goddesses and philosophers Noot, Isis, Ma'at the goddess of justice, Sekhmet the goddess of medicine and centuries later, Hypathia whose body was mutilated before she was killed by the Roman invaders who burnt her books.

Egypt is the burial ground of invaders. They have never ceased coming, occupying the land then leaving. They are always forced to leave even after centuries go by. They always find good reasons to come back. Reasons change with time and weapons too. The battalions of Napoleon shouldered muskets and used cannon, the British occupiers had machine-guns and artillery, the tripartite Anglo-French-Israeli invasion came with tanks and aeroplanes that dropped bombs.

In times of no war the invaders carry a message of peace and wear belts stuffed with hard currency. They come into Egypt tall, well-dressed, white-skinned, red-cheeked. They come from across the ocean or sea, proponents of universal theories. They are called 'experts', but they are like birds of prey coming in flights, their feathers puffing out as they walk the streets of Cairo like conquerors. They kill off dissidents, have pity on beggars and give them baksheesh, set up projects for the poverty-stricken dwellers of the City of the Dead, which lies below the Mokattam Hills behind the broad tarmac road leading from old Cairo to Cairo International Airport. This road carries the name of 'Salah Salem', one of the officer leaders of the July 1952 Revolution. He always wore dark glasses which hid his face like a disguise, and his photograph only appeared in the evening newspapers as though he were a bat and came out only at night.

Here in exile, my city Cairo stretches out in my imagination as far as the horizon. My feelings for it swing between love and hate, desire and refusal. It is peopled by the faces of my friends, men and women, whom I love and miss. And in my heart is a yearning to be with them, to walk with them through its streets, to stroll along the banks of the Nile with Raga'a and Safeya, and Samia and Rifa'a and Batta.

Five years ago I had to leave Egypt. It was the need to escape death, the legitimate desire to defend my life. They came to my home on June 9, 1992, just before the grey streaks of dawn started to creep across the night.

*   *   *   *

I was not acquainted with the men who were called 'visitors of the dawn'. It was only when I married Sherif in December 1964 that I began to hear about them. Sometimes he would mention things like how they went about breaking in through closed doors, the way they walked, how their eyes were always hidden behind dark glasses, their hands concealed in gloves, their shaven faces smelling of aftershave, their suits well-ironed, their shoes shining with a pointed tip protruding beneath the trouser leg, their steps silent as they moved through the night to pounce on him.

When they came for him the first time they were soft-spoken and polite. It was in the year 1948. He was twenty-five, had graduated as a physician with honours, was the son of a feudal family that exploited peasants on its land. They took him off to prison, then one morning brought him out to meet the judicial investigator responsible for his case. They said, 'You are the son of a noble family, forget about your comrades. They are nothing but a band of beggars, agents of Moscow, spies.' Then they took him back. A few days later they brought him out again to meet the same investigator. This time they said to him, 'Listen boy, you seem to be hard-headed but we are going to break this head of yours. We're giving you a last chance before we start on it.' Before they could break his head he escaped from prison. Only seasoned killers escaped from prison at that time, so the newspapers described him as some kind of phantom or myth. They published a sketch meant to illustrate how he had escaped. In this sketch he was portrayed as a red devil sliding down a rope from a high window with iron bars, then climbing walls. Together with the sketch was a photograph of him with a grim face and cold eyes like those of a killer. Children started to see him in their dreams and wake up shrieking, 'Help, help, Mummie – the Devil!'

My imagination would roam as he told his stories. The visitors of the dawn seemed to be spirits without bodies, gods or devils, until the day I came face to face with them.

It was September 6, 1981. I was alone at home sitting behind my desk, immersed in the *Fall of the Imam*, the new novel I was writing. The door-bell rang once, twice. I did not hear it. It rang again but I was far away with the Imam as he dropped dead, fell from his throne, then woke up and asked the gatekeeper of Paradise to allow him in so that he could have a meeting with God.

I heard what could have been the sixth or maybe seventh ring, got up and went to the door. I glimpsed them from behind the glass pane like phantoms in a childhood dream. I refused to open the door, so they broke in, filled their bags with my books and papers and took me off to prison after the officer-in-charge politely said to me, 'Just one or two questions and you'll be back home immediately.'

* * * *

The second time they came I was fast asleep. At the first knock on the door Sherif woke up. He could tell who it was from the way they knocked, from the timing shortly before dawn so that they could take whoever they had come for to a place known only to God and the Minister of Interior.

It was a dense black night with no stars or moon, in the month of June 1992. A thick fog lay over the city and the air was still with no breeze to alleviate the suffocating heat. I was immersed in a dream, swimming in the sea of Alexandria. The sea was as black as the sky above my head. I knew that my mother was dead, yet I could see her swimming in front of me, rising with the waves, threshing the water with her arms and legs. I swam strongly behind her, my head cleaving through water as though it were air. Suddenly I am flying up into space, hovering over a city that looks like Cairo, above houses and buildings that are unusual, their circular walls, characteristic of fortresses, pierced by lookout apertures.

From above I can see the three Pyramids, and the Sphinx standing on a hill of sand overlooking the Nile, which becomes so wide and vast that it is no longer the Nile but the sea of Alexandria with its deep blue waters. I ask myself how I can fly like this without wings? Will the earth's gravity drag me down? The question keeps going through my mind, so I flutter my arms like the wings of a bird, but I know that human beings do not fly and I am a human being not a bird. With that thought I start to drop gently until my body touches the surface of the water and I begin to swim towards a distant shore. I can no longer see my mother swimming ahead of me, and the waves, which are no longer blue but black, rise higher and higher, like mountains of black water coming towards me. I try to swim but my body is weighted by a stone and I keep struggling to be free. I open my mouth to scream but no sound comes out. On the distant shore I can glimpse a huge bell. It resembles the bell in my primary school years ago, hangs from a long rope and keeps ringing with a sound like thundering waves. A black flag signifying danger flutters high in the wind warning against entering the water, and on the seashore I can see my mother sitting on the sand. She is wearing black, in mourning for someone. I know she is dead, but she says to me, 'Your father died', and it sounds strange because my father has been dead for thirty-three long years.

I heard the door-bell at the second ring. I am sitting in the examination hall and the question paper lies on a desk in front of me. I do not know the answer to a single question and I am drowning under water. Only five minutes are left before the bell rings and sweat keeps pouring down my body. I read through the questions again. I cannot understand the language. It seems to be written in hieroglyphics. I am going to fail my exam and failing my exams is more frightening than death. My breath comes and goes in gasps as I write down the answers to the questions. I know the answers are all wrong – they are just a jumble of lines and scratches without meaning, Now I have only one minute to go and the pen keeps shaking between my fingers leaving waves of ink over the paper, smudged by the drops of sweat which keep pouring down from me, so that I cannot see what I have written. Then suddenly time is up and fingers of steel pull the sheet of paper from under my hands. I wake up suddenly wet with sweat, move my hand over the sheet which is under me. It is dry. I am not a child and I do not wet my bed, and there is no school and no examination haunting me. I am lying in bed and the door-bell is ringing.

I saw Sherif get out of bed, and suddenly realized that he was my husband, that we married twenty-eight years ago. Ever since we married we have slept in one room but in separate beds. We need freedom of movement whether awake or asleep. The night is dark. He searches for his spectacles on the table by his bed. He is not in a hurry, is in control of time, knows how to stop it from passing until he can find his spectacles, until he is set free from fourteen years in prison. I can see his back, his shoulders slightly bent as though he carries a load and walks with it, steadily, effortlessly, his head poised on a neck that refused to bow to the hangman's rope.

He goes out to the hall, his arms held in front of him as though walking in his sleep, moves steadily, neither slow nor quick, his gait almost dreamlike, unchanging, for even if all the bells in the world are ringing, he has known them all, can face them all, they will bring nothing new to him.

I heard him open the front door, speak to the people outside. I heard them answer. Their voices sounded strange to me, voices I had not heard before, and they crept under my closed eyelids like a dream within a dream.

They entered though the door into the small hall of our flat, sat around the circular table covered with a big brass tray. One of them was slightly hunch-backed, wearing civilian clothes with a coloured handkerchief protruding from his upper left pocket. He smelled of lavender. Everything about him seemed shaven, his face, his hair, his features, his expression, so that nothing looked different, expressed anything. No word escaped from his lips to explain what was happening. His voice was like a recording machine, metallic, emotionless, shaven, without character like everything else in him.

I heard Sherif ask them who they were, then request them to show their identity cards. No one ever asked them for their identity cards. They were the ones who asked others. They hesitated, looked at one another, then brought them out, reluctantly. He knew them, did not need to see their cards, but in every certitude there remains a grain of doubt and caution was necessary. He was more cautious than I was, had swum in the deep seas of political life, seen friends turn into enemies overnight and enemies become friends, seen intent hidden under a thick coating of slogans.

'Gentlemen, who are you?' he asked.

'Police,' they said.

The word 'police' echoed in my ears from a distance, as though I were hearing it in my sleep. I kept hanging on to a state of semi-consciousness as long as I could, kept holding on to the hem of my mother's skirt as she stood by my side. I was five years old when I first heard the word 'police' pronounced in front of me. We were living in Alexandria and my father said, 'The police have caught

Sadeya.' I imagined that police were people whose job it was to catch young maid-servants when they tried to escape, or thieves who took what did not belong to them. At that time I did not know that the police hunted down people who were revolutionary and had new ideas.

Sherif said: 'Let's hope that you are bearers of good news.'

'Is Dr Nawal El Saadawi here?'

'Yes, but she is sleeping.'

'Then it is our pleasure to speak with you, Dr Sherif.'

'No, the pleasure is mine.'

'We have instructions to put *hirasa*[2] on Dr Nawal.'

The word *hirasa* penetrated through the pillow I had covered my head with. The first time I had heard it used was thirty-three years before during the time of Nasser's rule. He had placed rich feudal landlords and capitalists under *hirasa* to prevent them from using the riches at their disposal against him. But I owned nothing. Even the three-roomed flat in which we lived was rented and did not belong to us. It accommodated our daughter and son in separate rooms, whereas Sherif and I shared a room in which we slept and worked.

'This *hirasa* is to protect your life,' they said to me when I joined them in the hall.

'To protect my life?!'

'Yes.'

'From what?'

'I do not know. I was ordered to inform you that the authorities will appoint guards to protect you and that is all.'

Knowledge is power. How was I to protect my life if I did not know what was threatening me? If the authorities really wanted to protect me why should they refuse to give me whatever information was available to them? In the past they had dealt me one blow after another, had continued to hunt me down in every activity I undertook. Just a few months earlier, they had decided to close down the Arab Women's Solidarity Association I had founded ten years before, and to ban the magazine *Noon* that we had been publishing for almost two years. How could a government that had fought me so persistently seek to protect my life?

---

[2] 'Hirasa' is used to indicate two different things. The most common is 'to place guards around a person for their protection', but in Egypt the authorities have had recourse to a financial measure against political opponents, which consists in depriving them of the right to dispose of their money or property.

'Thank you very much. I do not need your guards.'

'We are sorry, doctor, we have our instructions and must carry them out.'

'How can you protect my life against my will?'

'Your life does not belong to you, it belongs to the state.'

So from that moment onwards I began to live under the watchful eyes of guards, and, as the officer said, my life ceased to belong to me. Armed men stood in front of my door day and night. A bodyguard accompanied me wherever I went, young, tall, broad-shouldered carrying an automatic pistol and dressed in a parachutist's shirt. I used to feel that he would shoot me in the back as I walked in front of him, that the bullet that would kill me would come from him or from one of the guards. Guarded, I felt I was in danger at every moment.

At night I would hear silent steps creeping up to my bed and wake up bathed in sweat. I felt that at any moment I would glimpse the naked face of the devil or the masked face of God as he stood there holding a gun to my head. I would see shadows moving on the wall, like a child afraid that devils would appear in the dark of night. But in the morning I would regain my courage, put on my jogging shoes and together Sherif and I would walk at a fast pace along the Nile, resume the daily exercise we had maintained throughout the years no matter where we were. I used to stamp out my fear like a cigarette butt. I became a part of it and in order to forget no longer worried about guns being fired at me, no longer wondered whether the bullets would come my way or not.

I sometimes said to myself, all this is nothing but an illusion, just like the illusion my friend Raga'a was fond of talking about. Then my feet would tread firmly over the ground, my body move quickly through the air and the present moment would seem to stretch towards infinity. It became the only truth my mind could grasp. The past moments with their fear were gone and the coming moment was yet to come, and whether the bullet would be fired or would remain inside the gun mattered not. The future did not exist and the past had evaporated into nothingness so all I could do was to live in the present moment and forget.

*   *   *   *

I sent a letter to the Ministry of Interior asking them to issue a permit which would allow me to carry a gun. Since my life was in danger then I should carry a gun. But the authorities refused to give me the permit. It became clear that they were not really worried about what might happen to me and so I began to wonder what their purpose was.

The protection given to me was more of a dress rehearsal than anything else, and this I soon found out. One of the guards used to sit on a chair at the entrance to our building. The chair belonged to me, since the authorities could not provide him with anything on which to sit and there was no reason why the man should remain standing during the night hours of his shift. He was middle-aged, looked more like a janitor employed by a government department than a security guard, wore an old yellow jacket with frayed sleeves. He used to take tips from the other tenants in our building in return for carrying their parcels, fruit, vegetables and other things to the lift. If the tip was big enough he would ride up with them to their flat. At night when I walked in, if it was his shift I would find him sound asleep on his chair. I used to wake him up and say, 'Uncle, you're supposed to be on guard to protect me but here you are fast asleep.' He would laugh, show a row of perfect white teeth under his black whiskers and say, 'Forgive me, doctor. Sleep is a sultan' (meaning that it is powerful, irresistible).

'I wish you could sleep at home rather than on this chair.'

'I can't do that, doctor.'

'Why not?'

'If the inspector comes along what shall I do?'

'No inspector is coming. Go sleep at home.'

From June 9, 1992, the day when the guards were first sent, until I left Egypt in January 1993, the inspector never showed up once. But the guards would be changed quite often. Younger ones able to resist the sultan of sleep came along. I used to see them standing at the door of our building at night, so I sent them chairs, blankets, food and some of my books since they knew nothing about this woman doctor they were supposed to be protecting. I used to ask them, 'Do you know who I am? Do you know why you have been sent to guard me?' They had no clue for they had been told nothing. All they had were orders which they had to follow. They were soldiers whose duty was obedience, just like women under the marriage law.

*   *   *   *

Early in the morning the bodyguard used to ring the door-bell. Sherif would open and say to him, 'Good morning Rafeek.[3] Today is a vacation for you. Dr Nawal has no appointments, and will not be leaving the flat. Come tomorrow.'

Next day he would come along and Sherif would repeat the same thing. Escaping from the bodyguard became one of our main preoccupations, and every day we invented an excuse. Without the bodyguard danger seemed to go away and I felt free to walk in the streets, to forget my fears. I ceased to turn round to glimpse his hand before he fired the gun at my back.

*   *   *   *

In my life writing has remained my sole refuge. Nothing can replace the words I write on paper, can compensate me for them. For me it is like breathing. Through writing my self breathes, expresses itself. My pen breaks down the wall of isolation between my body and the world. I create words but words create me. Words are all I possess, yet I am possessed by them. Between words and me there is a love relation built on equality. Neither of the two partners dominates the other. Writing has been the antithesis of death and yet, paradoxically, the reason why in June 1992 I was put on a death-list.

The death-list is a new term that invaded our literary life in recent years. Names of men and women whose lives have been linked to literary production began to figure on these lists. When I walked down the streets a chance encounter with one of them would often lead to a question full of anxiety: 'Do you know who is on the list, Nawal?' Rumours went round, hung over our heads like the haze of smoke and dust that hangs over Cairo. Nothing was clear, no one knew the truth. We were like people walking in a fog. Is it the age in which we live that makes truth so difficult? At one time the enemy was visible, we could see him wearing a uniform, carrying a gun, occupying our land. He had a name and all of us knew it. But this hidden force, unknown to us, without a name, how could one fight against it?

At night I would hear a voice shouting out from a microphone. I wondered where it was coming from. From the minaret of the mosque? From the dome of the church? From the disco club, or may

---

[3] His name.

be from McDonalds? It was a strange voice that invaded the night. It said, 'Wherever they are, kill them, kill the enemies of Allah.' Then came a list of names, writers, poets, historians, philosophers. Thirty or forty names in a row. Suddenly I hear my name, 'Nawal El Saadawi'. It goes through my head like a bullet. The letters of my name echo loudly through the night followed by 'Kill her, the heretic, the enemy of Allah', and as I listen to the voice it sounds to me like the rattle of a snake rising louder and louder in the dark, and in my nose there is a fetid smell which reminds me of oil.

That month I was busy writing my novel *Love in the Kingdom of Oil*. Deep down inside me was the feeling that oil was the hidden factor behind all this. I gaze at the word 'oil', underline it and this gives me a feeling of relief as though I have taken the first step towards naming the unknown force operating without a name, as though I was revealing the relationship between oil and the death-list, pulling out the thread that will unroll the skein.

Were it not for oil the Gulf War would not have been waged in January 1991. Were it not for oil thirty-one armies led by the United States would not have reduced Iraq to ruins, and the Iraqi people to a nation dying of starvation. Were it not for oil British politicians and generals would not have planted Israel in the land of Palestine, nor would the world have turned against Mossadeq in Iran, nor would our region still be ruled by kings and emirs who can hardly read and write.

In my novel, oil is the hero. The island in the story is floating on a sea of oil, completely under the control of an oil consortium. The president of the consortium is a foreigner who cannot speak a word of Arabic and the Kingdom is ruled by the tribal Holy Family and Representative of Allah on earth.

The story begins with an ordinary woman of the people leaving her home for a two-day vacation despite a royal decree which says women are prohibited from going on leave and if a woman is caught infringing these rules she should be arrested and brought back dead or alive.

I was completely engrossed in my work, driven by a feeling that time was running out. The idea of death always haunts me when I am writing a work of fiction. I become anxious, feel that I have to hold the manuscript close in my arms like a child, afraid it might run away and be lost. When I walk in the streets, it's always on the pavement in case a car should run over me, for my only desire in the whole wide world is to live long enough to complete my novel.

This time death kept haunting me from the moment the guards were put in front of my house. Not a day went by without my hearing the words 'death-list' mentioned in front of me: 'Who is on the death-list now?' 'Who was assassinated by terrorists in Egypt and Algeria last week?' Now they had started to use machine-guns, were escaping on motor-cycles and the authorities had failed to track them down.

Almost every day the bodyguard would ring the bell and tell us that they had caught a stranger trying to come up to my flat. Every time the door-bell rang I imagined the assassin standing outside. I could not write with the fear of death hanging over my head. I tried to chase it away but it kept coming back like an obstinate fly. The fly grew bigger and bigger until it reached the size of a huge bird, its feathers all black. It resembled neither an eagle, nor a falcon, nor a hawk, nor any other creature I had ever seen. It used to spread its wings over my head as I sat writing. I would stop in the middle of a line or a word, the pen arrested in its movement.

Sherif would raise his head and look at me, then ask, 'Nawal, what's wrong?'

'I can't write, Sherif, my mind has become paralysed.'

Sherif goes off to the kitchen and comes back with a glass of juice, or a cup of tea, puts it on my desk and looks at his watch. 'Nawal, you've been sitting behind that desk for more than seven hours,' he says (sometimes it was eight or ten). 'Take a rest, go on vacation.'

'Vacations have been forbidden by decree of the King.'

'What King, Nawal?'

I was still living in the novel. Sherif brought me back to reality. I kept shifting between imagination and reality. Back in reality, I would stretch the muscles of my back stiff with pain, stand up with difficulty, my feet swollen, my bones creaking like the water wheel in my village. I had developed a prolapsed disc, and back pains were now a normal part of my life.

Every morning the newspapers were pushed by an unseen hand under the doormat of our flat. At the corner of our road a man called 'Muhammad' had set up a newspaper stall. Every morning, impelled by one of the unknown forces that rule our lives, he would pedal around on his bicycle distributing newspapers, lay them out on the pavement, or hang them up on his stall. In the morning when I passed near his stall on the way to my morning walk along the Nile, I would turn my head away to avoid looking at them. At home I kicked them away from the door, for when I read them in the morning their poison would seep into my veins, spoil my day for me, stifle the thoughts that were struggling to emerge from my mind.

Every morning I awoke with a headache, sat at my desk with a band tied tightly round my head. My mind was barren land, desert sand in which not a flower blooms. I sat there without adding a word to what I had written the day before, or repeated what I had already written. When I read the lines they seemed meaningless to me, dead words, flowers on a grave.

I used to tear my papers up, throw them at arms' length across the room, put my head under the shower, swallow aspirin, beat my fist against the wall, but nothing relieved the painful splitting headache I was suffering from.

I was receiving telephone calls at all hours of the day and night, hearing the voices of strange men insulting me in classical Arabic, in colloquial Egyptian or in words pronounced in the dialects typical of Saudi Arabia, of Kuwait, or even Algeria. In the mail came threatening letters, one of them said: 'You are a heretic, an enemy of Islam, an instrument of the Devil. You are the woman who caused Adam to be chased out of Paradise, and brought death and destruction with her. Through your Association you spread poisonous ideas. The authorities closed it down, transferred its money to the Association of Muslim Women and that is how it should be, for pious Muslim women have more right to this money than you do. The money of your Association is "haram"[4] because it is not used in the service of Islam. The slogan of your immoral association, "unveiling of the mind", is heresy. Do you not know that Allah commends all Muslim women to wear the veil? The veil is sacred and you are inciting women to disobey Allah. Women like you deserve only death.'

* * * *

One night I was alone at home. Sherif was on an urgent visit to his village Koddaba near the provincial city of Tanta. I sat at my desk trying to write. The building was plunged in deep silence. Mona and Atef had moved out of our flat to live on their own. For the first time in over twenty-five years, Sherif and I each had our own room in which to work and sometimes sleep if we wished. I liked to be alone with my thoughts especially when I was writing, to hear nothing but

---

[4] Illicit in the religious sense, not sanctified by Islam.

the sound of my breathing or the clock ticking when I came back to reality for a moment.

Suddenly the door-bell rang. I sat rigid in my chair. At this hour of the night who could be ringing the bell? My heart was pounding, cold sweat poured down my body as I sat there unable to move. Maybe someone had rung on the wrong door. But a moment later there was a second ring. My heart made a jump. I waited, then got up and moved silently through the dark out of my room into the hall. Behind the glass pane of the front door I glimpsed a shadow. I gathered up my remaining courage and asked: 'Who is at the door?'

There was no answer. The silence echoed in my ears, seemed to whistle like the rice mill near my childhood home in Menouf. I thought of running into the kitchen to pick up a knife. But what use was a knife if faced by a gun? If only I had a gun in the house! But why is the man silent? Why doesn't he say something? Why did the guards allow him to come up? And do assassins ring the door-bell?

There I stood in the darkness holding my breath. The shadow moved behind the window pane and disappeared. Strange. What was this shadow? Why had it waited behind the window pane and why had it gone away?

I went back to my room, my hands and feet were icy, my heart beat slow as though it would stop at any moment. I opened the window and looked out. Maybe I would see him emerge from the entrance to the building. If I did not see him coming out then perhaps one of the guards had come up and stood behind my door to make sure every thing was alright.

The minutes passed, ten minutes became twenty minutes as I stood there like a statue. Mourad Street was plunged into darkness. One of the cables was out of order. Every now and then a car sped along the road and I could hear the lion roar in the Giza Zoological Gardens. Police sirens shrieked in the night, the university clock chimed twice, followed by something like a sob or a moan coming from a distance, as if a woman were weeping. I strained my ears trying to hear where it was coming from. Was it the neighbour who lived in the flat above me? Was it coming from the flat below? Perhaps it was the that woman who lived above in the small flat to the left of the lift? At intervals the sobs were wafted to me by the night breeze blowing over Cairo, and the next moment it was as though I was hearing my mother dying of cancer, moaning with pain, calling out to me 'Naaawaal'. My head was buried under a pillow. I sobbed at the thought of her pain, my sobs rose higher than her moans, rising above the sound of the unknown woman weeping in the night.

When Sherif came home, he walked into the room, looked at me, put his hand on my head, then sat down near me and said: 'Nawal, you must leave the country.'

'Leave the country? Where to Sherif?'

'You are a well-known writer, Nawal, and have friends in many countries. I'm prepared to go with you if you do not want to go alone.'

*   *   *   *

I started to think about what Sherif had said. But where could I go? My previous travels had all been for a purpose: to attend a conference, to give a lecture, to launch one of my books. But now it was the threat hanging over my head which was forcing me to think of leaving the country. Was exile going to be my future, my fate? I had been through many experiences, had been in prison, had lost my job, my books had been censored or banned, my reputation sullied. Now I would no longer live in my own country and I had no idea what exile would be like.

One day the door-bell rang. Sherif opened the door. There was a young woman standing on the threshold, slim, brown with a satchel slung over her shoulder.

Her name was Elizabeth and she was a student at Duke University. She had read some of my novels in English, had come to Egypt to do some research and decided to try and meet me before she left. A friend of ours had spoken to us about her some weeks ago but the worry of recent events had made us forget that she was coming that evening.

As she entered the building she noticed there were guards at the entrance. One of them had insisted on going up with her in the lift to my flat. She asked me what had happened, why the guards were there. I said nothing had happened. They were there to protect my life. She looked at me, surprised to see me smile. 'Protect you from what?' she said.

'From a terrorist attack. My name has figured on a death list.'

'Why don't you leave for a while, Dr Saadawi?'

'But where can I go?'

'To Duke University. One of my professors there is called Myriam Cooke and she teaches your novels in a course on Arabic literature. I can call her tomorrow, explain the situation to her, and suggest that she phone you directly.'

*   *   *   *

Today is January 8, 1993. I take a last look at our small flat. I rented this flat in 1960 from the owner of the building, before Sherif and I were married. I have lived in it for thirty-three years.

Sherif is strapping our bags in the hall. Throughout the thirty years of our life together the authorities have given us no respite. They were after us all the time. If we published a magazine they closed it down. If we started a project they prevented us from carrying it through. If we established an association they told us we were breaking the laws and banned its activities. Now they were driving us out of the country.

I go through the rooms as though bidding farewell to the things I have lived with for so long. My daughter is waiting in the hall. She puts her arms around me and says 'Call us as soon as you arrive.' My son Atef is standing by her side. In turn he embraces me and says, 'Take care. Take care of yourself, Mummie.' In turn they hug Sherif, hold back the tears, smile.

Sherif carries the bags and lines them up outside the door. His movements are steady, remind me of my father. I was seven years old when I saw him strapping our bags as we got ready to leave Cairo. The authorities had decided to send him away from the city to one of the provinces because he had participated in demonstrations against the king and the British. He spent ten years in Menouf, from 1938 to 1948.

We walked out of the building carrying our bags. This was a farewell to family, to friends, to our homeland. In the plane Sherif put his arm around me and said, 'Nawal, we have a wonderful journey in front us, a new experience to live,' as the plane lifted us up above the clouds, banked and turned its nose northwards.

TWO

Spreading My Wings

I am in North Carolina. The sky above my head stretches towards the south-east coast of the United States of America and the night is a dense black. There is no moon but in the night the distant stars flicker as though they are about to go out. When I was a small child I would ask my father and my mother 'Who created all these stars?' 'God, my child' they answered. 'And who created God?' I would ask. There would be a stony silence which lasted a long moment. My father would swallow his saliva. I could see his Adam's apple move up and down at the front of his neck. His voice sounded hoarse as he answered, 'Nobody created God. He created himself.' My child's mind could not imagine someone creating himself.

My father would point to the sky. His finger was the finger of God. I watched it big and long as it pointed to the stars. 'That is Mars, and over there is Saturn, and Neptune; the bright one there is the North Star, Al-Zahra.' My eyes would remain fixed on Zahra.[1] It was the only female star, the others were male. She was my star born with me, and destined to die with me. My grandmother Sittil Hajja used to say that each one of us has his or her star in the sky, that it is born with us and dies with us.

My eyes single out the North Star, Zahra. Is she the same star I used to see in my village? Between me and my village there now lies half a century and ten thousand miles. When I look at Zahra she fills me with a deep yearning for the years of my childhood, for my

---

[1] 'Zahra' means 'flower' and in Arabic is a feminine noun.

girlhood. I lived my first love at the age of ten. I was twenty years old when I met my second love, so the first and second loves were separated by ten years. But it took thirteen years before I fell in love for the third time.

Each time I asked myself: why him? I never found the answer, as though not knowing is a condition for love. Moments in my life have made me stop to think, moments which were difficult to understand. Maybe the understanding of the heart requires no words, needs no language. In history love was born before language. It was a knowledge arising from the body, feeling taking precedence over reason, over mind.

Writing destroys these moments of love. Writing is like a surgeon's knife. It tears the body apart, kills the moment, cuts the head off from the neck, from the heart, the chest, the guts, the belly.

When I was still twenty it was not difficult for me to write words like 'head' or 'heart' or 'chest' in my secret diary. They were innocent words referring to innocent parts of the body. But I never pronounced the word 'belly', even after I became a student in medical school and dissected the bellies of dead bodies in the anatomy hall. I never pronounced the word 'sex', even after my first marriage, even after I used to sleep in the same bed with a man, even after marriage had made of us a single animal with two heads. Even after all that had happened, I never pronounced the word 'sex', and the word 'husband' spoken in colloquial Arabic remained for me a dirty word that I avoided carefully.

In medical school we were never taught anything about sex. We studied the reproductive and urinary systems, pregnancy and childbirth, diseases of women, cancer of the uterus and of the testicle, but never anything about the subject that occupied our minds most of the time, namely sex. Medical science was completely cut off from our daily lives.

At the age of twenty something very important happened to me. I was given a room of my own, with my own little library and my own desk. My younger sister Leila no longer shared a room with me. When I introduced a dead man's skull into the room we shared together Leila departed in haste, taking her bed with her. My greatest happiness at the age of twenty was this room of mine, this new-found freedom. When I was still a child cutting dolls to pieces with my sister Leila I used to dream of freedom. These dreams haunted me throughout primary and secondary school, and in the Helwan

Boarding School for Girls. My yearning for freedom was much greater than my desire for love. For what was love if I had no freedom?

In the autumn of 1951 for the first time in my life I began to enjoy some freedom. When I opened my eyes in the morning I felt a wave of strange happiness sweep over me. I used to jump out of bed as light as a small bird. Everything filled me with wonder. The lightness of my body, the sound of water falling from the shower, the feeling of my hand rubbing my body with soap. My heart fluttered with joy under my ribs and I sang, 'When night falls and stars scatter in the sky, I ask the night where is my star, when will it shine?' There seemed to be a relationship between the stars and the pulsations of my heart.

Now at the age of sixty I know matter is one: quarks, electrons, atoms; that stars and human bodies are different combinations of the same – so step by step the mystery, the wonder of the child has gone.

For the first time in my life I had a space of my own on which I could close the door. It was a small room, just big enough to accommodate a few bookshelves and a small desk behind which I could squeeze myself only if the door was closed. I could write whatever I wanted in my secret diary without anyone prying into what I wrote, drink glasses of tea with mint without anyone to count the number I had drunk, lie on my bed and wander to my heart's content, stare into space for hours with no-one to say that something strange was happening to me, that my head was not right.

The window in my room looked out into a small back garden. Rising in it was a tall palm tree with a head of fronds jutting out in all directions, and with branches of dates dangling down from above very much like my untidy mop of thick black hair always blowing in the wind.

The small desk had been bought for me by my father. It had three narrow drawers on the right side and two on the left. The top drawer on the left had a key which locked both drawers at once. My library was composed of three shelves jutting out from the wall above my desk. They accommodated my medical books, lecture notebooks, some novels and collections of short stories, books on history and philosophy and other books sometimes borrowed from a library. On the wall between the shelves and my desk was a wooden board on which I pinned my timetable.

From the front window I looked out on to a lane which branched out from the main street running parallel to Toure't Al-Zoumour

(*zoumour*: stream) Road. The district, called Al-Oumraneya, was quiet, and was located at the beginning of a broad road leading to the Pyramids.

The window looking out on to the small back garden also faced the house of our neighbours. It had a small balcony and at certain hours of the day a boy would stand on it with a mirror in his hand. He was fat and had a round white face like King Farouk. He used to catch the sun in his mirror and direct it at my window. I would close the shutters and peer at him through them. I could see him watching my window through binoculars, so I stuffed up the cracks with old newspapers and went back to my desk with the skull on it to study, read, or write.

Otherwise I wrote always with the front window wide open to the sky. If I did not see the sky I found it difficult to write, so I got into the habit of writing in the open air, or near a window looking out at the sky as far as the horizon. My eyes need to wander in infinite space, with nothing to obstruct my vision.

The skull on my desk kept me company, reminded me of death, made the feeling of being alive more vivid. The proximity of death filled my being with the joy of living.

Next to the skull stood a small fan which made a slight whirring noise, as though it were whispering to me, dispelling any feeling of loneliness. I had only to close the door on myself and a wave of happiness would go through me. No-one in the house disturbed me whether I was asleep or awake. I could read in bed until dawn, close myself up in my room for two or three days, writing, put on my clothes and go out without anybody asking me where I was going, or when I would be back. Classes and rounds in medical school lasted all day, demonstrations could break out at any time. Student meetings were very frequent, and I never missed any of these activities.

Every day I walked from home to the School of Medicine in Kasr Al-Aini Street. Often I walked back at the end of the day. If I was very late I would ride home in a tram. When I bought shoes I made sure their leather was strong, their heels low. I avoided shoes with a shine, made of patent leather, did not like clothes made of shining silk, jackets made of what we called sharkskin, hair greased with brilliantine, patent leather shoes which were named after the French word *aglacé*, skins anointed with creams, whiskers that were oiled and neatly clipped, smooth silk neckties knotted with care. I disliked 'gloss'. Nature, spontaneity, the chaos which should accompany any system, the ugliness that is a necessary part of real beauty were always close to my heart. I did not like make-up, did not paint my face, or put lipstick on, or varnish my nails. I wore dresses made of cheap rough material, with a high bodice so that my breasts would not show. My body was mine and I did not need to exhibit it to people's eyes.

Sometimes I wore men's shirts or jackets, for to me masculinity and femininity enhanced one another, made each other more beautiful. Beauty to me was nature.

Deep down inside me I could feel the full vigour of my femininity, ascetic, struggling not to show itself. The more it flamed, the more ascetic it became, hiding deep in my body, refusing to reveal itself except rarely in a look, a sudden glitter in the eyes.

I used to wake up early in the morning when everybody else was still asleep, eat breakfast alone: a cup of very hot tea with milk, a small piece of white cheese, a spoonful of honey, and half a round loaf of thin flat bread. In the middle of the day, or in the afternoon I drank a glass of tea with mint. I began to drink coffee during the nights when I stayed up late preparing for exams. Most of all I liked to sleep, a sleep so deep that it was like a kind of death from which I resurrected in the morning ready once more to embrace life with open arms .

I had small whims and I loved these whims with all my heart. Staring at the sky for hours without moving, sometimes during the day, but preferably at night. The universe enchanted me, the planets, the stars, and each time it was the same question: where did all this come from? When did it all begin, and when will it all end?

The second time my heart beat with love I was sitting in a small underground auditorium near the anatomy hall where we used to dissect dead bodies. Here student leaders met to discuss how they were going to organize strikes and demonstrations against the British occupation.

The autumn of 1951 was crowded with political events and demonstrations. After the abolition of the Anglo-Egyptian Treaty by the Wafdist government in October 1951 there was a series of demonstrations against the British occupation forces. The Wafdist government headed by Mostafa Al-Nahas Pasha encouraged popular resistance against them, and secretly armed guerrilla fighters called *fida'iyeen* who were operating in the Canal Zone.

A colleague of mine called Ahmed Al-Menessi had joined one of the guerrilla groups. The weeks passed and one day we heard that he had been killed in a skirmish, would never come back. He and I used to talk to one another sometimes while working in the biochemistry lab. One day he wrote me a short letter and slipped it into the notebook of lectures he had borrowed before returning it to me: 'Your image will always be before my eyes as I fight our enemies in the name of God.'

I remember his sharp hooked nose making a small arch in the air as he stood beside me at the bench, his shining defiant, black eyes, yet too shy to meet my look. Rigid traditions separated the sexes, forbade us to talk or look at one another, even though we studied together in the same university.

After the day he had slipped his short letter into my notebook, I met him only once before he went off to meet his death and become a martyr in the struggle against British colonialism. The School of Medicine organized a meeting to commemorate his death, and his name was engraved on a stone placed in the courtyard a short distance from the entrance. Now the stone is no longer there, and nobody remembers him. He is no longer a part of our history, has been forgotten like many other guerrilla fighters who lost their lives in the struggle for independence, or who came back to be hunted down by the Egyptian police with a zeal greater than that of the British. These young men were transformed by some hidden will from heroes fighting for their country into criminals to be tracked down by the government, or into terrorists to be shot by the British.

*   *   *   *

Ahmed Helmi was a freedom fighter. The first time I saw him was in the small underground auditorium near the anatomy hall. I was the only girl student to be invited to meetings held by the student leaders, probably because I used to participate in the anti-colonialist demonstrations, and write in the magazines published by the students in our school. I had inherited my father's childhood dreams, wrote poetry and prose, dreamt of carrying a gun and fighting the enemies of my country. In my dreams I never saw myself wearing the veil and long dress of a bride. A husband had no place in my dreams, no man could change my name to his, or invade my body.

This sudden leap of my heart, what was it? Did it really happen, or was I imagining something as I sat in the meeting held to organize the largest demonstration we had ever organized? I pressed my bag against my ribs as though trying to contain my heart. My heart had not pounded behind my ribs like this since my first love when I was ten years old. The child had become a girl of twenty, a student who took her studies seriously, followed courses in anatomy, biochemistry, physiology and pathology. She had read the Qur'an and parts of the Old and New Testaments, as well as other books on philosophy, religion, and especially history, starting from the time of the Pharaohs and the ancient Egyptians up to the Khedive Ismail, the British occupation, King Fouad and King Farouk, and the birth of political parties in Egypt.

I used to walk to save the tram fare and buy books with the money. My colleague Samia lent me books about Marxism. In my father's library there were the works of Ibn Rushd, Ibn Khaldoun, Ibn Seena, Al-Gahiz the physician, Al-Razi, and the philosopher Abou Al-Ala'a Al-Ma'ari. I had read *Risalat Al-Ghofran*[2] before falling on *The Divine Comedy*. Dante was born in the year 1265 and had read about the cultural heritage of Egypt, about Christianity and Islam. Probably he had also read Ibn Arabi Al-Soufi and the 'Elegy' or 'Epistles of Forgiveness' written by Abou Al-Ala'a Al-Ma'ari. Is that why the image of the afterworld in Dante's *Divine Comedy* was very similar to what was described in the 'Elegy' or 'Epistles of Forgiveness'?

I used to hear my father say that Dante had copied from Abou Al-Ala'a Al-Ma'ari, but when I mentioned that to Samia she pouted in disgust, and said 'Ma'ari my foot, Nawal. He was nothing but a nobody, a half-naked beggar. That's why he was called 'Ma'ari.[3] How can you compare him to someone like Dante?' She would pronounce Dante with her tongue inside her mouth thickening the 't' as though it were an Arabic name. My colleague Batta on the other hand pronounced the 'r'[4] in Ma'ari like a Parisian but made it more substantial. She cared little for what we were talking about, was bored by it and heaped insults on Dante, Ma'ari, Marx and all the rest. She waxed sarcastic when mentioning Marx, called him

---

[2] The 'Elegy of Forgiveness'.
[3] In Arabic, 'ma'ari' means 'not covered'.
[4] There is a letter in Arabic which sounds thicker than the Parisian 'r'.

'Morcos'[5] like the man with whom our friend Safeya had fallen in love when we were still in secondary school.

None of the girl students in the medical school participated in demonstrations or attended the political meetings in the small auditorium. When I spoke to her about such things Batta would twist her lower lip and say. 'Politics, Nawal? It's *kalam farigh*',[6] not forgetting to pronounce the Parisian 'r' whenever she had a chance.

Safeya's reaction was different. She would look the other way and say, 'Isn't it enough that politics has landed my brother in prison and ruined our lives?' At which Samia would give us her usual pout of disgust and chime in: 'Those students are no more than agents of the political parties competing for power. The only people with any loyalty to the country are the Communists'.

The word communism was fraught with danger, surrounded by dark clouds of suspicion and rumour, and the Communist Party operated underground. The student who led the Communists was in the final year of medical school. His name was Ismail Shalaby. He came to school driving a dark Buick car, and wearing dark glasses with a golden chain hanging down. He was short, and made long speeches about the poverty of the workers and peasants. The students listening to him shifted uneasily on their benches, and looked at their wrist-watches.

There came the turn of the leader of the Muslim Brothers. He was called Omran Abdel Mawgood. He wore a tight suit into which he squeezed his square body and sported a waistcoat with a silver chain crossing over from the watch pocket. The silver chain was holy, for it had come from Mecca, the city where Prophet Muhammad was buried in the land of Hejjaz. He stood on the platform, his body leaning to the right, his left hand held to his waist, his right arm up in the air, his thick lips parted as though he were smiling up at some force hidden in the heavens. He maintained this posture for a long moment without moving, as though a magic lens up there in space were taking a picture of him, then turned slowly to face the audience and his voice would thunder out. He always began his speech in the name of Allah the Supreme who knew all things, and ended it with a prayer for the Prophet of all prophets after whom no more prophets would come.

---

[5] 'Morcos' in Arabic is like 'Mark' in English.
[6] 'Nonsense', literally 'empty talk'.

The students would again begin to shift on their benches. Some of them would sneak out of the back door, others would stand up and say, 'Brother, we've had enough of your blather. We want to hear something useful.' Then Fouad Mohieddin[7] would stand up. He was already a resident doctor at Kasr Al-Aini University Hospital, taller than anyone else, thin as a cane stick, wearing a smart well-pressed suit, a snow-white starched shirt collar, with a brightly coloured necktie carefully knotted in the middle exactly in line with his chin. He kept pulling at it with the tips of his long thin fingers, stretching his long thin neck with a movement resembling that of a turkey or a peacock. I could not tell whether this was out of conceit or the result of the stuffy atmosphere in the underground auditorium, for all the windows were closed, and cigarette smoke rose up in the air to the ceiling. All the students here smoked, blowing the smoke from their nostrils as though this were one of the rituals required in politics, or an irrefutable indication of their masculinity.

Fouad Mohieddin pounded on the pulpit with no less vigour than the leader of the Muslim Brothers. His voice thundered out in the same way as he quoted the famous saying of Mostafa Kamal Pasha: '"If I had not been born an Egyptian my one desire would have been to become Egyptian." Colleagues, we all belong to Egypt, whether Muslims or Copts.[8] Our constitution is the supreme law which governs all Egyptians, not the Qur'an. Religion is God's domain but our country belongs to all its citizens irrespective of religion. We are all brothers.'

After that it was the turn of Yusif Idris.[9] He was in his final year in medical school, was of middle height, neither thin nor fat, dressed rather carelessly in a suit too big for him, his necktie loose around his neck, hanging to one side as though he had knotted it hurriedly without looking in the mirror. He walked to the platform taking big rapid strides, his head bent slightly forwards as though he were butting the air with it. When he spoke he kept his right hand in his pocket, and waved his left hand in the air, fixed the audience with his deep-set glittering eyes as though he were trying to hypnotize the students sitting in rows. He shouted just as loud as the previous speakers, but mixed classical Arabic with colloquial words.

---

[7] Later prime minister under Sadat.

[8] Egyptian Christians belonging to the Eastern Orthodox or Protestant Church.

[9] Later well-known as a short-story writer and novelist.

'Colleagues, our country is passing through a phase fraught with danger and we must all take up arms, become freedom fighters, force the colonialists to evacuate our land. But to defeat the imperialists is not enough, we need a people's revolution to build a system which will ensure justice and freedom for all, equality between the toilers and those for whom they toil.'

A wave of murmuring flutters through the audience. A voice rises above the others in a shout: 'That is Communist talk.' Another voice says, 'Shut up! We want to hear what is being said.' 'What do you mean, shut up? I won't shut up!' The voices mingle and a fight breaks out in the far corner of the auditorium. The leader of the Wafdist students seizes the opportunity and climbs on to the platform, but Yusif Idris refuses to budge, and both of them occupy the platform together. The Wafdist leader is shorter than Yusif Idris, his suit is even more crumpled, and it hangs even more loosely on him – as though he had inherited it from his father or an elder brother. His shirt collar is slightly blackened with dust and sweat and his faded tie hangs down unknotted. But his fist pounds the pulpit more ferociously than any of the previous speakers, and he shouts much more loudly than anyone else, for that is as things should be. He is the representative of the majority party, and, to boot, that party is in power, rules under its President Mostafa Al-Nahas Pasha.

Some of the students begin to shout 'Al-Nahas! Al-Nahas!' Pandemonium breaks out and the leader of the Wafd stamps his foot down on the platform trying to control the situation. His shoes have thick heels with a crescent of iron nailed to them and make a shattering noise. He bellows out like a bull louder than anyone else, 'Long live Nahas, leader of the nation.'

I used to sit in the last row near the door, so that I could leave whenever I wanted without drawing attention to myself. But that day the stifling atmosphere, the smoke, the lack of oxygen and the increasing amounts of carbon dioxide in the air had deadened my senses, put me in a kind of daze made worse by a painful headache running down at the back of my head to my neck. Suddenly I became aware of a voice rising out of the haze, a voice which asked, 'Where is Ahmed Helmi?'

I opened my eyes and saw heads turn around to look at him. Like me he was seated in the last row, but on the opposite side near the window. Between us was a long row of empty seats. He wore a white shirt with an open collar, no tie or jacket or sweater. He stood up, walked without haste up to the platform and stood behind the lectern. When he began to speak it was in a quiet voice full of feeling, there was no hint of rhetoric, no special emphasis on words, no pounding of his fist on the pulpit. He went straight into the subject, into what was necessary, important. 'Colleagues, the freedom fighters in the Canal Zone need ammunition and rations, their rear lines have to be stable to protect them, there is no time, no room for partisan struggles. We need unity of the people.'

He walked back to his seat in the same way without haste. Our eyes met across the long row of empty seats. He did not wear sunglasses, so I saw his eyes as they met mine for a short moment. But in that moment I saw light in them leading to more light, two open windows leading to his depths, to an ocean where I would drown, to a world unknown.

I walked back home. It was an autumn day in the month of November 1951. The sun was setting or had set a few moments ago. I reached Abbas Bridge as the rays of the setting sun spread over the sky in a carnival of colour: blue, green, indigo, orange, gold and silver, intermingling in the clouds, taking on different shapes that resembled the many heads and arms of the dancing goddesses in ancient India and Egypt. The shapes kept changing, moving in waves with the movement of the clouds, disappeared in a great splash of deep crimson red as though consumed in a huge fire that burnt across the sky then slowly died down, fading into hues of orange and pink before the grey of dusk and black of night took over. I continued to walk through the night as it enveloped the world in a thick blanket of dark silence where nothing moved except a soft breeze and the occasional flutter of leaves.

The waters of the Nile flowed by, calm and unhurried, the way he walked. His voice echoed in my ears, wafted through the silence. My feet continued to move over the ground at the same pace, as though I could go on and on until I reached the end of the world.

I arrived home later than usual. My mother lit the stove to heat a dinner of chicken broth, fried rice and chicken for me.

I devoured the meal like a hungry child. She sat in front of me watching me eat as she used to do when I came home from primary school. Her eyes seemed to see into me. Her voice penetrated through the barricades I had carefully built around myself. I heard her ask, 'Tell me, Nawal, how was your day in school?'

It was a routine question, one she asked me almost every day. I buried my face in my plate trying to avoid her eyes. Something like a cloud, a shade of doubt passed over her face. She repeated her question, 'How was your day, Nawal?' I answered, murmuring the words as I chewed the food, 'Nothing special to tell about, mother.'

After eating I went straight to my room, closed the door on myself with a sigh of relief, opened the window and stood there staring at the sky. Did my mother have a special sense organ like the tactile horns of some insect through which she could feel certain things? Or was it my eyes she read into like an open book. I went up to the mirror and stared at my face. My eyes looked the same. A deep black with a sparkle in them. Maybe the sparkle had increased a little. This girl standing in the mirror, was she same girl I saw every day? A voice within me whispers, 'What has happened to you, Nawal?' Back comes the answer: 'Nothing at all, just a silent encounter across a long row of empty seats.'

Between the moment of this silent encounter in November 1951 until the day we divorced in January 1957, there were many encounters. We talked, lived through the experience of love and marriage and of having a child. Yet from it all, what remains in my memory is this silent encounter lasting no more than a second, this moment which can never be lost, will never die. I always remember this particular moment – of all the moments we passed together – as the most important, the most lasting in the six years between our meeting and our separation. We met and parted, met and parted again and again, yet each time what brought us back to one another, despite everything, was this single silent moment when we had looked at one another across a long row of empty seats in the small auditorium next to the anatomy hall.

Was it a language, a magic code that belonged to another world, to a world which is not ours, expressing itself away from time and place and words? A moment outside the universe, outside all natural law, outside the logic of reason and mind? Yet to me it seemed the most logical, the most natural moment of all, a moment which forced its way into mind, into memory, into time and place, into history. Otherwise how can I explain that in all of those six years, this is the moment I recall, although it only lasted for a second or maybe half a second of time.

Between our meeting in November 1951 and our divorce in January 1957, my life was changed more than in all the preceding years of my life. In those same years Egypt also underwent important changes which ended in the collapse of the ruling system.

Ahmed Helmi was one of the freedom fighters who took part in the guerrilla attacks on British troops occupying the Canal Zone. With others he helped to pave the way for a change in the system. The freedom fighters were the fuel of the revolution. They were the unknown soldiers who fought and fell in the front ranks, who paid for the revolution with their blood. Some of them died in battle, others survived. Yet when it was time to celebrate the revolution and its victories, no-one remembered them. Unknown soldiers have no names, no faces. They become a piece of stone engraved with a few words that crumbles into pieces with the passage of time.

In the small auditorium the student leaders made fiery resounding speeches calling on the students to join the ranks of the freedom fighters. But they themselves never travelled to the Canal Zone to fight. Not one of them was hurt, or received so much as a scratch despite the battles that were going on. They made speeches, then went on their way to graduate on time, rose up to be ministers, to be rulers wielding power.

Sometimes I run into one of them by accident in a meeting or a conference. We exchange a few words about the old days, but not one of them ever recalls the freedom fighters who interrupted their studies and went off to fight in the guerrilla war.

Before leaving to join the freedom fighters, Ahmed Helmi asked my father for my hand in marriage. My father had always supported the struggle against the British, always waxed enthusiastic when mention was made of the freedom fighters, but marrying his daughter to one of them was another thing. He said to Ahmed, 'How can you abandon your studies and go off to fight the British? Marriage, my son, is a responsibility.' I could see him shoot side glances at me out of his black eyes as he pronounced these words, for he could see that I was deeply disappointed by his stand. Was it not he who had filled my child's mind with stories of his heroism during the revolution of 1919? But a moment later, to regain my confidence he beat a retreat and said, 'All right son, I agree to an engagement, but marriage must come after you have finished your studies and graduated as a doctor.'

So one day a golden engagement ring engraved with the name of Ahmed Helmi was slipped around the finger of my right hand. My mother insisted that apart from the ring around my finger something else called *al-shabka*[10] should be tied around my neck or encircle my wrist. The word *shabka* filled me with terror. Was I being hooked to the bridegroom? Ever since I was a child the word 'bridegroom' had sounded terrible to my ears. At the age of ten I had learnt how to drive bridegrooms away. Not once had I dreamt of myself wearing a wedding dress. But love was a different matter. It carried me up into the sky on wings like a bird. I became Zahra, the North Star, full of light, and by my side up there in the heavens was suspended another star full of light, a spirit without body, just two eyes, and nothing else material that would touch my body, apart from the ring around my finger with his name engraved on it.

My mother's voice echoed in the hall: 'A bridegroom always buys a *shabka*[11] for his wife. What will people say if he marries you without buying one?'

'People? What people, mother?'

'Your Aunt Hanim and Aunt Fahima and all our relations will certainly ask about the *shabka*. What shall I say to them, Nawal?'

'Tell them there won't be any *shabka*, that Nawal doesn't believe in *shabkas*.' My mother's face turns pale, as though I had said I did not believe in God.

The value of a bridegroom was measured by the price of the *shabka* he bought for his bride. This was the case in all families, including that of my father and mother. In the School of Medicine, when my student friends heard that I was refusing to accept a *shabka* they gasped. 'An engagement without a *shabka* and to a man who is a guerrilla fighter! Nawal, you are absolutely crazy.'

In the students' room my eyes sparkling, my cheeks flaming, my imagination flying up to the seventh heaven, I would give them lessons in love. 'Girls, you don't know anything about love. Real love is more important than a thousand *shabkas*, than all the gold in the world.' Batta would gurgle with laughter. Her laughter sounded like water pouring out of a narrow-necked earthenware[12] jar. 'I can die for love for a man, as long as he is a professor in the School of Medicine, owns a posh clinic, a luxurious building, a big farm, and a smart car, not a down-and-out guerrilla fighter.' Safeya as usual would repeat the story of her old love for Dr Morcos. He fulfilled Batta's

---

[10] 'The hook'.

[11] 'Necklace', 'bracelet', 'earrings'.

[12] Earthenware jars are used by poor people, especially in the village, to cool their water. When water is poured out of them it makes a characteristic gurgling sound.

conditions, except that he was a Copt, not a Muslim like Safeya. He was prepared to give up Jesus Christ for his love, but his mother was adamantly opposed to that and he was not prepared to give up his mother for Safeya.

Samia also had been bitten by the bug of love. She had fallen for a colleague of hers. He was a student in the School of Pharmacology, a Communist like her. 'How can I love someone who is not a Communist?' she would say. 'You don't expect me to fall in love with one of those bourgeois men, do you!' Batta would break out into her gurgling laughter and say, 'I adore bourgeois men. As a matter of fact the more bourgeois they are, the more I can die of love for them.' This was enough to provoke hilarious laughter from the girls, all except Samia who pouted her thin lips to emphasize her disapproval for what had been said and commented, 'A bourgeois man can never really fall in love. All he knows is his own self-interest – exactly like the imperialists.' Safeya would go red with anger. 'Do you mean to say that only a Communist can really fall in love? To hell with you and your Communists.' A quarrel would break out only to be cut short by Batta. 'To hell with both the bourgeois and the Communists. May Allah make them all die a premature death.'

At the end of 1951 the Egyptian people were living under a corrupt system headed by King Farouk. The situation was aggravated by the struggle for power being waged by the political parties, with the British colonialists pulling the strings from behind. The majority party, the Wafd, vacillated between the interests of the Egyptian people, as voiced by an underdeveloped national bourgeoisie, and those of the king and his English masters, and the minority parties manoeuvered for power backed by the king and the British colonialists. Anger was mounting and the country was pregnant with revolution. University students had for a long time been the first to rebel, and the first to be consumed by the flames of revolution.

Ahmed Helmi and I used to meet near the tennis courts. He would wait for me on a bench until I finished playing, or I would wait for him until he had finished rewriting the issue of a magazine called the **Spark of Liberation** before it went to print. Then we would sit together and talk. Ours was not the usual conversation exchanged between a boy and a girl. We were more like colleagues talking of things they had in common.

The hours would pass as we sat there oblivious of time, drinking glasses of mint tea and lemonade, and talking. The sun would swing down from above our heads, hover above the horizon and sink behind it. Suddenly it was night, time to go home, yet it seemed as though only a few moments ago we had heard the call to prayer.

The first days of winter arrived and brought the cold with them. Cairo was covered in a thick grey mist. We sat as usual on the wooden bench, Ahmed leaning against the armrest smoking a cigarette, his eyes wandering, as though searching for something beyond the horizon. The call to prayer reaches us from a distance: 'Rejoice, it is the time of prayer! Rejoice, it is the time of salvation!' The words rise up from the minaret into the sky, cling to the mist, reverberate. The muezzin recites words from the Qur'an: 'Hail to Almighty Allah the one and only.' The words cut through my wandering thoughts as his voice rises from one level to another, and as I listen to them the heavens seem to become covered in dark clouds of doubt.

I listen to Ahmed as he talks about the armed struggle against the British in the Canal Zone. He tells me he will be travelling next day, to Tel Al-Kibeer, with a group of freedom fighters. Speaking in a quiet voice, he blows out his cigarette smoke with long slow deep breaths, like a lion containing its anger but ready to pounce. He has a large hand like my father's, stretches it out towards me and takes hold of my hand. I close my eyes as though in a dream. In my dream I see him firing his gun, attacking the British camps. freeing our country. Back home the whole village comes out to meet him, the women shrilling 'yooyoos', the men carrying him up on their shoulders. Then suddenly I hear an explosion followed by the whine of bullets. He falls to the ground bleeding and I can see a red ribbon of blood creeping over the dark tarmac of the road. I wrench myself out of my dream, open my eyes and there he is sitting beside me. In his hand he is holding a ring of keys and with the pointed tip of a key he carves a heart on the tree trunk and inside the heart engraves our names. I feel that, as he whittles away at the bark of the eucalyptus tree, he is engraving our names in history and that they will be carried down by it for all time.

The tree lived on for twenty-three years with our names engraved on it. I used to pass close to it sometimes during the time of our marriage, and later after we divorced. The letters continued to embrace one another after we had separated. Then other youths came along and carved their names with a key or a knife and the pointed tips erased the two names. In 1974 the whole tree was destroyed. A bulldozer uprooted it from the earth and in its place rose blocks of cement.

Before Ahmed left with the group of freedom fighters I asked myself whether I should not go with him. But armed struggle was only for men. Women were not eligible for the honour of freeing their country. If a woman volunteered, she could go as a nurse, or to entertain the fighters. If she died in a battle, she was never described as a martyr. Her only glory was to be sought in nursing the wounded, or entertaining the men who fought. These two vocations seemed insulting to a young girl who, when still a child, had dreamt of carrying a gun rather than a chamber pot, wearing fatigues rather than dancing tights.

I loved my country and was prepared to sacrifice my life for it. But my self-respect, my pride, was more precious to me than my life. I could not sacrifice that for anything, even my country, could not think of carrying chamber pots full of urine and excreta, or of dancing to entertain the fighters.

Yet the battlefield attracted me. Words like 'sacrifice', 'my country', 'martyrs', 'danger', 'death', had a magic ring in my ears. They meant the exhilaration of probing the unknown. They were the desire to display my abilities, to show people what I was capable of, to be a hero. They indicated a self-confidence that excluded the possibility of death. Others could die but not me. Was this the blindness, the lack of understanding common at this age? Yet even today, although I am over sixty, I cannot imagine myself dead. I have often tried, lain down in my bed again and again ready to die, but have never succeeded.

Winter winds started to blow. They came from the North, bringing with them cold and frost. The city of Cairo was grey, colourless, depressing. The School of Medicine seemed to be plunged into silence, as though everybody in it had died since Ahmed had left, as though the whole universe had been abandoned. Dark clouds hid the sun, and the air was heavy, saturated with sadness and defeat. I used to wake up to my voice crying out in a dream: 'Down with the British! Down with Dr Derry!'

Dr Derry was the only English professor who had stayed on in the School of Medicine. The others, faced by the rising tide of struggle for independence, had all left. The doctor looked like a tiger ready to pounce on us at any moment, his body enveloped in a white coat which reached to his knees. From his upper pocket protruded a huge black pen that looked like a gun. He used to point it at me when he asked me a question. In my dreams he would fire it at me and I would wake up screaming, 'Down with the British! Down with Dr Derry!'

After graduating in 1954 I never saw him again. Forty years have gone by since then. His face still remains with me, his fair complexion, his ruddy cheeks fed with our blood, blooming with the prosperity that the British colonialists enjoyed in our country. His body short and taut and slim, his jaw big and square, his hands joined behind his back. He gave his lectures in sharp, staccato sentences, like shots fired from a gun. After every sentence he would look at us and say, 'Ask why? Never stop asking why.'

That day Dr Derry was facing the blackboard, his back turned towards us as he prepared to write the word 'why' in big capital letters. The students sat on the benches, their heads bent over their notebooks writing down the last sentences he had pronounced. In the big auditorium not a sound was to be heard, as though they were all holding their breath. Suddenly out of the middle of the throng seated in the auditorium a voice speaking in bad English shouted 'Why you English here in our country?' Then there was a silence, as though the person who had shouted these words had evaporated into thin air.

Dr Derry's body went rigid, then he turned round to face the students. He stared at them with his blue eyes, at the faces rising in crescent-shaped rows right up to the ceiling. His eyes circled over them like searchlights, in the same way as the torch in the hand of the superintendent used to travel over the faces of the sleeping girls in the dormitory of Helwan Boarding School. His voice resounded like the lash of a whip as he said, 'If you're a man stand up.'

No-one stood up. Not a sound could be heard; it was as though every one in the auditorium including Dr Derry had been struck dead all of a sudden. I could hear the bell of the tram clanging its way through Kasr Al-Aini Street. In the silence it sounded like the repeated screams of a suffering child. Then slowly life began to stir in the auditorium. The first to move was Dr Derry. He pulled a big silk handkerchief out of the pocket of his short white coat, wiped his forehead and his big red nose with it, wiped off the sweat and the chalk sticking to the palms of his hands, folded the handkerchief four times and with a theatrical flourish put it back in his pocket. His lips parted in an ironic smile, as he closed the book which lay in front of him, put it under his arm and then walked to the door, stopped, turned round to stare at the silent faces for a moment and shouted, 'We are here because you are cowards.'

The word 'cowards' shot out from between his lips like a stone from a sling, a blob of spit, white and frothy. I saw it emerge from his mouth the size of a bean, move through the air and split into hundreds of tiny blobs of spit, into as many blobs as there were students. I saw the spit land on the face of every single one of them. Not one of them raised a hand in protest, or wiped it off. In the night when I slept I used to wake up suddenly shaking with anger. What angered me most was that a blob of spit had landed on my face also, that my hand had not lifted to wipe it away, that it would remain stuck to my face, no matter how many times I washed it with soap and water.

*   *   *   *

It was not long before I heard the news of Ahmed Al-Menessi's death. When I heard it my ears began to whistle like the rice mill used to do in Menouf. I had time only to hear the name 'Ahmed' before my ears became blocked and I could hear no more.

A huge marquee was hoisted for him in the courtyard of the School of Medicine. It resembled the circus tent I used to see in Menouf, made of thick canvas cloth with red and blue designs, like the marquees in which people gather to celebrate a wedding or mourn their dead. Under these marquees yellow cane chairs are placed in rows. The men sit on them, drink bitter black coffee in small white cups if it is a death, or a red syrupy liquid in tall thin glasses with a gold rim if it is a celebration. Their heads nod with the slow rhythmic chant of the Qur'an, or with the ring of brass castanets when there is song and dance.

But this marquee had been erected to mourn the death of Ahmed Al-Menessi. Students from the School of Medicine and from all the university colleges flocked into it. The dean sat in the middle of the front row flanked by the professors, and the student leaders dressed in grey suits and black ties kept coming and going. Fouad Mohieddin had covered his eyes with dark glasses, and his lips were tightly closed to indicate sorrow. Ibrahim Al-Sherbini followed behind, his body not as tall, his suit not as smart, his sorrow greater. Yusif Idris wore a black tie knotted untidily around his neck, and shouted angrily at Omran Abdel Mawgood, the leader of the Muslim Brothers:

'Al-Menessi's martyrdom does not concern the Muslim Brothers alone. It concerns all Egyptians'.

'Al-Menessi's martyrdom is certainly a matter that concerns all Egyptians, brother Yusif, but the programme is full and there will be plenty of occasions for mourning in the future at which you can make a speech.'

Menessi had been transformed into a word, that of 'martyr', into a word composed of six letters. It kept echoing in my ears, sticking in my throat. I sat in the marquee, held my icy cold hands in my lap, trying to keep them warm. A cold wind was blowing through the gaping holes in the marquee and the canvass kept shaking with every gust of wind. The leader of the Muslim Brothers was making a long speech but I did not hear a single word. Menessi's image hovered before my eyes, stood by my side in the biochemistry lab, his long strong fingers trembling slightly as they held the test tube between them. His voice whispered to me: 'I leave you in God's hands'. His eyes black and shining with light looked out from between their thick lashes. He was tall, taller than Ahmed Helmi and more handsome, yet my heart never beat for him in the way it had for Ahmed. It rejected the traditional values related to what was called manhood, or masculinity, or presumed good looks in a man. It was attracted by unknown elements hidden somewhere in the blood, in the chest or the body, in my subconscious, or in the way my consciousness understood things when I was still a child, to the childhood dreams of the seven-year-old girl, to that image of the man of my dreams woven over the years by the stories of my father, my mother and grandmother, to the hero carrying arms and fighting to free his country, to a man who resembled any father, or Saad Zaghloul,[13] but whose head was lifted even more proudly, whose will was even more unbreakable.

Ahmed Al-Menessi, despite his shining jet black eyes, had a defeated beaten look, a look full of humility. He never raised his eyes to mine. His eyes resembled those of his leader Omran Abdel Mawgood, resembled the eyes of all the students who belonged to the Muslim Brotherhood. They never looked straight at you. They always looked down, or were raised up to the heavens, never seemed to be able to see anybody except Allah, were always staring into space.

---

[13] Leader of the 1919 national revolution in Egypt.

As I sat in the marquee everything seemed unreal, bathed in a dense mist. Only death was real. I was seeing faces around me as though in my sleep. Every one was talking at the same time. The speeches sounded like explosions coming from the military training camp nearby. Coming from a distance the shrieks of women mourners following a dead body being carried out of Kasr Al-Aini Hospital in a coffin seemed no different from the 'yooyoos' celebrating a wedding.

I awoke from my reverie to the sound of my name being called: 'Sister Nawal El Saadawi'. The word 'sister' sounded strange in my ears. I was not a member of the Muslim Sisterhood, had never joined a political party. My name was called out again, this time preceded by 'our colleague'. I stood up like one resurrected from the dead, walked cautiously down a long aisle covered in red carpeting, as though stepping on blood that had not yet dried on a tarmac road, climbed the few shaky stairs to the platform, felt my knees go weak under me as I stood in front of the microphone and heard someone announcing in a loud voice, 'Now we will hear our colleague Nawal El Saadawi.'

I stared at the faces, paralysed, unable to pronounce a single word. I had never attended what people called a 'celebration for the dead'. The word 'celebration' was the antithesis of death, for how could one celebrate death? Ahmed Al-Menessi for me was still alive. He lived in my imagination, moved, spoke to me. The ink with which he had written his letter to me had not yet dried. His face was there, right in front of my eyes on the sheet of paper I kept folded between the pages of my notebook. What could I say to the men seated on their chairs staring at me?

Suddenly the words came tumbling out one after the other.

'Yes, Menessi is dead. He died for what he believed, for God and his country. But why are we alive? What are we living for? To make speeches from the top of a platform? To celebrate the dead, hold meetings to mourn them? This meeting means that Menessi is dead, yet Menessi is still alive. He is here, present in front of my eyes, more than any of those present in this meeting, than those who glorify the dead but do not die like them, fighting. Would not silence be more eloquent than words? What use is our presence here today? Why are we not over there at the front, shedding our blood on our soil like others have done?'

I had been thinking of Ahmed Helmi and maybe that is what put these words into my mouth. He was at the front with other freedom fighters and we had no news from them. Were they still alive? Were they dead like Menessi, or taken prisoner by the British? Had they been arrested by the Egyptian authorities and thrown into prison? Anything could have happened to them. How were we to know? We could trust neither the British colonialists nor the Egyptian government. Both of them had a dark history. In secret they collaborated but publicly they pretended to differ. Their interests coincided most of the time, were rarely at odds, but their antagonism towards the Egyptian people was unchanging. Was the blood of Menessi and others being shed in vain?

When I had ended my speech one of the leaders of the Muslim Brotherhood, a student in the School of Law named Hassan Douh, replaced me on the platform. He was known to be the most talented speaker in the university. He stood behind the microphone silent, his head bent. A thousand eyes stared at him, a thousand chests held their breath waiting. He looked at the rows of students then said, 'Brothers, after listening to our colleague Nawal El Saadawi I have nothing to say.'

After the meeting a number of my colleagues gathered around me. 'Your speech was wonderful, Nawal,' they said, 'straight from the heart, straight into our hearts. It was the shortest and the best. Even the most eloquent orator in the whole university had nothing to add after you.'

Their eyes stared at me full of admiration, lifted me to new heights as though I had suddenly become Saad Zaghloul or the martyr Ahmed Al-Menessi. Had they already forgotten Ahmed Al-Menessi? Were the dead forgotten as soon as they had been mourned?

I walked to the bus station carrying my bag. This was the bag that Ahmed Al-Menessi had held in his hands just a few weeks before. I had forgotten it in the pharmacology lab where a fire had broken out. He rushed upstairs, went into the lab and brought it back to me. I could almost see his fingerprints on the leather. They had left a deep groove like a wound. The bag was black, the colour of death, the colour of my guilty conscience. Why had my heart refused to beat for him? Had he gone to war out of despair? The world around me seemed like a dream. People walking in the streets were figments of my imagination. The buses went and came from nowhere to nowhere, and the students rushing to the school were just phantoms. They looked at their wrist-watches with bulging eyes, squeezed their bags tightly against their chests, squeezed their wallets into their pockets, imprisoned their souls inside their bodies, and their minds inside their skulls. They pushed one another with their elbows, jostled to get in first through the doors, stepped on one another's feet, competed over the dead bodies available for dissection, over the front row in the auditorium, over grades in the examinations. They rushed from home to school, from school to home, graduated as doctors, set up a clinic, bought cars, buildings, farms, married, had children, then died just like Menessi. But Menessi, like all martyrs for a cause, is not dead. He continues to live with the prophets in the house of eternity.

I stood at the bus-stop holding my bag. The bus arrived but it was crowded with people and I could not get in. Buses kept coming one after the other, all crowded. I stood at the stop for a full hour. Was this the day of judgement when all the dead would be resurrected? Was there another life in the hereafter? Menessi died at the age of twenty. He flitted through the world like a shadow. Was life just a short dream from which we awakened after death? Was it just an illusion, and the life hereafter the only reality? My mind was giving way under the weight of sadness. There had to be a life in the hereafter or else Menessi would have died twice, once in the world and once more after he had left it.

It had been a long sad day. I had left home in the morning without breakfast. Night had fallen and here I was still waiting at the bus-stop. I leaned against the lamp-post, closed my eyes for a moment. I heard a voice call out, 'Sister Nawal'. I recognized the face. It was Omran Abdel Mawgood, leader of the Muslim Brothers, standing in front of me, his square body squeezed into his tight suit, the silver watch-chain crossing over his waistcoat. He stood on the pavement leaning slightly to the right, his left arm held to his waist, his right hand holding out a small folded piece of paper, his full lips parted in a smile as he looked up at someone in the heavens. He stood silent for a long moment as though posing for the magic camera lens hovering somewhere in space ready to take a picture of him, handed me the piece of paper and said in a slightly embarrassed voice, 'This letter is for you, Sister Nawal.'

I finally managed to get into one of the crowded buses, pushed my way through bodies exhausted from a long day's work. I could smell the acid odour of sweat in the old clothes covered with oil stains. The passengers stood leaning against one another, holding on to the supports like fillets of sardine hanging in a tin box, but they kept at a distance from me and whenever the bus made a leap or jerked to a stop made sure to keep their balance so that our bodies did not touch, their eyes fixed to the ground, their features emaciated like those of my relatives in the village. They respected women much more than did the smartly dressed young men walking down the streets of the city centre. Was it real respect or just the fear that comes with poverty?

I got down at the bus-stop at the beginning of Al-Haram Street, and walked over the small bridge which crosses the stream of Al-Zoumour. The road that follows the stream was never lit and the district of Omraneya where we lived was enveloped in darkness as soon as night fell. All I could hear was the sound of my footsteps on the road.

I wanted to open my bag and read the letter but it was too dark. I felt a kind of exhilaration. The female buried inside me since childhood was like a sleeping giant. She woke up sometimes and poked her head out to look at the men around. But the face she was looking for was the product of her imagination. It resembled none of the students, and certainly had nothing in common with the face of the Muslim student leader. Besides he had a small fleshy hand, his body was fat, compressed inside the tight suit. His vacant eyes looked into vacant space. What could he have written in his letter?

When I got home my father was sitting in the hall and my mother was preparing dinner. I told my father what had happened at the meeting organized to mourn Al-Menessi. I heard my mother say, 'Poor Al-Menessi, he sacrificed his life for nothing.' My father was silent for a long moment then he said, 'No Zaynab, it was not for nothing. The British fear nothing as much as they fear freedom fighters. Nahas Pasha is just a scarecrow.'

I wanted to ask my father whether Menessi's name would live on in history through eternity. I venerated the word eternity as I venerated God, sacrifice, and history. They were words that had a magic ring to them and that I would never forget, and they kept coming and going in my mind as I sat at table. Then my mother brought out a big bowl of steaming chicken soup and I breathed the delicious smell, filled my lungs with it, felt it creep up my nostrils to my brain and envelop it in a kind of torpor, and the sacred words evaporated from my mind.

After dinner my eyelids were heavy with sleep, but in bed I dropped into the lost moments of time that intervene between wakefulness and sleep, for then I suddenly remembered the letter. My memory seems to function best at such moments. Omran Abdel Mawgood reappeared in front of me. I stretched out my hand, opened the envelope with fingers numbed by approaching sleep and looked at the half-page of lined paper torn from a lecture notebook. There was nothing on it except two lines of neat tiny characters, so small that they were hardly legible, as though he were trying to conceal them in the lines on which he had written: 'Before I heard you speak at the mourning of the martyr Al-Menessi I believed in Allah, my country and myself. Now I believe in Allah, my country, you and myself.'

The letter seemed innocent to me so I showed it to my father. I felt quite proud. Here was a human being whose faith in me was only slightly less than his faith in God and in his country. It was as though I had been promoted to a very high status equal to that of God and country, or at least just one or half a degree below them. Yet my heart missed not a single beat for him. Sometimes I used to cross him in the school courtyard. We used to shake hands and I could feel that small flabby hand of his in mine as his eyes stared into space. He graduated one or two years ahead of me and specialized in obstetrics and gynaecology. After Ahmed and I were divorced he wanted to marry me. I could not imagine him as a husband, could not imagine his small flabby hand touching my body. The mere idea made me shiver as though I were being touched by the tail of a catfish.

Twenty years went by before the day when I saw him on television. During Sadat's rule he became an important Islamic figure, travelled to Saudi Arabia and came back carrying gold and silver, bought a luxurious mansion in Heliopolis, and built a mosque in Old Cairo. Another twenty years went by and I ran into him in Zurich where I was attending an international congress on religion. He read a lengthy paper on Islam and Democracy. After I gave my talk he came up to me and shook hands. His hand had not changed in all the forty years. It was the same small flabby hand, slightly moist with sweat. His face however had changed a lot. It was pale and his jowls hung down. The hair on his head had fallen off, but his beard had grown long, dropping down to his chest. He stood on the platform in exactly the same way as he did when still a student, leaning with his body to the right, his left hand at his waist, his right arm up in the air, and remained silent for a long moment as he stared into space as though posing in front of that magic camera in the heavens.

*   *   *   *

Ahmed came back from the Canal Zone and started to attend classes. But he came back another person, his face thin and haggard, his eyes hidden behind dark glasses. A wounded lion, broken, defeated. The features of his face seeming to hang down. The freedom fighters had suffered a resounding defeat.

The winter was freezing, the air thick with a dark, damp mist. Northern winds bent the tree tops, women in black clothes walked behind their dead letting out terrible shrieks. The sports grounds were deserted and the cafeteria was closed. Uncle[14] Mahmoud was at home sick in bed. We sat on the wooden bench in the tennis courts. Dark clouds hid the sun and sadness hung heavy in the air. Ahmed had become very silent, rarely spoke, and his mind seemed to wander. The silence echoed in my ears. A tram clanged its way through Kasr Al-Aini Street, its bell sounding like the shrieks of women mourners. The call to prayer rose from the minaret of the mosque into the dark clouds. Raindrops wet the wooden bench. I felt them with the palm of my hand, wiped them off with my white handkerchief. The golden engagement ring still encircled my finger. On it was engraved the name of Ahmed Helmi. It gave off a pale thin glimmer in the half light of winter, was smooth like a thread of silk, and I could hardly feel it, yet it seemed the only thing to have a material consistency in a world that had become unreal. Thin as a fine hair it had the solidarity of gold and linked us together for ever.

For him defeat was worse than death. He could not forget the blood shed on the soil of the Canal Zone. His voice still speaks to me today although more than forty years have gone by. 'Can you imagine, Nawal, that the freedom fighters who fought against the British are now being hunted down like criminals by the government?'

This sentence has lived on in my memory ever since. The first time I heard what had happened to the freedom fighters was from Ahmed Helmi after the burning of Cairo on January 26, 1952. I heard

---

[14] A term of respect for elderly men.

exactly the same words a second time after the invasion of Egypt by England, France and Israel in 1956. Youths had volunteered by the thousands to participate in the popular resistance against the aggressors and then had been hunted down once the war was over. The third time was after Egypt's defeat in the 1967 war. During the Six Day War, as it was called, a small number of medical doctors had volunteered to give services in the war zone of Port Said, Ismaileya and Suez, only to pay a heavy price later on. The fourth time was in the October war of 1973.

Each time our country went through difficult times, young men and women volunteered to fight or to serve in zones that were exposed to danger. Each time the same tragedy was repeated. Once the crisis was over, these men and women, these heroes and freedom fighters, became criminals to be hunted down and put in prison or forced into exile, or obliged to hide unless they agreed to surrender to the ruling system and become the instruments of those who wielded power. The ruling classes in Egypt at all stages could not bear young people who organized for a cause. They could be used when needed. After that they had to be suppressed, called back to the house of obedience like a recalcitrant wife.

* * * *

After January 26, 1952, the day on which the city of Cairo was burnt, King Farouk dismissed Prime Minister Nahas Pasha and the Wafdist government. The new government presided over by Ali Maher directed all its efforts towards combating the movement for independence and the freedom fighters.

The prisons were filled with young nationalists belonging to different political currents, Muslim Brothers, Communists, Wafdists, young workers from the trade union movement, students who did not belong to any particular political party and freedom fighters back from the Canal Zone. Martial law was declared and the Federation of Trade Unions dissolved.

The city of Cairo lived its days in an atmosphere of dark defeat and silence. The smell of smoke rose from the charred walls.

By that time I had moved from the anatomy hall to the hospital. On July 23, 1952 I was attending a round in the surgical wards of the new Kasr Al-Aini Hospital. The professor teaching the round resembled Mahatma Ghandi. He was short with a thin, almost emaciated body, large black eyes that looked out from behind the glass of his metal-rimmed spectacles, and a broad forehead extending far back because of his baldness. His voice was soft, barely audible, his features like his voice neutral, unattractive. He was giving us a long talk about cancer of the bladder. A patient lay on the bed, his body thinner than that of the professor, the bones of his face showing from under the skin. The students in the round jostled about him, their stethoscopes hanging over the emaciated body. They competed for a chance to examine the 'case' like flies with truncular probosces settling down to suck a dead body.

The smell of pus and blood in the bedding nauseated me. I stood right at the rear, paralysed, unable to participate in what was going on. My eyes travelled over the long ward, over the thin haggard faces of the patients, most of them poor peasants who had come from villages like my village Kafr Tahla. The worms which caused bilharziasis had sucked the life-blood out of them, and what was left of it was sucked out by the eminent medical doctors to whose clinics they thronged, only to end up lying on a bed in Kasr Al-Aini University Hospital, where the endless rows of students kept jabbing their fingers mercilessly into their flesh in order to learn how to follow in the footsteps of their professors. Once finished off by them they ended as dead bodies to be carried to the dissecting hall, or put in a wooden coffin carried by a few men, with the women walking behind dressed in black robes and shrieking loudly until they arrived at the cemetery.

After the round was over we went out of the ward into the long wide corridor of the hospital. Batta and Safeya were with me. We walked along looking at the Nile through the big, tall windows covered in dust, their glass all broken. I stood at one of the windows for a moment breathing in the fresh air, ridding my lungs of the germs and the smell of disease. The golden sunrays danced over the small waves on the water, and a pure sky extended to the horizon. Nature seemed so full of beauty, so full of the joy of life, yet my heart was heavy with sadness. Why did joy always bring a feeling of sadness with it? Was it the sadness built up since I was born? Was it the pain and suffering I saw every day in the wards? Or was it because Ahmed continued to be absent from the school? I had no idea where he was. In prison? A dead body lying on the bank of Ismaileya stream, or hiding in one of the caves in the hills of Lahoun?

Suddenly as we stood there the patients rushed out of the wards shouting 'Long live the revolution!' I could see their mouths wide open, their arms waving in the air, their tattered shirts fluttering around their bodies. It was as though the corpses from the dissecting hall had suddenly risen from the dead and were shouting 'Long live the revolution!'

A youth whose legs were amputated had jumped out of bed leaving his crutches behind and was sliding on his buttocks over the floor of the corridor shouting madly 'Long live the revolution!' An old peasant stumbled along with the others shouting at the top of his voice. A woman, her belly big with child, let out long shrilling 'yooyoos' as she ran on bare feet. A small girl, her arm in plaster, lifted it high up above her head like a banner and walked along with tears streaming from her eyes as she shouted in her thin voice 'Long live the revolution!' In the wards the patients had been listening to the radio. Suddenly the music broke off for an important announcement which said that the army had taken over control of the country and that Farouk was no longer king.

From the men's wards arose a clamour of voices hailing the revolution. From the women's wards came the sharp shrilling of 'yooyoos' rising over the roar of male voices. Patients continued to stream out dressed in white cotton shirts, walking in their rubber slippers. The hospital nurses and cleaners were not long in joining the demonstrations of joy. They could be seen running amidst the throngs in the corridors dressed in their white uniforms and caps, wearing white rubber shoes or sandals. After a moment's hesitation the doctors joined in. They did not run but walked to preserve their dignity, dressed in their short white coats with stethoscopes dangling down from their necks. The crowds flowed into the front courtyard of the hospital. After a short while the students arrived followed by the nurse trainees, the cooks, the workers in the laundry section, and the janitors from the dissecting hall.

My body propelled itself into the crowd, moved by a will of its own. I began to shout with them 'Long live the revolution!' Batta waddled along in her high heels echoing 'Long live the revolution?' (with a Parisian 'r'). A funeral coming out of the hospital came to a stop. The men carrying the coffin put it down on the pavement and mixed with the crowd shouting 'Long live the revolution!' and the women who a moment ago had been mourning the defunct started to shrill out 'yooyoos' instead of shrieks.

I kept looking among the crowds for Ahmed's face. I wanted him to share in my joy. I spotted him advancing over the small bridge that linked the old with the new hospital. He had come out of the caves of Lahoun when he heard the news. The revolution brought with it a new hope. For the first time since we had met our arms stretched out to one another in an embrace, for the first time we discovered that we had arms and that arms could embrace. Before that we had only shaken hands, but later after we married and started to share the same bed my body no longer trembled the way it had trembled when we shook hands. I tried to understand why. Had it been my young imagination multiplying my feelings a hundred times? Or was it because sex proved to be no less disappointing than joining in the freedom fight?

That day when we embraced I realized that Ahmed was not the Ahmed I had known before. It was not my mind that told me that. It was something deeper, more genuine – the spontaneous feeling of my body not yet distorted by knowledge and reason. Ahmed had lost something, and that something would never return. He had left something behind him on the shores of Ismaileya. Was it his heart? Had he come back without a heart?

We went back to our eucalyptus tree. With the tips of our fingers we touched the names carved inside the heart, caressed the golden rings worn on our fingers. These rings remained the only material solid things in a world in which everything seemed to have become amorphous, to have lost its shape, or become enveloped in a mist which hid it from us. We clung on to our rings like a drowning man hangs on to anything in his reach, like a blind man searches in the darkness for a ray of light.

On July 26 King Farouk boarded his royal yacht for the last time. He stood on deck dressed in his white naval uniform looking down at the sea of Alexandria, the sea in which I had swum when still a child. I could remember my father standing on the northern balcony and saying 'Down with the King'. Now the king had fallen from his throne. He had been replaced by his infant child Ahmed, with a Tripartite Trusteeship Council to manage court matters until he grew up.

I was five years old when King Fouad died in 1936, and the young boy Farouk came back from England to inherit the throne. The streets of Alexandria resounded to the shouts of 'The King is dead, Long live the King!' The radio was singing King Farouk, King of the country, light of our eyes, flower of our nation. From the balcony the white round face of the child-king looked out over his people. He had become king overnight, knew nothing about the dark corridors of power and politics, was quickly surrounded by the three forces that wielded power: the court, the British and Al-Azhar,[15] by the three men who embodied these forces: Ahmed Hassanein, Ali Maher and Sheikh Al-Maraghi.

How did the child Farouk develop into a king no different from his father, into a corrupt, licentious assassin? Now here he was standing on the deck of his yacht taking a last look at Egypt, a look full of sadness and regret. Maybe he would have been better off had he not been born the son of a king. People in my village used to say: 'To be a sultan keep away from the sultan.'[16] Do sultans and kings suffer from a disease which is like cancer, where the sick cells devour the healthy ones, where greed and madness devour the self? King Farouk's greed and ambition knew no limits. He even tried to become the Caliph of all Muslims and receive his crown from the hands of God.

After King Farouk was forced to leave Egypt, Muhammad Naguib became the first Egyptian to rule since King Mena in ancient Egypt. He had the features of a peasant, rough and simple with an open smile. His voice was gruff, which made him sound like a man of the people.

At the beginning of the revolution, an amnesty was decreed for all political prisoners and colleagues of ours who belonged to the Muslim Brothers, or the Wafdist Party, or to no party at all. They were all released from prisons and concentration camps, all except the Communists who were not included in the amnesty. Safeya's brother Asaad and Rifa'a who was engaged to Samia remained in prison. Zakareya Mohieddin who was one of the Free Officers in the revolutionary movement that came to power made a declaration in which he said that Communists were social criminals and not members of a political movement. Samia pouted in disgust and said, 'You call this a revolution, Nawal? They're no more than a bunch of soldiers who carried out a putsch to replace British colonialism by American imperialism.'

One of the first measures carried out by the new regime was the promulgation of an agrarian reform which fixed the ceiling for land

---

[15] The thousand year-old theological university considered to be the centre of Islam.
[16] To be free, able to decide your own life, keep away from those who wield power.

ownership at 200 feddans. In addition, each child was allowed to own fifty feddans.[17]

In the month of July 1953, that is one year later, titles, political parties and the monarchy were abolished and Egypt became a republic.

The atmosphere in the country changed. People used to walk along with grim, silent faces. No-one said good morning or smiled at passers-by. Now the streets had changed. People there behaved as though they were at home. They chatted, smiled, said good morning, shook hands with complete strangers, asked about one another's health, about recent events, congratulated one another for the change of regime, discussed, tried to foretell future events, kept expecting changes to happen every day.

In the morning on my way to the medical school my ears would pick up some of the comments people made: 'At last God has set us free.' 'Could anyone have believed that the king's throne would collapse overnight.' 'Now, uncle, there is nothing called Pasha or Bey. Pasha is not an Arabic word, it is Turkish, we inherited it from the reign of the Osmanlis and the Mamelukes.' 'Do you mean to say that from now onwards we'll really be free?' 'Long live Muhammad Naguib!'

But as expected, the old forces and their political parties refused to surrender. The Pashas and landlords were not prepared to give up the land they owned without a fight. They gathered around Muhammad Naguib. They formed a powerful front which claimed that its aim was to defend democracy, freedom and the right to form political parties. This front grouped together leaderships from the Wafd, the Muslim Brothers and the Communists despite the feuds that had always existed between them, for in the political game enemies often unite against a common enemy who has become a danger to them. The same thing happens in children's stories. The cat and the mouse join hands against the lion or the tiger.

But the lion in this story had not yet appeared openly on the scene. The revolution was announced on the radio by Anwar Al-Sadat and at the same time many pictures of Muhammad Naguib were published in the newspapers. But my father spotted the lion standing in the photograph next to him. He pointed at him and said, 'This man is the real leader of the revolution, Nawal.'

---

[17] Around 80 hectares. Land in Egypt is very fertile and grows three crops a year.

At the beginning people used to hail Muhammad Naguib, proclaim his name. No-one knew Gamal Abd Al-Nasser. I asked my father, 'How did you discover that?' He answered, 'From his eyes.' So I looked at his eyes in the photograph. Big, dark, wide open eyes looking straight out of the picture from under a broad obstinate forehead. His sharp nose stood out in his face, slightly hooked. His thin lips were pressed together with determination or in anger, an anger that had kept growing since he was a child. Muhammad Naguib's features next to him looked ordinary, childish, as though he had not seen very much in his life.

I met Gamal Abd Al-Nasser face to face for the first time in 1962 during the National Congress of Popular Forces. The revolution was moving forwards, mobilizing to strike down the remaining bastions of feudalism and comprador capitalism and had announced what were called the Socialist Decrees. But my father did not witness these events. He had died three years before. When I looked into Gamal Abdel Nasser's face I found him more attractive than in his pictures. The cameras could not catch the strong glimmer in his big, black eyes. His skin was brown, the colour of fresh silt brought down by the Nile. He was tall, very tall, with a slight stoop to his shoulders like my grandmother and my father, walked slightly bent, taking long strides. Was he carrying the same load they had carried throughout their lives? They had never bowed under it. He too looked as though he could carry it with the same dignity with which my father had carried the load of feeding nine children, their mother, his mother and a sister who was divorced and lived in the village with her.

Now it was my time to take over the load. Normally it should have reverted to my elder brother, but my young brothers and sisters held a meeting after the death of my father and decided that their sister Nawal be nominated as trustee over them. My father's pension was not enough to support all these young girls and boys, most of whom were still either in school or at the university. I had to work to support them and to be able to care for my daughter Mona who continued to live with me after Ahmed Helmi and I had divorced.

Sometimes I feel that as a result my hair went grey at a very early age. But I rarely feel that way. Deep down inside me I know that I inherited quite a lot of things from my father and one of them was my white hair. When I was a child I used to watch the white hairs creep stealthily through the mass of thick hair which covered his head. His hair was black as the night and my hair was just as black when the white hairs started to steal through its strands like the light of dawn steals across the dark night, at the beginning of each day.

I graduated from medical school in 1954. My studies lasted six-and-a-half years. To me they were like a sentence of hard labour through which I had to live. Lectures were lengthy and boring, and we were supposed to memorize everything as through studying the Qur'an. We used to learn them almost by heart, spell them out in the exams and then forget them.

The results were hung on a board at the main entrance, and as we stood staring at them we would discover all of a sudden that the sons of our professors were all geniuses, since their names always came at the top of the list. Having scored the top marks they then went on to occupy the top posts in the university hospitals and on the staff of the School of Medicine. The throne was inherited from father to son in the Kingdom of Medicine as it used to be in the Kingdom of Egypt.

Nervous breakdowns amongst the students during and after the final exams were quite common. They often had recourse to the use of stimulants (amphetamines) or tranquillizers (valium) to overcome insomnia. While preparing for the exams, to keep awake for long hours some of them would use maxitone. The professors had little pity when they dealt with poor patients, and much less when they were dealing with those who would be their competitors in the future.

I was very attentive, and never failed to turn up to a lecture or a round, or for work in the laboratory. My professors and teachers expressed their admiration for my assiduous performance. I was always on the alert, my five senses tuned to every word, every gesture, ready to divine what was going to be said even before the words dropped from their lips. During the holidays too I was to be seen doing the rounds of the hospital wards, looking over the diagnosis and treatment written on the sheets, checking them by examining the patients. I wasted no time, heading straight for what I wanted, never dawdled in the courtyard to talk to a colleague or one of the staff, went in and out of school like an arrow, looked straight in people's faces and did not sway on high-heeled shoes.

One of the assistant professors who made the rounds with us in the surgical wards was called Dr Rashad. He had long fingers, as tough and strong as nails, and when he percussed a patient's chest or his abdomen I felt as though they could easily pierce it. He used to press his stethoscope down on a patient's ribs as though pressing down on the ground with his shoe. There was a small child in the ward called Mostafa whom I always remember. His features resembled those of my cousin in the village, the son of my Aunt Nefissa. He was ten years old, the same age as me when I first fell in love in Menouf. His skin was brown like mine, his eyes like mine, large and black, shining brightly. A few days after he entered the hospital the sparkle in his eyes had gone, to be replaced by a dark cloud of sadness. He stifled a moan of pain every time some one pressed down on his chest with a stethoscope. Every day forty or fifty stethoscopes would press down on his chest. During rounds the students pushed against each other as they tried to hear the blowing murmurs in his heart. He held back his tears but sometimes I could see the glimmer in his eyes as he did so, watch him choke a sigh of pain under the stern gaze of Dr Rashad. If he hesitated to lift his shirt, the commanding voice would ring out: 'Take off your shirt, or I'll take out your eye.' If he struggled to keep it on, down would come Dr Rashad's iron hand with a resounding slap on his cheek, and up would come the little faded peasant robe he wore over his shirt. His ribs were small, fragile, his chest like that of a small chick. I could hear them crackle under the metal of the stethoscope. Were all these ears deaf, blocked by the rubber tubes they had pushed into them, at the end of which dangled a rounded piece of metal like a bell that they pressed down heavily on a small area below the left nipple, leaving a round pit below the rib, over the heart where the murmur was to be heard?

Their ears failed to hear the murmur no matter how hard they tried, no matter how hard they pressed the heavy metal bell down on the little chest. Maybe their ears were blocked by the dust of the streets, of the lecture rooms or hospital wards, or by the dust that had accumulated in them over the years. They used to clean their ears with a matchstick and yet they still could not hear the murmur. It was a faint murmur, the almost inaudible sound of blood moving over a roughened valve which could not close fast or well enough. Like the whisper of a spring breeze moving over a newly born leaf.

Dr Rashad would extract a silver coin from his pocket and throw it out on the table, just as you would bet on a horse, or on a poker table. 'This shilling will be won by whoever succeeds in telling me what kind of murmur you have heard in the boy's heart.' He would pronounce the sentence in English like everything else in the School of Medicine. We were taught in English, lectures were in English, books in English, diseases and murmurs described in English. Even our jokes were made in English.

The students rushed forward to crowd around the little patient again. They stepped on one another's feet, they jostled with their elbows, their shoulders, their arms. One of them would push his elbow into someone's belly and finally get through to reach the boy's chest and plant his stethoscope valiantly on the designated spot like a victorious flag. The metal bell came down like the head of a cobra snake attacking with its writhing body to plunge its fangs into the little groove below the left nipple. From the child arose a silent cry which no-one heard.

The girl students had no place in these competitions, for how could a virgin girl push her body through between the bodies of these males to listen to the murmur and win the silver coin?

I used to stand right at the back and look between the bodies crowding round the bed at the little boy's face. Our eyes would meet, and his eyes would hold on to mine, as though my eyes were those of a mother, an aunt, or an elder sister. He would stare at me with a long beseeching look. It reminded me of the way a lamb would look at me when the butcher's knife was ready to descend on its neck as a sacrifice for the Great Festival (Id Al-Kabir).

There I stood, silent and helpless. The eyes would follow me in my dreams. They looked the same. Big eyes, glistening with suppressed tears, dark and slightly bulging, the whites a little yellow, shot with fine threads of blood. They stared at me out of the night, wide open, without lids, or lashes. Not a sound, not a movement, just that dumb, beseeching look that made me awaken suddenly, bathed in sweat.

Dr Rashad behaved in the surgical wards in exactly the same way as Dr Amr did in the dissecting hall. In front of the head of section he stood at attention, his arms and legs rigid, like a polite student or a young virgin. But once his superior was out of sight, Dr Rashad would stretch his arms and legs, walk up and down the ward with his head tipped backwards on his neck like a peacock or a turkey cock in exactly the same way as the head of his section. He imitated him in everything, even in the way he pronounced certain words, or letters, to give the impression that he came from the upper classes who were in the habit of speaking French. Like him he would laugh out loudly, throw his head backwards, eye the girl students and say in the same sarcastic way, 'Young beautiful vases, why are you all so silent? Doesn't one of you want to win the shilling? Come on, Batta, do something, Safeya, Fawzeya, Samia, Nabeela, any one of you, come on now, what's wrong with all of you?' But when it came to mentioning my name in the same tones he would hesitate and move on to someone else. I do not know why. Maybe because I would be staring at him with a look full of anger. The word vases sounded to my ear like the word slaves. My unblinking black fiery stare perhaps scared him away.

Never in my life have I detested a man the way I detested Dr Rashad. At the time I did not know that a man is often attracted to the woman that refuses him, that he has no peace until he overcomes her resistance, wages a battle to the last breath, mobilizes all his weapons to win her over.

Dr Rashad's weapons were a tall building overlooking the Nile, a big farm in Al-Sharkeya Province, a clinic in the centre of Cairo, and his long blue Chevrolet car. He used to sidle over to me in it as I stood at the bus-stop, jut his head out of the window and say, 'Come, Nawal, I'll take you home.'

I pulled on the muscles of my face to extract a smile from it and answered 'Thank you, Dr Rashad, it's a short ride on the bus.' But he would not accept my polite refusal. 'Come, Nawal, I'll take you home. Better than pushing yourself into a crowded bus.' 'Thank you, Dr Rashad, thank you,' I would say shaking my head in refusal. I kept refusing, and he kept insisting.

Deep inside me something held back. My body said no to him when we shook hands, said no to the iron grasp of his fingers. My mind said no, and so did that strange intangible obscure thing, half-angel, half-devil that dwelt within my body and that we call spirit.

To this very day I do not know why I detested him so violently. But hate like love happens without reason, or has a reason of its own which does not belong to the mind, nor can be fathomed by it. They are like all the important truths in life which the human mind fails to understand. Like the existence of God. These important truths are always surrounded by doubt, but I never doubted my feelings towards people, the feelings born in a first encounter. I like or dislike a face at the first look. Eyes for me are like windows. Through them I look into the depths, into what other people sometimes call the soul, and once I have looked I know. After that the bones of the face and the mouth complete the picture I form in my mind.

Since I was a young child of seven and throughout the years this feeling for people has not changed. I have never lost faith in my first impression. It suggests all sorts of things to me, things that my conscious reason often fails to see. Yet for a very long time I knew nothing about what is called the subconscious, even after reading Sigmund Freud. This area is still surrounded by clouds of mystery, but the clouds are dispersing the more we find out about the human mind, the more science tells us about the brain cells and how they function. Nevertheless, experiences in life often unveil more of the truth than science is able to reveal.

In the summer of 1957, before my mother died, Dr Rashad paid us a visit at home. He came to ask my father for my hand. It was a hot and dusty day. He stopped his long blue Chevrolet in front of the house, and the eyes of our neighbours peered out at it from their windows. The relatives of my father and mother who were staying with us at the time were bowled over by his car, watched him as he got out of it, tall and upright and dressed in a shark-skin suit.

My father received him in the drawing-room. Everything about him seemed to shine. His hair, his shoes, his ring, his necktie, and his dark glasses, which he took off once seated in the chair. Everything except his eyes. They looked dull. I kept searching for a spark in them, asking myself when the shine had gone. Had it happened during his childhood? When he was a young student? Or later on when he became an assistant professor in the School of Medicine?

My father said, 'Welcome, Rashad Bey.'

He answered, 'I am happy to meet you, Saadawi Bey.'

They kept exchanging titles although all titles had been abolished by the revolution, sat stiff and upright in the chairs of the brightly lit drawing-room. The servant girl walked in carrying the old tarnished silver tray with the coffee cups on it. I remember tripping over with the tray at the age of ten and spilling the contents on my suitor's lap as he sat in a chair. The small servant girl almost tripped over too, her slipper caught in the flayed threads of the carpet bought for my mother's wedding. It had been worn away by the years like the features on my mother's tired face.

The tray tipped over and almost fell into Dr Rashad's lap, but at the last moment the poor girl regained her balance. A half-suppressed laugh escaped me as I sat in a corner of the room. My mind kept going back to Menouf, to the days when my music teacher Miss Yvonne used to visit us at home. As I sat in front of her, my foot would move stealthily over the carpet to hide the hole in it.

But the revolution had changed many things. Now I was no longer ashamed of the signs of poverty in our home. Now I no longer tried to avoid my colleagues seeing my peasant aunt when they visited me at home.

'Welcome, Rashad Bey.'

'Welcome to you, Saadawi Bey.'

They seemed to be stuck with their welcomes. I was wearing an old frock made of gabardine. It was a sad grey. My heart was heavy with sadness, but my father's eyes were shining with joy. This was a suitable husband for his daughter, not that bogus guerrilla fighter who had failed to finish his studies.

My mother had not come to the drawing-room. It was three months before her death and she was lying sick in bed with breast cancer. My Aunt Ni'mat, who had come on a visit that day, was sitting on the edge of her bed when Dr Rashad arrived. She peered out through a crack in the door and came back to my mother gasping with excitement. 'A medical doctor as big as life and handsome as the moon. Any girl in the world would hope for nothing better. Yet I hear Nawal doesn't want him. Why Zaynab, why?'

'I don't know why, Ni'mat. Ask her,' my mother said. That day Aunt Ni'mat asked me why I did not want to marry Dr Rashad. I did not know what to answer. There was nothing that seemed wrong with him. 'I don't know, Auntie Ni'mat. I don't love him.' Aunt Ni'mat waved her hand derisively in the air. 'Love? What nonsense. All you got out of love is what you are now, a divorced woman.'

The word 'divorced' pronounced in Aunt Ni'mat's voice pierced my ear like an insult. Nobody marries a divorced woman. People describe her as a 'second-hand' woman, something that has already been used. They say that if a man marries her it is like drinking out of someone else's cup. That is how writers like Abdel Halim Abdallah, Yusif Al-Siba'i and Naguib Mahfouz described her.

I fought hard at home to avoid being married to Dr Rashad, just as hard as I had fought to marry Ahmed Helmi. I believed that the only reason for which I should marry was love. Ever since I was a child the word 'marriage' or 'bridegroom' sounded repugnant to me. Love had wiped away this feeling, had helped me embark on a first marriage. But love seemed to be short-lived, like the first flowers of spring that die early. Or maybe marriage destroys love in one way or another. There was something unnatural in the institution. Was it the law of obedience? One of the stipulations in the marriage law said: 'A husband possesses his wife, but she does not possess him.'[18] The duty of the husband is to provide for his wife. The duty of the wife is to obey her husband.

The word obedience had an ugly ring to it. To me it sounded like an insult, a characteristic of slaves. People kept saying that obedience was a virtue, but to me it seemed the opposite, for it required that I abolish my reason and my will, do what other people told me to do. It would lead me to lose my quality as a human being, to become what was called a 'female', like obedient wives or domesticated animals who live locked behind closed walls and dare not disobey their masters.

There was another stipulation in the marriage law that was worse. A husband had the absolute right to divorce whenever he wanted, or to marry a second wife. On the other hand, a wife could not divorce her husband except in court, and the judges who decided were all men. If she married a second husband while she was still married to the first, she was considered an adulterer, but a man could marry four wives and yet be considered a law-abiding and moral person. No one could describe him as having committed adultery.

I felt that the marriage law was immoral, a law against true morality, since all people should be considered equal before the law irrespective of gender, class, race, colour or religion. Moral principles should apply to everyone without distinction between male and female, rich and poor, rulers and ruled.

Whenever I read the law I became full of anger. Marriage under it would be against all reason even if I loved the man, so what if I did not even love him?

The first divorce in my life had been a unique experience, like a slave freed of his chains, like a bird let out of its cage to fly, or a prisoner released from behind iron bars. I held the divorce papers in my hand as though clutching on to a lifeboat that had saved me from drowning. It was a glimmering, shining moment in my life, like that moment when I held my graduation certificate pressed under my arm, or when I held the first salary envelope in my hand. That moment too was one of freedom. Now I was independent, could provide for myself, no longer needed money from my father, no longer had to obey him, even though he never made me feel that he expected obedience in return for my keep. Throughout his life he

---

[18] At that time.

taught me self-respect, taught me to argue with him, tell him what I thought, discuss my feelings even about the existence of the God in whom he believed.

I did not need a husband to provide for me. I was a medical doctor. I had become a different being, neither male nor female. I examined men and women, rose above the distinctions imposed by gender, overrode laws that governed the life of women, was no longer subject to what was called the 'personal law'. Under the personal law an independent woman was reduced to dependency, could no longer decide for herself, was like a child below the age of full citizenship, or a mental case requiring supervision.

Once married a woman had to accept her husband as a trustee. He possessed her body and her mind. This was enshrined in religious jurisprudence. It allowed him to beat her as a means of correction if she disobeyed his orders. It allowed him to marry three other women, but if he saw her with another man, he could shoot her with a gun and be declared innocent by a court, for he was a forthright man who had insisted on defending his honour.

The word 'honour' rung strangely in my ears, filled me with a dark anger. Honour was always linked to the behaviour of women, to a particular part in the lower half of their bodies. Honour was never linked to the behaviour of men. The only thing considered unworthy in a man was an empty pocket. If his pocket was full of money then he was respectable and honourable even if he had sex with several women who were or were not married to him.

The voices of the men and women in my father's and mother's families rose in a single clamour. What's wrong with Dr Rashad? What's wrong with him? The only thing which makes a man unworthy is his empty pocket. Dr Rashad owns a building, has a farm, runs his own clinic and rides a beautiful Chevrolet car. What more do you want?'

The question went round and round in my mind as he sat in front of me in the drawing-room. My father was engrossed in a discussion about politics. His enthusiasm for Gamal Abd Al-Nasser had increased tenfold after the nationalization of the Suez Canal in 1956. He had almost enlisted as a volunteer in the popular resistance against the tripartite invasion.

'Right from the beginning of the revolution I kept insisting that Gamal Abd Al-Nasser was the real leader, even when Muhammad Naguib was in power. Or do you see things differently, Rashad Bey?'

'No, I agree with you, Saadawi Bey. The problem with Abd Al-Nasser is that he's turning more and more to the left, moving closer to the Soviet Union, and that puts our country in great danger.'

'What is the danger, Rashad Bey?'

'Communism. Communism is a great danger, Saadawi Bey.'

'Gamal Abd Al-Nasser is not a Communist. He is a Muslim who believes in Allah and the Prophet. The problem is that America refused to fund the Aswan High Dam project and he was left with no alternative other than to nationalize the Suez Canal Company. We just managed to get rid of the British colonialists so why should we allow the Americans to come in, Rashad Bey?'

'I am against American imperialism, Saadawi Bey, but I also oppose Russian imperialism.'

'Gamal Abd Al-Nasser is a nationalist who believes in independence and has refused to join any alliance or pact, and he will never allow the imperialists into our country, whether Russian or otherwise.'

I sat silent in my corner following the discussion. Neither of them asked me what I thought. The discussion went on but I was out of it, as though not there. Why did a woman always disappear once the husband appeared on the scene? Dr Rashad was not my husband yet. He was still a potential bridegroom, a suitor who had come to ask my father for my hand, yet he had already abolished my existence, and here was my father ignoring me too, not asking me what I thought of Gamal Abd Al-Nasser or even of Dr Rashad himself, whereas until then he had always encouraged me to voice my opinion whenever a question arose.

After the visit was over my father asked me, 'What is it that you find missing in Dr Rashad, Nawal?' I was unable to answer. Throughout the visit I had sat there looking at him as he talked to my father enveloped in a shining shark-skin suit, his shoes made of shining leather, his tie of shining silk, the ring on his finger, the pin in his necktie, his teeth when he smiled, his well-greased hair, everything I looked at was shining, everything except his eyes. How could I say to my father that what attracted me to living creatures was the shine in their eyes. Not any shine. The eyes of a wild cat or a tiger were shining. What I was looking for was a special shine that could be found only in the eyes of some human beings. I felt that Dr Rashad's eyes were full of cruelty, that now and then I could spot a glimmer, but it was always sharp and short and calculating despite the soft, delicate way in which he was saying things to my father.

This time no-one in the family told me off when Dr Rashad disappeared from the scene. But the atmosphere at home was heavy with silence, a silence which lasted several days broken only by my Aunt Ni'mat. She stopped me one day in the hall, gave me an owlish stare and said: 'You should not be so blown up with conceit, my girl. Marrying a woman who is divorced is like partaking of a stale melon. It wouldn't be so bad if you were only divorced, but into the bargain you have a small girl!'

The word 'girl' shot out from her lips like a slug of lead, like a frozen piece of heavy sadness which had accumulated in her ever since she was born, then trapped in a loveless marriage, to become a divorced woman and already dead before the time for her to die had come.

The word flew out of her mouth like a heavy spit, as grey as the grey of the pupils in her eyes. It went through my head, carried my memories way back to that day when I was born a girl, when a silence descended over the whole universe, stifled the 'yooyoos' of joy in the throats of the women, made my appearance in this world a cause for sadness in the family rather than a cause for joy.

Ever since I was a child a question had never ceased to hammer in my mind. Why should my presence in the world be a cause for sadness in the family? I loved my parents even though I knew how they felt about me. But later on another question started to occupy my mind. How could my presence be transformed from a cause for sadness into something that could bring them happiness? How could I extract a smile or even a laugh from their lips pressed so tight together? The only moments of joy in the family were when a bridegroom appeared on the scene. Features would relax, laughter would ring out and the 'yooyoos' would follow in cascades. My moments of happiness were linked to other things, to my achievements in school, or in my medical studies, or in my writing. These areas were considered by them to belong to men. The female areas were elsewhere, where they had always been: in the toilets cleaning the bowls, in the hall washing the tiles, or in the kitchen peeling onions and garlic.

I kept asking myself how could their hearts change and feel joy at my success as a doctor or a writer rather than at how well I cleaned the toilet bowls? How could the dreams of my father and mother begin to see me dressed in a doctor's coat, or a writer's cloak rather than in a long wedding dress and satin shoes?

It turned out to be a long and arduous process full of obstacles and retreats. At times my father and mother would be happy at my success in medical school but the happiness in the family would evaporate as soon as I did not yield to their will in other matters concerning my life, or when I gave birth to a girl instead of a boy.

The word girl when it emerged from their lips had an intonation which filled me with anger especially when Aunt Ni'mat pronounced it. Deep inside me I had decided that if I gave birth to a girl she would be, in spite of whatever they said or did, a real cause for joy. I would celebrate her coming into the world with happiness no matter how they felt. I would let out a 'yooyoo' lasting for a thousand years, rising in space to the seventh heaven, piercing through the ears of even gods and devils – if they had ears. I would proclaim from the rooftops that I had delivered a girl, that with her I would challenge the whole world, make it change so that people would rejoice at the birth of a girl even more than that of a boy.

In the middle of spring, on April 8, 1956 my daughter Mona was born. My labour pains disappeared as soon as I went into labour, as though they were nothing but an illusion imposed on women by the verse, 'They shall give birth in pain and suffering and shall lust after thine husband but he shall possess thee.'

I had read this verse in the Old Testament in primary school when we were still living in Menouf. My father told me the Old Testament, like the New Testament, was God's book and that God had sent them down to light the way for all people, that, as well as the Qur'an, Muslims should also believe in these two books. But my child's mind found it difficult to accept what this verse said. When I read it, it seemed to form a small pebble and stick in my throat.

When I gave birth to my daughter a wave of extraordinary happiness swept over me, a feeling which I had not known before and which is called motherhood. In my dreams I had never seen myself as a mother carrying a child on her shoulder, or feeding it from her breast. I used to dream of myself carrying a gun to free my country, or grasping a scalpel to dissect a body, or holding a pen to write stories. But when I gave birth to her something in my body changed, something like a river started to flow through it, a feeling called motherhood created over centuries of history, stored in the body, in the mind and in the spirit. The three were now united in one thing called motherhood. My mind, my body and my spirit fused into a solid, strong being called a mother. In this mother's arms lay the new-born child.

This ability to repeat myself in another body, which had my features, my fingers, my eyes shining with the light of sunrise, this discovery of motherhood flowing like a river of warm milk from my body to hers seemed to me like a miracle. It reminded me of my mother when she used to hold me in her arms. She and I were one being. I used to open my eyes, wake up as I lay on her breast, as though it was the only shore in a vast sea where I could rest.

The beat under my child's ribs kept time with the beat of my heart. She stretched out her little hand and held on to mine. Her eyes were like the eyes of my mother, honey-coloured. They stared at me with amazement, with the joy of discovering her mother. The small fingers curled around my thumb in the same way as my fingers used to curl around that of my mother.

I can see her face now as she looks at me and laughs. I do not remember when she laughed for the first time. She had a laugh that was all her own, different from that of any other child. It rang out in our home, went through the walls into the street, filled the whole universe with its ring. I could hear it when I walked the streets or stood in the operating theatre, or sat writing at my desk in the office, or rode in a train, or a bus or a tram. It had such a wonderful ring in my ears, like pure water splashing in a silver vessel. I hear it in my sleep and it seems real, hear it when awake and it seems like a dream.

I hold her to my breast and feed her like my mother did with me. The smell of her body in my nose resembles the smell of my mother when I was a child, when the warm milk flowed through me like life-blood.

When it is my birthday her voice comes to me over the telephone. It crosses the Mediterranean Sea, Europe and the Atlantic Ocean, then flies over from the south-east coast of America to the small town of Durham. It travels across space and distance unhindered, for nothing can stop it, neither on land, in the sea, or in the sky. It comes right up to my ear as I lie in bed at dawn, goes through me like the first rays of the sun. 'Many happy returns of the day, Mummie.'

Every year she reminds me of my birthday. She never forgets. Her voice reaches me no matter where I am, wherever the winds of chance have carried me in exile far away from home. The telephone will ring and her voice will come to me as though in a dream. 'Many happy returns of the day, Mummie.'

I forget my birthday, never celebrate it. So I say: What day are we Mona?' I can hear that special ring coming to me across the lines as she says 'Today is your birthday, Mummie.' Her laugh goes through me as I lie half-asleep in bed, like a warm flow of feeling. It brings me back to life. 'You're kidding, Mona. D'you mean to say a whole year has passed? Time is flying so fast, it seems like only yesterday when you last wished me Happy Birthday.'

My peasant grandmother used to say: 'He whose body is covered by the days is naked.'[19] I repeat the proverb on the phone. I hear her laugh, the same unchanging laugh I used to hear when she was a child, jump out of bed the way I used to when I was seven years old, open the windows wide, let the sun and the air flow in. This is the beginning of another year in a life which has lasted so long. And this is my daughter remembering me, despite distance and time, taking me back to where I belong, embracing me with a motherly warmth. Her voice comes to me even when all other voices have become silent. Even if everybody else forgets me she will not forget. She always makes room for me in her bed, her door is always open to let me in, her heart has a place for me no matter how full it is. If I am tired or sick she is there by my side, for me to rest my head on her breast, just as she rested her head on mine when she was a child. Now she has grown up and become the well-known writer Mona Helmi. Her fingers look like mine as they curl around her pen. Her letters are bold, engraved on the moon, and her name printed on the page makes my heart beat so strongly.

When I was a child I thought that my father's heart was bigger than that of my mother, big enough to hold within it his love for God and his country. I never heard my mother speak about God or country. To me it seemed that fatherhood was superior to motherhood, something at a higher level, in the same way as men were superior to women and told them what to do. Then as the years went by I discovered that a mother's heart is bigger than that of a father, that nothing in the whole world is bigger than a mother's heart for she does not expect obedience in exchange for her love.

---

[19] A popular proverb which means that a person who depends on time to solve his/her problems will be disappointed because time flies by.

Motherhood goes back in history to a time when a father had no way of knowing his children. Fatherhood only became known when class patriarchal society had established itself and imposed monogamous marriage on women. Motherhood is like sun and rain and plants, a quality and product of nature which does not require laws or systems in order to exist.

My daughter was born in the spring of 1956. Two months later the country witnessed changes which were welcomed with joy by the great majority of people. On June 8, 1956 a new constitution was proclaimed and martial law abolished. On July 2, all political prisoners, including the Communists, were set free. It was not long before other momentous events took place. On the July 23, 1956 Gamal Abd Al-Nasser's voice resounded on the radio as he announced the nationalization of the Suez Canal. My daughter was four months old. It was as though her birth signalled the inauguration of a new era of happiness in every home. The prisoners were received with open arms. Their return contributed to the general joy, to the optimism which everyone felt at the time. Safeya's brother As'ad came home. His sister had become a medical doctor in the University Children's Hospital and had married its assistant director. Rifa'a came out to marry Samia and I attended their wedding. Batta married a professor in the medical school, and started to share a big clinic with him in Dokki Square.

But I was looking for something different, a place that would take me away from the routine drudge of work in Cairo to where I could live a new experience. I was yearning to go back to the village. Perhaps the birth of my daughter and the loss of interest in the things which made Cairo attractive to others made me remember my childhood.

Since my daughter was born I had begun to ask myself whether she had not become the most important thing in my life, whether she was not the only justification for my having fallen in love, married and then divorced. Nothing apart from this small being seemed to have any significance in my life, not even her father. It was as though he had never existed, as though there was no need for his existence, like the drone which dies off once it has fertilized the queen bee.

THREE

The Village Doctor

It was a warm September day in the year 1956. I turned my back on Cairo, left it behind. Cairo was not the soil from which I had grown. Not a flower bloomed on its tarmac roads, and if it did, heavy heels, or iron wheels would run it over. My stride on the earth was powerful, big like my village grandmother. I needed space, yearned for the smell of green fields, of mud ovens baking bread.

I held my daughter in my arms, wrapped in a pink shawl knitted for her out of soft wool, and ran to catch the train as I had done when still a child. I had a child's heart inside my woman's body, enjoyed riding in a train, and sitting near the window. I sat watching the schoolchildren as they ran over the platform towards the doors letting out cries of joy. The picture of Gamal Abd Al-Nasser rose high up on the wall. He was the hero of many battles fought since his speech on March 17, 1953, one year before I graduated.

On that day we sat around a radio in the School of Medicine listening to him: 'We reject foreign military pacts that hide their real aims behind what is called mutual defence. The defence of our region is a matter which concerns us alone. A people that lives under the yoke of imperialism cannot be expected to defend its own oppression, to accept it and maintain it, because it fears a hypothetical aggression from some other sources. We demand the complete, unconditional withdrawal of all foreign troops from our country.'

It took another three years and three months before the British forces were finally withdrawn from Egypt. On June 17, 1956 the ship

Ivan Gibb left the port of Suez carrying the last contingent of British troops. British occupation had ended after having lasted for seventy-two years, only to attempt a return four months later with the tripartite invasion of Egypt.

On the train seat in front of me sat a young schoolgirl about ten years old, wearing a cotton uniform with small blue squares printed on it, her satchel held tightly on her knees. Four years ago I had taken my first train ride from Menouf to Cairo wearing a primary school uniform very much like hers. At that time I was escaping the village to go to the city. Now I was a young woman going back to the village to escape the city. On the first trip I had nothing apart from a pencil with which to write and my blue notebook. Now I had a graduate degree and people addressed me as 'Doctor'.

But we graduated as doctors without having given a single injection. During my year as trainee in the university hospital I taught myself how to do minor operations, including evacuations (abortions) and appendectomies. All these were done behind the back of the resident doctors who insisted on monopolizing all operations.

I used to hear my father say 'The university is no different from our schools. It does not teach anything. If people were given real knowledge none of our rulers would remain where they are. Our military academy produces people who are ignorant, and now they are ministers, so what do you expect?' My mother would ask him laughingly, 'Sayed, if they made you Minister of Education, what would you do?'

The name 'Sayed' never escaped the lips of my mother until after she had given birth to her fifth child. Before that she had always referred to him as 'he'. Her ninth child was born without her ever having undressed in front of her husband, and when I married for the first time, I too never took off my clothes in front of my husband. I laughed at these thoughts as I sat in the train and the little girl sitting in front of me looked at me with her shining black eyes and smiled. I opened my bag, brought out a small mirror and took a quick look at my eyes. My eyes were shining. The train was taking me further and further away from Cairo. I felt like a prisoner breaking out from behind iron bars. The houses, their walls black with smoke, were retreating quickly into the background and the world was opening up towards the horizon, with a blue sky above, and green fields below getting wider and wider on either side as the train moved north into the delta.

My big bag lay beside me on the seat, half of it filled with clothes, the remaining half with new books on medicine and philosophy, novels in Arabic and in English, and my secret diary.

The train entered Benha[1] station. Mona woke up and smiled at me. Whenever she looked at me her eyes filled with light. Before she was born my mind had always been occupied with ponderous thoughts and I missed many small wonderful things around me, but now I was living intimate feelings that had never before been reflected in my diary.

I got down at Benha station. The platform was crowded with people: civil servants dressed in suits, some of them wearing fezzes, peasants wearing long *gallabeyas* and skullcaps, city women in short dresses reaching above their knees and village women in their long black robes with a *tarha*[2] wrapped around their heads, the younger ones in coloured robes with their hair hanging down in long braids. The station chief blew into his whistle, his cheeks full of air, the vendor of sesame bread and Greek cheese called out in a characteristic clipped tone 'Sameet, sameet', and the schoolchildren kept shouting with joy as they raced across the platform, throwing their satchels at one another or into the air.

Railway stations filled me with a feeling of joy, with the bustle of life, with the smells of smoke, and fresh sesame bread, with a desire to challenge the world, to be on the move, to see places and people I had never seen before.

I walked with a light step, carrying Mona on my arm, and with the bag held in my hand. She looked at me in wonder. Why was her mother walking so fast, where was she taking her at such an eager pace? I sang to her, 'Run, run, run, take me quickly to where I want to go,' and she shook her head to the rhythm of the song the way my mother said I used to do when she sang to me.

I took a taxi from Benha to Kafr Tahla,[3] ten kilometres away. The streets in Benha were dusty, full of potholes and bumps. Our route took us up to the banks of the Nile. The taxi was old and decrepit, the glass of its windows all broken, the doors rattled, and the wheels made a loud noise on the road. It kept going up and down with the bumps like a swing and Mona kept gurgling with laughter. Every time she laughed the driver was delighted and said with amusement:

---

[1] The provincial capital of Kalioubeya Province.
[2] A long veil or shawl that does not cover the face.
[3] The author's village.

'This car is blessed. It's like a cat with nine lives. Before it I had a cab with a horse. What a cab, and what a horse, a real horse! But God suddenly remembered him, decided to take him away. I buried him close to my father. When he died I was much sadder than when my father died, because he was really of good descent, ate little and worked very hard. Maybe that's why God took him away. You know, God always takes away things that are genuine and have value.'

'May God prolong your life and that of your car,' I said.

'This is a very old car almost from the days of Noah but God wanted to compensate me for the loss of my horse. It runs as well as a horse even though it's made of tin and neither eats, nor drinks, nor dies. God put his spirit into tin, not one spirit but seven of them.'

Mona kept staring at the driver. His head was wrapped in a white scarf with red fringes. She kept putting out her little hand to pull on the fringe and laughed whenever he moved his head to make the fringes dance or pointed to the Nile and said 'Look at the sea, how beautiful it is. You don't have a sea like that in Misr![4]

The air was fresh, smelt of silt and green fields, and the smoke of the city was being cleansed by it from my body and my lungs. The past kept moving further and further away and after a while had disappeared with the city. It was as though I had never lived anywhere else except in this particular spot on the banks of the Nile, in a moment of time which seemed to extend to infinity.

The men and women of the village had gathered around the door of the health unit to which I had been posted. As soon as I got down from the car the 'yooyoos' of the women shrilled out. I heard voices shouting: 'A thousand greetings to our lady, the doctor. You have brought light with you to Tahla, Kafr Tahla, Digwa and Al-Ramla[5] all the way as far as Benha. She is our doctor, the Saadawi daughter of Sayed Bey, may God prolong his life for his good deeds have been showered on all of us. A thousand greetings, doctor. You have brought light[6] to the health unit!'

The combined health unit was a complex of newly constructed small white buildings that lay like pigeons in the midst of green fields. They housed three distinct sections: the health unit, the social services unit and the educational or school unit.

---

[4] 'Misr', meaning 'Egypt', is sometimes used to mean Cairo. Villagers call the Nile the sea.

[5] Villages in the area where the author was born.

[6] Light, the antithesis of darkness, is a symbol of everything that is good.

One of the projects implemented by the revolutionary regime in 1956 was the establishment of combined health units in rural areas. It was run by a bureaucratic administrative apparatus based in Cairo called the Supreme Council for Services, headed by a man called Fouad Galal. The headquarters were housed in a luxurious palatial building on Kasr Al-Aini Street right behind Parliament House. Later on, at the time of Sadat, it was turned over to a new institution known as Majlis Al-Shoura (Consultative Council) which people called sarcastically Majlis Al-Shourba (literally, Soup Council, meaning a place where you cook things up in a corrupt and chaotic way without rules or regulations).

I had met Fouad Galal only once, during a big meeting held to celebrate the dispatch of the first group of doctors to the combined health units. The doctors being sent were all males since the Supreme Council had refused to nominate women to rural areas.

Fouad Galal sat on a very high platform surrounded by the other members of the Supreme Council. Above his head hung a picture of Gamal Abd Al-Nasser in a gilt frame. The wall was decorated with designs painted in gold and the high-backed chair on which Fouad Galal sat resembled a throne. Before the revolution, on the same chair, in the same palace, had sat another man, and hanging over his head was a picture of King Farouk. After the death of Gamal Abd Al-Nasser the man sitting on the chair was replaced by another man, and the picture hanging over his head became that of Sadat. Today on the same chair, in the very same palace there sits another man with the picture of Mobarak hanging over his head in the same gilt frame.

As the years go by the picture in the gilt frame keeps changing as one ruler replaces another. There it hangs high over the head of one man after the other, over the heads of men who bow down before it as though worshipping a pagan god, who speak in low tones lest the man in the picture hear what they say, shoot quick glances at it as though he is watching them as they move around, imitate the way he walks, the way he talks, his voice, his gestures. The prayer beads slip through their fingers as though they are slipping through his fingers and if he has any particularity, a special way of pronouncing certain letters, a stammer, or a tic it immediately becomes theirs. If he says 'Wallah' they say 'Wallah'. If he says 'Bismillah' they say 'Bismillah'[7]

---

[7] Meaning 'By God', a stock phrase of Gamal Abd Al-Nasser.

and whenever they make a statement it begins with the phrase, 'In conformity with the directives of the President'.

Fouad Gallal sat looking down on us for a moment from the high platform, then he began his speech. 'In conformity with the directives of the President we are launching a project which aims at the establishment of combined health units in all rural areas. Under the regime, which is now no more, peasants suffered poverty, disease and ignorance, but the blessed revolution has now come to bring justice to the suffering toilers living in the villages and hamlets. Our first duty in this Supreme Council for Services is to serve the people!'

The faces of the men sitting high up on the platform did not indicate in any way that they were there to serve the people. Their rigid expressions gave me the feeling that their features were fixed with wiring. Their suits made of English wool were carefully ironed, their shoulders stuffed with cotton by the tailor to make them look broad, the way my mother used to stuff the shoulders of the bridegroom doll she made for us to play with when we were children.

The hall was crowded with the doctors who were being sent to the health units. There were about three hundred of them sitting in rows shoulder to shoulder, their hair cut short, their faces raised to the rostrum as they listened to the speech.

When it ended they clapped dutifully. Clapping was a proof of loyalty to the government, of patriotism. If someone's hands did not clap, or clapped feebly, he or she would be looked upon with suspicion. His or her name might even appear on a list at the Ministry of Interior.

Other speeches followed delivered by the other members of the Supreme Council, four of whom were sitting on the right side of the chairman and four on his left. I began to doze. Pictures flitted through my mind, took me back to the day when I was interviewed for a post in one of these health units. The committee that interviewed me was composed of two assistants to Fouad Galal. One was dark and the other fair but they looked like twins. One of them was called Muhammad Bey and the other Mostafa Bey.

'Is Captain El Saadawi a relative of yours, doctor?'

'No. We don't have a captain in the family.'

'And where is Kafr Tahla, doctor?'

'In Kalioubeya Province.'

'Dr Nawal, we know you are excellent in your work, but to work in a rural area is not an easy thing for some one who belongs to the fair sex. Don't you think so, Muhammad Bey?'

'I agree with you, Mostafa Bey. And Dr Nawal certainly belongs to the fair sex.'

He pronounced the words 'fair sex' in a voice softer than that of a woman. The hand he waved in the air was smaller than mine, its fingers delicate and smooth, his complexion fair. He had cheeks like a young blushing bride, and he wore a silk shirt with golden buttons. My skin was brown, burnt by the sun and I wore a blouse made of rough calico.

'A member of the fair sex cannot stand the rough life of a rural doctor. He is often deprived of electricity and clean drinking water. What do you think Muhammad Bey?'

'Of course Mostafa Bey. I would like to ask you, Dr Nawal, supposing you are called upon in the middle of the night for an urgent case, can you venture out into the dark? Wouldn't you be afraid that the wolves might attack you as you walk through the fields? If your high heels get stuck in the mud or in a heap of manure, what will you do?'

That day as usual I was wearing my flat, thick-soled shoes and they were covered with the dust they had picked up as I walked from our home in Giza down to where the meeting was being held in Kasr Al-Aini Street. Every now and then these men would let out one of those small bursts of licentious laughter which men allow themselves in the absence of their wives and their bosses.

I came back from my ruminations to the sound of loud clapping from the rows of doctors sitting in the hall. When it subsided I heard a voice ask from the platform: 'Doctors, have any of you got questions you would like to ask?' There was a deep silence. All of them sat without movement almost holding their breath, then I found myself standing in the middle of the hall with my hand held up in the air. A voice coming from somewhere inside me said, 'Yes, I wish to speak.' I walked to the microphone. Hundreds of eyes stared at me as they waited to hear what I had to say. My heart beat violently under my ribs. I felt a wave of anger rising within me. It caught me at the throat, but I made an effort to speak calmly the way my father did.

'The revolution you keep mentioning in speeches has declared that it aims at ensuring equal opportunities for every one, yet you are depriving women doctors from working in rural areas, from being posted like their men colleagues in the combined health units. I belong to a village called Kafr Tahla, and in my village women leave their homes before dawn to hoe the fields. They labour in the early morning frost or under the burning heat of the summer sun. At the end of the day they come home to cook, and wash, and bake bread. They eat only when every one else in the house has had their meal. They wear only a *gallabeya* throughout the year. walk bare-foot over the rough roads and pathways, work more than the men. Are not these women members of what you call "the fair sex"?'

After the meeting was over Fouad Galal descended from the platform surrounded by his coterie of government employees and walked up to where I was standing amidst a group of doctors. He shook hands with me and said, 'I liked what you said, Dr Nawal. I have decided to appoint you to the combined health unit of Kafr Tahla. You can come to Dr Abdou Salam's office tomorrow morning and there you will be given your letter of appointment.'

My new small two-storeyed dwelling looked like a white pigeon that had settled amidst green fields. Village people called it the *filla*, pronouncing the 'v' like an 'f' because in Arabic there is no letter 'v'. The health unit was composed of three such two-storeyed villas. The first one situated near the outer gate was the home of the social security worker, the next was supposed to be occupied by the director of the primary school but he preferred to live in the village with his family. The third became my home. It was composed of a hall, a dining-room and a kitchen on the ground floor; the two bedrooms and the bathroom were on the first floor and looked out over fields reaching to the horizon.

On the morning of the first day after my arrival I heard knocking at the door. When I opened it, standing on the threshold was a tall village woman who reminded me of my grandmother. She had tied her white-coated donkey near the entrance then walked up to my door and slammed on it with the palm of her large sunburnt hand. There she stood, her head held upright, wearing the same long black *gallabeya* as my grandmother always did, with the same familiar smell of green fields, grilled corn, baked bread and mulberries all mixed together. She had the same way of laughing that went on until it brought tears to her flashing black eyes, and the same way of holding the tip of her shawl over her mouth to conceal it as she laughed before she pronounced the phrase I had heard from my grandmother so many times in the same hoarse tones.

'May God bestow his bounty on us. My name is Om[8] Ibrahim,' she said to me. 'We are related, Dr Nawal, through your deceased grandmother, Sittil Hajja Mabrouka, may God have mercy on her. I am all on my own. The children are all grown up and have left home and my husband has gone off I don't know where. Take me into your home and I will serve you with both my eyes.'[9]

I bestowed the name Dada Om Ibrahim on her and she took over everything, the keys of the house, the care of my baby daughter, the cleaning, washing and cooking. I even left my secret diary with her. I taught her how to read and write, gave her a big wrist-watch and a small notebook in which she used to note down my appointments, and all the running expenses. I bought her coloured *gallabeyas* and white kerchiefs with which to tie her long black hair. She used to comb it into a single braid which kept tossing over her upright back as she walked. She walked with a long, firm stride. Her voice rang through the house greeting every new day with joy. 'Our day will be full of light, doctor, and sweet as honey.'

A smell of jasmine and Arabian jasmine filled the house. I planted three bushes in the small garden in front of it: jasmine, Arabian jasmine, and scarlet bougainvillea.[10] I slept in the big bedroom, and my daughter slept in a small swinging cot next to my bed. Om Ibrahim slept in the other bedroom. She woke up to the chirrup of birds at dawn, put a big tin of hot water for me in the bathroom, and then went downstairs to prepare tea and breakfast in the kitchen. Sharp at seven her voice would rise up from below to reach me as I lay fast asleep. 'It's seven o'clock, doctor. The sun is up and it's a beautiful day, with the flowers blooming.' Then she'd go round the house opening the shutters and the windows and the sun would come streaming in up to my bed. When she reached the window on the first floor which looked out on to the compound I could hear her call out to me: 'May the prophet bless you. There are lines of patients waiting for you outside the door of the unit. Wake up doctor, tea is ready and I've heated a pastry for you in the oven.'

I left the house at eight in the morning, walked through the garden and the big plot planted with vegetables, then under the

---

[8] Mother of Ibrahim. A woman is often addressed in this way in poor urban and rural areas if she has a son.
[9] Faithfully (sacrifice even my eyes for you).
[10] In Arabic 'the colour of gazelle's blood'.

grapevine to reach the outpatients' clinic. Waiting at the door would be Abdel Fattah, the male nurse, slim and straight in his clean white apron. He was always on the move, fast as an arrow, bringing order to chaos, silence to noise, always calm and in control. Under his quiet admonitions the ragged lines of patients straightened out. And voices died down. Even babies stopped crying.

Usually there would be about a hundred patients but with more women than men. With Abdel Fattah's help it became possible for me to examine this number. It took four to five hours after which I would go upstairs to the small inpatients' ward and the adjoining operating theatre. There were three nurses whom I had trained to do a lot of the work. They lived in the wing opposite to that of the patients ward. The most active of the three was called Zeinat, so I appointed her head nurse. She was a young woman about thirty years old who had been trained at the nursing school of Kasr Al-Aini Hospital and who had not married after leaving school. She was of middle height, fair-skinned with round green eyes like those of a cat At night she did her rounds, holding a small torch in her hand, walking silently in her white rubber shoes, her hair showing in a bun from under her nurse's cap, her white uniform reaching down to her knees to cover the short dress she wore underneath, a narrow belt tied around her waist.

There were a number of men employees with me in the health unit. I trained one of them to work in the pharmacy, to be able to read prescriptions and distribute drugs to patients. I taught the second to do health education work, to go round visiting the village houses and talking to people about the prevalent tropical diseases such as bilharziasis, ankylostomiasis and malaria, as well as intestinal and respiratory disorders which affected children. He had been trained in a health institute, was married with two children and lived with his family in the village. Very much a government employee, he was short and fat, always dressed in a suit and tie.

Saturday was when I did operations. Thursday was consecrated to visiting village homes. The rest of the week there were the outpatient clinics. Friday was the weekly holiday, and on that day I walked along the bank of the Nile in the sunshine, pushing the pram with my daughter in it, her round baby's face looking out, her honey-coloured eyes shining with light, her white skin showing a healthy flush in her cheeks. I could hear her laugh with a chirrup like that of the birds, feel her little hands curl round my fingers when I lifted her out high into the air to look at the Nile.

Abdel Fatteh, the male nurse, lived in the village with his wife and three children. Once, in the middle of the night, I was up in my room when there came a knocking at the door. Om Ibrahim opened up, and when I went down Abdel Fatteh, slim and straight in his long white apron, was standing there waiting. I was surprised because he usually came to the unit at dawn, not leaving until midnight, so what could have brought him back again?

He said, 'Mahmoud the son of Haj Hassanein from the Abou Hisham household is in a very bad way, doctor.'

'What do you think is the matter with him, Abdel Fatteh? You are as good as I am at diagnosing, or may be even better.'

'That's kind of you doctor, still, I can never be like you where making the right diagnosis is concerned. But it could be an appendicitis, or a stone in the right kidney. He's got severe colic and his body is on fire.'

'Open the operating theatre and get it ready, you and nurse Zeinat.'

I slipped on my clothes, put on a white coat, and walked quickly across the garden and the vegetable plot, lighting my way with a hand torch. At the door of the health unit there had gathered what was almost a tribe from the Abou Hisham family. The mother was there in a long black *gallabeya* and with a *tarha* around her head, wiping her tears with its corner. She accosted me beseechingly.

'May God give you a long life, doctor! Mahmoud is my only son in a family with six daughters. May God put blessings in your hand.' Next to her stood the father, Haj Hassanein, wearing a long caftan with a big turban around his head, and standing around were tens of relatives from the huge family spread over the area between Tahla and Kafr Tahla, looking at me with veneration as though I were a god with the power to cure all ills.

After examining the patient carefully, I put on the long white sterilized apron, and my face disappeared behind the mask. I felt relieved when no-one could see my face. Deep down inside I felt uncertain, for in medicine one can never be absolutely sure of the diagnosis. I had no X-rays at my disposal, no laboratory where I could examine his blood or anything else. I was depending on my senses, on the touch of my fingers, and on my imagination as a writer and a doctor, on a kind of sixth sense functioning somewhere inside me. In medical college we had not been trained to do any surgery, and during the year I spent as a trainee at the university hospital I had done only a limited number of small operations for hernias, or appendicitis, or to evacuate a uterus, or a tonsilectomy. The scalpel in my hand did not tremble when I dissected a dead body that did not move, that had been drained of its blood, injected with colouring matter, and preserved in formalin. Then I had nothing to fear, could cut deep down into the belly of the dead body and explore without a blink. But now my body was trembling as I cut into the wall of the abdomen, felt the intestines move with life under my fingers. Any small movement of the lancet brought out gushes of blood like a fountain, and I had to search for their hidden source to damp it down. Each gush of blood was like an electric shock, welling out in a deep vivid red that almost dazzled me. I felt my breath coming and going with the movement of blood inside the body as though it had an existence of its own, as though it were made of a different matter, more spirit than body, which gushed and flowed endlessly. I kept putting out my hand to catch hold of it, to stop it, to block it at its source. I fought against it with all the abilities I could muster, but it resisted me, fought back at me, and the struggle went on between me and this jet that kept shooting out towards my face like a tongue of flame.

Blood was considered the sacred spirit by the peoples of Ancient Egypt. Hippocrates maintained that the secret of life was to be found in the blood, and that the human body was composed primarily of blood, with other secondary elements like water, bile and salt. If blood was affected by any malady, then the human being died with it.

'Sweat!'

My voice rang out in the small operating theatre the way the voice of our professor used to ring out when he was doing an operation. His name was Dr Ahmed Abou Zikry. The beads of sweat would stand out on his forehead as he lifted his face from the open belly bathing in blood that lay on the table before him. The hand of the head nurse would move out with a piece of gauze to wipe the sweat off his forehead, before it fell into the open wound.

'Sweat!'

The nurse Zeinab who was standing at my side moved quickly to pick up a piece of sterile gauze and wipe the sweat from my forehead. I was happy that she could not hear the sound of my heart beating under my ribs as though the belly lying open on the table before me was mine, and not the patient's. Could it be just a temporary obstruction of the large intestine, the huge quantities of pastry and roast stuffed duck he had been fed by his mother to celebrate his visit to the village on a short holiday from the Al-Azhar Theological University in Cairo where he was studying? He was twenty years old, the only son amongst half a dozen daughters. So I kept glancing anxiously at the breathing balloon attached to the anaesthesia apparatus as it contracted and expanded with the movement of his lungs, kept lifting my nose up in the air like professor Abou Zikry used to do and saying:

'Sweat!'

My voice echoed loudly with the upward movement of my nose as I tried to hide the mounting panic that was taking hold of me. Maybe the balloon would stop moving all of a sudden? Why had I not sent him off to the central hospital? There was no ambulance in the health unit. The only means of transport available were a donkey and an old rusty bicycle with no brakes, which I sometimes utilized for emergency visits to patients in their homes. I had asked the Supreme Council to send me a truck several times, and after a year had passed they sent me an old van with a closed 'box' fixed to it at the back that worked for a day and remained out of order for months. We ended up using a donkey to drag it into a corner of the compound where we left it to rust away. But in Cairo, at the headquarters of the Supreme Council, a whole caravan of gleaming cars was lined up near the pavement. Each of the responsible officials was allotted two cars, one for office work and the other for personal use.

'Sweat!'

The balloon was still moving. I remembered God during those moments, prayed that he might save Mahmoud's life. He was the creator who gave life, and took it away. Everything depended on His will, so who was I to interfere? I could have sent Mahmoud by donkey back to the Central Hospital in Benha. If he died on the way it would have been God's will and His responsibility not mine. I wished I had evaded the responsibility and passed it on to God.

My fingers were now steady as the scalpel cut into the inflamed and swollen appendix. How had my fingers become so steady? Deep down inside me my mother's voice was echoing as she said, 'You can throw Nawal into the fire, she will come out of it unscathed. No-one in the world is cleverer than she is.' The voice flowed through me in a stream of self-confidence that seemed to infuse me with life and energy. I held the appendix with the forceps, lifted it high up in the air for the nurses to see. There it hung for a moment like a swollen bleeding worm before I let it drop into a pail.

Mahmoud came to from the effect of the anaesthesia after about half an hour. The first sound he uttered was an 'Ah' of pain. It sounded to my ears sweeter than the refrains of my first love. He opened his eyes to find me standing near him. He had big blue eyes, bluer than the sky. He closed his eyes, opened his lips and murmured, 'Ama'.

The word escaped from his lips with the village pronunciation, 'Ama'. People remembered their mothers when death hovered over their heads, they would remember them also on the day of judgement, for on that day they would be called by the names of their mothers.

The nurse Zeinat laughed happily as she wiped his dry lips with a piece of gauze wetted in water. 'Do you want your mother, Mahmoud?' she said. 'She's standing outside the door with your father Haj Hassanein, your sisters, aunts and uncles, and the village folk are all gathered in the compound, with their donkeys too.'

Forty years have gone by since that night, when I stood there by his side and saw his lips open in a weary smile. I cannot remember a smile that seemed to me more beautiful. I cannot forget his smile, the way it lit up in the pale, worn face surrounded by thick locks of smooth black hair, one of which had dropped over his white forehead.

'His mother is dark-skinned with black eyes, his father's skin even darker, his eyes even blacker, so where did he get his fair skin and blue eyes from?'

'You know, Zeinat, maybe his grandfather was fair-skinned, or he had a grandmother with blue eyes and he inherited their genes.'

'What do you mean by genes, Dr Nawal?'

'Genes are proteins in the cell that carry the hereditary characteristics.'

'No, Dr Nawal, it's not the genes but the genies from the sea. Om Mahmoud must have had an affair with a fair-skinned, blue-eyed genie.'

Om Mahmoud came into the ward and when she saw her son she let out piercing 'yooyoos' of joy that rose high up to the heavens. The news spread with the 'yooyoos' from Tahla to Kafr Tahla, to Digwa, and Ramla, and went on to Benha. For village people, to be cured from disease or illness was like a miracle, like being resurrected from the dead. Death was common, but to be cured was rare, and an occasion for great rejoicing in which everyone joined. Death was an occasion for great sadness and shared by everyone. Men put on solemn faces, and sat in silent rows to give their condolences. The women beat their faces, shrieked with grief, and ripped open the bodices of their long robes. Joy and sadness were always shared in a communal way, which helped to increase the joy or mitigate the sadness.

So the women gathered around and their 'yooyoos' filled the air. As I walked through the compound people kept expressing their gratitude. I could hear them say: 'May Allah protect you and give you long life, Dr Nawal.' 'May Allah help you to overcome your enemies.'

I became a subject of conversation whenever people met and sat together. In the evenings after sunset the men gathered in front of their homes, drinking tea, smoking their water-pipes, and talking of different things. My name would crop up: 'Dr Nawal is the daughter of our village, and Allah has blessed her hands. Who would have thought that a woman, not a man, could do what she did, but Allah can do anything and Allah has bestowed these blessings on her hands. A thousand prayers for the Prophet. Do you remember when she first arrived at the health unit, how we all agreed that a woman should never be allowed to examine us? Yes, by Allah, that's what we said, and now look what has happened. The column of male patients waiting in line to be examined by her is longer than that of the women.'

Dada Om Ibrahim used to keep me informed of the talk in the village, for I did not go out at night, nor could I find out what the villagers were saying in private. There was no electricity in the village and the nights were pitch dark. Om Ibrahim used to light a kerosene lamp and I would sit in bed and read. My library had grown, its shelves now rose up to the ceiling carrying old and new books on medicine, philosophy, literature, history and the arts. I devoured one book after the other, happy to have this chance to be alone, to read and think and write.

I continued to keep in touch with my school friends, especially Samia and her husband Rifa'a. Sometimes I visited them in the pharmacy they owned on Kasr Al-Aini Street. From them I picked up news about what was happening in the country, and a few things concerning the political situation. Within short walking distance of the pharmacy was the University Children's Hospital where my friend Safeya worked as a doctor. The assistant director of the hospital, Dr Mostafa, was her husband. Further away in Dokki

Square was my third friend, Batta (Camelia), and her husband, Dr Hamdi, a professor in the Kasr Al-Aini School of Medicine from which we had graduated. Now Batta drove a Buick, and sometimes she would drive down in it with Safeya and Samia to visit me at the health unit. On rare occasions their husbands would come too, and then the villa would be full of guests. Often relatives from my family would come to see me.

On such occasions Om Ibrahim would be in her element, her voice rising joyfully from below together with the smells of her cooking – pastry, roast rabbit, *mouloukheya*,[11] or pigeons stuffed with green wheat.

When we had no visitors the house would be very quiet. I enjoyed the silence after hours or days of noise, enjoyed getting into bed with a book, or a new novel, or to write a short story for a magazine, or note down my impressions in my diary.

Sometimes I took my daughter out of her cot and let her sleep in my arms. Om Ibrahim would come along with a basin of hot water in which she had put some salt and massaged my feet that were tired from tramping the rounds in the village, or she would bring me a hot drink of aniseed, or fenugreek, or herbs gathered from the fields and a concoction of which she usually poured into a small earthenware basin.

Often before sunset I would go for a walk, watch the sun as it dropped down towards the earth, spreading its colours over the sky, over the clouds and the waters of the Nile, follow them as they changed, immerse my eyes in the hues and shadows and shapes, let my senses dissolve into space before the night dropped its cloak of darkness over the village.

Once a fortnight I used to put on my white coat and take the nurses on a round of the village. We would sit with the men on mud benches outside their homes, or with the women in an inner courtyard or on their doorsteps. If I felt like walking through the village without being recognized I put on a *gallabeya*, tied my head in a black kerchief, put on a *tarha* and went through the lanes, certain that no-one would speak to me, that the men would not stand up as I approached and invite me to take a glass of tea with them: 'A thousand welcomes, doctor, please join us. You have brought light with you.'

---

[11] A thick greenish spinach type of soup made with stock from chicken or rabbit and fried garlic.

I enjoyed these 'free' strolls through the village where no-one stopped me, spoke to me, or recognized me. I could go wherever I wanted, stride along freely, swing my arms, embrace the world, forget who I was, be nameless, and discover myself, discover who I was, as though to do that I had to forget the outer self that people knew, and remember the one I was looking for.

The school attached to the combined unit had a headmaster called Ostaz[12] Abd Al-Moneim. He was short with grey hair, wore a suit and a fez during working hours, but changed into a *gallabeya* when he got home or was on holiday. On winter days he wore a caftan over the *gallabeya*, and wound a grey scarf around his neck. He always mentioned my father with deep respect and would say: 'Saadawi Bey was a great man. If there were only ten men like him the educational system could have been reformed.'

The social security worker was according to the statutes the director of the combined unit. His name was Ostaz Khairallah. He was bald with a tonsure of rough dark hair around his head, a yellowish complexion, a big nose, thick black whiskers, and, like the members of the security police, he wore dark glasses hiding his eyes.

Newspapers and magazines came to us only by mail, and usually a month or a month and a half late. I had no idea of what was going on in the world except through a small radio which worked by battery and which Om Ibrahim used to call 'radion'. She reminded me of my grandmother, Sittil Hajja. Like her she used to say 'Open the radion, doctor, I want to listen to Om Koulsoum',[13] and like her she was fond of a particular Om Koulsoum song which went, 'Since you love, why deny, love shows in the lovers' eyes'.

I asked her the same question that I used to ask my grandmother when I was a child: 'Have you ever been in love?' She looked at me with her dark, deep-set eyes from under a broad sunburnt forehead as she stood with my daughter in her arms near the balcony door, her body strong and youthful, her powerful arms swinging Mona up and down to the rhythm of a song, her voice warm and full of joy. 'Yes, doctor, like every one else I did know love,' she said, and I watched her tall and graceful body move under the folds of her colourful cotton *gallabeya*.

'Who did you love, Om Ibrahim?' I asked.

---

[12] Mister.
[13] A famous Egyptian singer.

'I loved God the Almighty up on High, and his Prophet Muhammad, a thousand prayers for Him, and Imam Al-Shafei[14] and Sayeda Zaynab,[15] and the Virgin Mary.'

'I mean the other kind of love.'

'What other kind of love, doctor?'

'The one Om Koulsoum sings about.'

Her body went rigid, a cloud passed over her eyes, and I saw wrinkles gather in her face and creep over her forehead. She undid the kerchief around her head, pulled it tight and knotted it three times over her forehead. She was not more than thirty-five years old but now she looked over fifty.

'Yes, doctor, I lived the other kind of love you asked about. Twenty-five bitter years with a man, and four children, two boys and two girls. If God hadn't taken him away I would have killed him with my hoe.'

'Why do you call them bitter years, Om Ibrahim?'

'He used to beat me. Every night he would beat me with the donkey-stick just out of habit. Starting from the wedding night a man must beat his wife if he's a man, so that she should not forget that God is supreme in the heavens above and her husband supreme here below. I was a small child playing with other children, my breasts were still buds and my periods hadn't started when they decided to marry me off to Abou Ibrahim. I ran off and hid in the fields but they pulled me out, tied me up and brought me back, all of them, that horrible brazen village *daya* (nurse), my mother, my aunts. They trussed me up like a chicken, put a towel around my head and took me to Abou Ibrahim so that he could deflorate me before I became his bride. I bled so much that my wedding was very close to becoming my funeral.'

In medical school we were taught nothing about the unhealthy and often dangerous habits and rituals practised in both rural and urban areas, including circumcision of female and male children. When I graduated as a medical doctor I knew nothing about the hymen or the clitoris, or the practices related to them that were encouraged by *dayas* and village barbers, who made more money out of them than out of any of the other functions they fulfilled. So I began to go round with Om Ibrahim, to attend weddings and

---

[14] One of the four leading theologians of Islamic doctrine and jurisprudence.
[15] One of the Prophet's wives.

funerals, circumcisions and deflorations. The *dayas* and village barbers did not welcome my presence, but they could do nothing about it since I was the medical authority in the village.

One day I caught a village barber giving an injection to a woman through the cloth of her *gallabeya* so as not to expose her thigh. I protested and told him off. 'How can you do something like that? Don't you realize you can give her a serious infection!' He answered, 'What can I do, doctor? She doesn't want to show her thigh.' On another occasion the village barber cut off the head of the penis instead of just removing the foreskin of a small boy being circumcised. The child almost died of haemorrhage, but we took him quickly to the operating theatre and were able to save him. At a wedding ceremony the fingernail of a bridegroom penetrated into the bladder of his young bride when he tried to deflorate her. They carried her to the health unit on the back of a donkey and I repaired the organs that had been damaged.

Bleeding after female circumcision was very common and even commoner was infection since the *dayas* did not sterilize their instruments (mainly a razor) and did not disinfect the wound. Often they used dust to stop bleeding.

Every Thursday was devoted to health education in the homes. Together with the nurses I went round teaching people about hygiene, cleanliness, nutrition, the most common diseases and their prevention. After a while I began to tell them about the effects and dangers of the customs and habits they tended to follow. The *dayas* and village barbers started to campaign against me, so I organized health education sessions for them in the health unit. But it was like trying to inflate a balloon that was torn. Om Ibrahim summarized the situation when she said to me, 'How will they buy food for themselves if circumcisions and deflorations are no longer done in the village?'

FOUR

The Tripartite Invasion

Abd Al-Nasser's voice echoed loudly from thousands of radios in the houses and on the streets: 'We shall go on fighting until the invaders leave. We will never surrender.' It was October 29, 1956. The armed forces of England, France and Israel had attacked by air, land, and sea. Popular resistance was being organized everywhere. Samia, Rifa'a and Assad, Samia's brother, joined up in Cairo to be trained.

I took off my doctor's coat and put on fatigues. What had happened to the freedom fighters under Farouk was now forgotten. We were living under a new patriotic regime. A group of soldiers travelled from Benha to our village. The health unit was transformed into a training camp for armed struggle. The male and female nurses volunteered to form first-aid groups, and we hoisted the flag of Egypt over the white buildings.

At night I sat on the balcony embroidering a badge with the words 'We will fight on until victory.' Ten years before at the Helwan Boarding School I had stood at the window with my friends Fikreya, Fatma, and Safeya, embroidering a badge that said 'Evacuation, through blood and struggle'. Over my fingers I could still recall the singe of the ruler, in my ears I could still hear the warnings of the headmistress, and in my heart was a wound that had never healed, the face of Ahmed Menissi now dead, the voice of Ahmed Helmi coming to me as though from the bottom of a pit: 'They abandoned us, left us to face the bullets of the enemy on our own. They became heroes, and we who had shouldered arms and fought became criminals, to be hunted down and caught.'

Om Ibrahim used to see me carrying a rifle as I walked through the compound. 'Why do you care about the war, doctor? You have nothing to do with it. To hell with war and with those who brought it. My heart has been broken by war. My eldest son Ibrahim was in Fallouja with Gamal[1] and it's eight years now since I last saw him. Every night he comes to me in my dreams, and in all these years I have never found out whether he's dead or alive.'

I was twenty-five, and the idea of death to me was as far away as the stars in heaven. In my mind war was not linked to death, but to a childhood dream of freeing my country. Painful moments in my life were forgotten. Memories of death or the disappointments of love did not last. Sadness dissolved in my body and was excreted like acids and toxins. Only the child in me continued to live. The young virgin girl remained intact, untouched by evil. I woke up in the morning radiant as the rising sun, sang to my daughter as she lay in her cot. 'The sun has risen. How beautiful is her light. Let's go out to fill our pots with water. Let's milk the buffalo waiting in her shed.' She would gurgle with laughter as I lifted her up out of the cot and embraced her.

I used to feed her with fresh buffalo's milk diluted with water. My aunt Fatma, who lived a short distance away in Tahla, used to milk her buffalo and send the milk to me on a donkey together with butter, cream and cottage cheese. I fed my daughter on wheat grains mashed with honey and milk, powdered rice cooked in diluted milk with sugar, half the yellow of an egg mashed with cottage cheese, and grape or orange juice.

She sat on a high chair playing with the coloured balls, moving them over the wire, knocking them together as she imitated the songs I used to sing to her. And from below I could hear Om Ibrahim singing one of those old folkloric songs as she prepared breakfast.

I did not abandon you on land,
Yet you abandoned me in the middle of the sea.
I did not barter you for gold,
But you bartered me for straw.[2]

---

[1] Gamal Abd Al-Nasser.

[2] Gold in colloquial Arabic is *tibr*. Straw is *tibn* whence a rhyme and a sort of play on words.

Her sweet and powerful voice rose up to me with the smell of freshly baked pastry and tea, reminding me of my mother when she used to sing to me.

'A morning of bounty to you, doctor. Breakfast is on the table.'

Dada Om Ibrahim had become a member of my small family. She surrounded me with warmth and affection, held me in her arms, compensated me for the loss of my mother, for the disappointments of love. She used to sit on the floor near my bed with a cushion under her, and tell me the story of her life, as well as that of her mother, her grandmother and the women of Tahla and Kafr Tahla. Before going to bed she took a quick look at my daughter to make sure she was all right, closed all the doors and windows, then came to my bed and wrapped the blankets around my body carefully. Sometimes if I was still awake she massaged my tired feet with her big, strong hands.

'Doctor, you stand on your feet all day long and now in addition we have this training camp. May Allah help you to overcome all your enemies and above all that man called Khairallah. He is full of evil, he should have been called Shar[3] Allah. He should pick up a rifle, and go off to fight instead of hiding here like a woman.'

The word woman pierced my ear. The greatest insult to a man was to describe him as a woman. I said to her, 'How can you say that when you yourself are a woman? It's an insult to both you and me since you and I are both women.'

'Please forgive me, doctor. My tongue is used to the bad language of village people. May God cut off my tongue if I ever say anything like that again. Yes, what's wrong with women? There are women that are worth twenty of that unspeakable Khairallah.'

The training camp in the health unit had become as active as a beehive. The youth in the different villages were competing to be trained in the use of arms. The young women joined the first-aid unit. Zeinat was the only woman who agreed to carry arms. She attended target-shooting sessions with me. One of the officers who trained us was called Captain Ala'a. He was fair-skinned with broad shoulders and rather stout. The three brass stars shone on his shoulders and he had a thick black moustache and blue eyes. Every day he rode to the camp in a jeep. When he laughed his eyes were slits, his cheeks wobbled up and down, and his face became round

---

[3] Meaning 'evil' – Allah's evil instead of Allah's good, since *khair* means 'good' or 'bounty'.

like that of a child. He spoke through his nose with a kind of upper-class insolence. Sometimes I thought he must be suffering from sinusitis.

'Doctor, our people are poor and ignorant. If they are given arms the first thing they will do is to turn them against their rulers. I have orders not to distribute arms to the youth in the camp.'

He was enthusiastic about training me in the use of arms, but not happy with the idea of my going to join the ranks of the popular resistance in Port Said. 'Are there no men left in the country to fight the invaders? Women are delicate, like fine thread. D'you think it reasonable for a woman like you to go to war. Do you think you can kill like a man?'

He kept on saying such things in a stupid flirtatious way that was nauseating. He used to let his hand rest on my shoulder when he taught me how to shoot with a rifle, steal glances at my breasts through the open neck of my fatigues, and his fat hand would keep trembling for no obvious reason when he came close to me. When I looked him straight in the eye he would cringe like a mouse facing a cat. He sometimes addressed me as captain and at others as the 'wild cat'.

One day when I had just finished with the outpatients' clinic Captain Ala'a came up to me and said, 'I would like to have a talk with you, Dr Nawal.' I brought him a cup of coffee and prepared to listen. He began to tell me about himself, about his heroic record in the army, the decoration he had received from Abd Al-Hakeem Amer, the Defence Minister and Chief of Staff, the certificate of outstanding performance in the military academy from which he graduated, the prizes he had won in the Ibrahimeya Secondary School, the records he had broken in athletics, and so on and so forth. At the end he pushed his fat white hand into the inner pocket of his tunic and brought out a swollen wallet. From the wallet he extracted a photograph and said, 'This is a photograph of me when I was in the Mère de Dieu School.'

The name 'Mère de Dieu' emerged from behind his thick black moustache in excruciatingly delicate tones that reminded me of my friend Batta. She was particularly fond of pronouncing her words with a pseudo-refined French accent since she too had been to the Mère de Dieu School. She was very proud of the fact, would stretch her neck, and curl her lips as she pronounced the Arabic letter 'ghein' like a Parisian 'r'.

The term 'Mère de Dieu', meaning 'Mother of God' or 'Mother of Allah' by Islamic standards, was nothing less than a heresy, for in Islam Allah had no mother, had not been born, or given birth. Captain Ala'a had told me that at one time he had joined the Muslim Brothers with Kamal Al-Deir Hussein,[4] so I pounced on the opportunity to turn the tables on him. 'You are a Muslim and a believer in the one and only Allah. So how on earth did you go to a school called the "Mother of God".'

He was taken aback, blushed furiously, and pulled out another photograph from his wallet. This time it was that of his father. 'I was a child at that time, doctor,' he said, 'and of course it was my father who sent me to that school. You see the level of education there was much better than in government schools, and all respectable families in Egypt used to send their children to this school, or to other foreign schools. My father was a colonel in the army at the time of Farouk, and after the revolution he retired and stayed at home. He was bitterly opposed to Abd Al-Nasser and almost every night he dreamt that he had shot him, then in the morning he woke up to find him still alive so he would take it out on my poor mother, and one day he beat her. So after thirty years together she insisted on a divorce.'

He went on telling me his story, as he sipped a second cup of coffee. I examined the photograph of his father, registered the cruelty of the eyes that stared out at me. 'Did your father beat you when you were a child?' I asked. He put the photo back in his wallet, smiled and said. 'My father was an army man and believed in punishing any disobedience.'

The head of the military unit stationed in Benha used to visit the camp, but Captain Ala'a had been sent from headquarters in Cairo, and so he used to behave in front of the Captain like an obedient schoolboy, stamp the ground and raise his hand to his cap in a forceful military salute, making sure that his thumb was exactly in line with his eyebrow. But with the young trainees from the village the docile lamb become a lion, throwing orders right and left in a loud imperious voice, insulting their fathers and mothers at the slightest mistake. He always carried a cane with which he beat the trainees on various parts of the body.

---

[4] One of the Free Officers and later Minister of Education under Gamal Abd Al-Nasser.

One day as I was crossing the compound I saw him beating one of the village youths, a slip of a boy who had volunteered to join the popular resistance. His thin body was dressed in an old *gallabeya*, his skin a dark brown with whitish patches due to a disease called pellagra which affects the nerve endings and is accompanied by severe anaemia. The disease leads to a slowness in understanding, and to slower reactions, so the boy was not responding quickly enough to orders. Captain Ala'a took the cane from his subordinate and started to land it on the thin body, not deterred by the beseeching cries that rose from the boy as he beat down with a ferocity that increased at every supplication from his victim. The cane held in the fat thick fingers of his hand kept descending like a whip, his big square body jerked up and down like that of a white bear giving vent to an anger that had accumulated over the years and was imprisoned deep down in the flesh, waiting to break out against a creature whom he had no reason to fear. The two bodies, that of the man and that of the boy, kept jerking up and down as though the body of the punisher and the body of the punished were one, separated by the cane and yet tied to one another through it, as though the punisher were punishing himself, directing his hatred at himself. He kept closing his eyes, clenching his teeth, lifting the cane up in the air, threshing the heavens with it, as though looking for the face of his father hidden up there behind a cloud with the name of Allah inscribed on it.

The tripartite attack on Egypt began with the armies of Israel overrunning Sinai. This was followed by the bombing of Port Said in which British and French planes participated, the dropping of paratroops to occupy the city, bombardment from the sea by naval ships, and the landing of tanks and artillery. Since the partition of Palestine the new Israeli state had continued to serve the interests of imperialism in the Arab region. After the nationalization of the Suez Canal Company England had been waiting for an opportunity to strike back and regain control of the Canal Zone. France was seeking vengeance against the revolutionary regime for two reasons: the support given by the regime to the Algerian national liberation movement, and the loss the French capital had sustained as a result of the nationalization of the Suez Canal Company. So the agreement reached was that Israel strike first and occupy Sinai. This would give the other two powers an excuse to intervene, to pretend that their aim was to separate the two opposing forces, end the hostilities, and protect Egypt against further attack.

On Fridays I continued to take a walk on the banks of the Nile. It was the month of October and the autumn air was pleasantly cool, so that day I went out quite early. I had reached the banks of the Nile and was pushing my daughter's pram at a steady pace, my shoulders enveloped in a light blue shawl, when, almost at the confines between Tahla and Kafr Tahla, I saw a demonstration coming in the opposite direction. There were about one hundred people, mainly schoolboys and students from the university and from Al-Azhar who were back in the village on vacation. They were carrying a long white banner attached to two poles on which they had painted in black 'Down with the tripartite invasion'. Some of the demonstrators were carrying a picture of Abd Al-Nasser. Two students walked in front holding up a big painting that was supposed to represent England in the form of a white bear. Standing on the head of the bear was the drawing of a woman wearing shoes with long thin pointed heels. The demonstrators kept shouting at the top of their voices:

'Down with the people who are ruled by a *mara* [woman].'[5]

'Down with the army led by a *nitaya* [woman].'[6]

The words *mara* and especially *nitaya*, both used to degrade women, struck me like a blow. If England was ruled by a queen, why should all women be insulted for a crime they had not committed? It was like the story of Eve. Adam and Eve both ate from the tree of knowledge, but all women were made sinful because of Eve.

I stood without moving, like a statue, swallowing the humiliation and the dust raised by the demonstrators as they went on their way. I was no longer the doctor who treated them when they were sick, no longer the freedom fighter ready to go off to the front. I was a mere woman, a hussy, a bitch. I was just a *nitaya* to be reviled like all other women in this world. I was a word shooting out from the mouths of the boys like a gob of spit.

A sudden gust of cold wind blew the shawl off my shoulders. It flew away and landed on the water like a dead dove.

By the time I got home I was numb and trembling with cold, and my daughter had started to sneeze and cough. We were met at the door by Om Ibrahim who bustled around us anxiously. 'I told you not to go out today. I was sure the weather was going to turn bad. The poor child has caught cold and you look as pale as death, doctor.'

---

[5] The colloquial word is '*mara*' and implies disrespect (much like hussy or tart).

[6] Literally 'a women's army'. The word is in colloquial Arabic and is habitually used for animals. Stops short of 'bitch'.

* * * *

Abdel Fatteh, the male nurse, came into my office that day all excited.

'It's his excellency the Pasha.'

'Which Pasha, Abdel Fatteh?'

'The big one, the head of the Abd Al-Aleem household.'

A moment later a tall, thin man dressed in a smart suit walked into my office. Following behind him was another man wearing a caftan made of English wool over his silken *jibba*,[7] and a huge white turban wound around his head. Following behind both of them was Khairallah, the social security worker, and last of all came the headmaster of the school, Ostaz Abd Al-Moneim. The latter two were both gasping as though out of breath.

I was dressed in my army fatigues since I was expecting to receive a message summoning me to the front in Port Said at any moment. The Pasha or the Bey stared at me in surprise, but Ostaz Khairallah volunteered to clarify the situation by saying in a mildly sarcastic tone, 'Dr Nawal, your excellency, is an enthusiastic supporter of the revolution and of Gamal Abd Al-Nasser.'

Abd Al-Aleem Bey's face went pale at the mention of Gamal Abd Al-Nasser's name. His long thin features seemed to grow even longer and his lips curled derisively exposing small pointed teeth stained with tobacco. He extracted a thick dark evil-looking cigar from one of his pockets, stuck it between his lips, and struck a match with trembling fingers, but its flame went out. After a second and a third try he was finally able to light it. He blew out smoke from his nose and mouth, murmuring in a voice that could hardly be heard, 'That man is going to lead us into trouble.'

The headmaster's body shrunk into his suit. He hid his face in his scarf and lowered his eyelids as though he had not heard anything. In those days it was enough to hear something against Abd Al-Nasser without reporting it, or at least protesting, to land in trouble.

Ostaz Khairallah was a government official like the headmaster, perhaps one or two grades above him in rank. He belonged to the social category of educated university graduates. He owned a piece of land and had close relations with the landowners in the village including the household of Abd Al-Aleem. The family of Abd Al-

---

[7] A long robe, often made of striped material, with small embroidered ball-like buttons running down for a distance from the neck.

Aleem was rich, owned land, and had influence. At the time of Farouk some of its members had been in parliament. After the revolution they became linked by marriage to the new class of military officers who had come into power. They owned a huge mansion near the health unit that remained empty most of the year, but was filled with people at harvest or election time.

During this visit, which turned out to be a short one, Abd Al-Aleem Bey informed me between puffs of smoke that he had heard of my prowess as a doctor, that he had come on holiday for a week to relax with his wife in the village, and that suddenly she had started to bleed severely from her uterus. Then he added, 'I wish you would open a private clinic in the village.'

'Why do you think I should do that, Ostaz Abd Al-Aleem?'

'There are people who refuse to go to a government clinic or hospital.'

'Why is that so?'

'The level of service is always much lower than in the private clinics.'

'This health unit is well-equipped and is regularly supplied with the drugs we need. The service here is better than in the private clinics.'

Ostaz Khairallah was obviously not happy with the way the dialogue was going, nor with the way I was answering our visitor, but he kept quiet. Later on, after the man had left, he said to me: 'How can you address his excellency as Ostaz and not show him the due respect owed to him? Don't you know the harm he can do us?'

'What business of yours is that, Ostaz Khairallah?'

'I am the responsible head of the combined unit.'

'I know that, but I am solely responsible for whatever I say or do.'

Using the excuse of his responsibility as head of the unit Ostaz Khairallah kept interfering in my work. But he did nothing all day except sit in the shade of the grapevine, where he would drink tea, smoke and chat with his guests, and exchange stories interrupted by bursts of laughter and puffs at a water-pipe. Or he would walk around the garden and the vegetable field as though he owned them, staring down his nose at the labourers, as they bent to hoe the ground, in the same way as an estate owner would with his slaves. Most days I could hear him showing off his authority by shouting at the other employees. Often he would invade the health unit accompanied by a few guests and show them round, so that they could see for themselves how well the unit was run, how spotless everything was, how efficiently the staff worked and went about their jobs clad in their white uniforms. Sometimes he even opened the door of my office and walked in as I was examining a patient.

'Ostaz Khairallah, this is a room in which I examine my patients, and you have to respect their privacy. It's not a vegetable field.'

'I am the head of the combined unit, Dr Nawal, and it is my right to carry out inspections anywhere in the unit, and at any time.'

'No, Ostaz, you have no right to walk into the examination room, or to inspect the health unit. The health unit is my responsibility.'

The differences and struggles that kept arising between us were always related to matters of this nature. The statutes said that the social security worker was responsible for administrative matters in the combined unit, and he kept using this as an excuse to interfere in matters that were not in his domain. He kept boasting that he had influential connections and could get rid of anybody he did not want.

On November 6, 1956 the city of Port Said was transformed into a mass of flames. Rockets and bombs were dropped by thousands from planes, naval ships bombarded it from the sea, tanks roared through the streets, and sharpshooters were parachuted on to the roofs of houses. They fired at people standing in their windows or walking down the streets. Men, women, and children fought back with sticks and stones and knives from lane to lane, and house to house. Groups of guerrilla fighters, most of them very young, were formed and began to fight with guns, grenades and molotov cocktails. A young boy caught by British soldiers was tortured but refused to give information about his group. Another young boy from the district of Manakh was shot in front of his mother, then they tortured her, but she refused to open her mouth. Om Ibrahim followed what was happening and asked me questions as she sat on the floor in my room.

'She died, Dr Nawal? Her heart must have stopped beating when she saw them kill her son. I wonder where my son is now. Maybe they are torturing him in an Israeli prison.'

Many women lost their sons in the five wars I lived through in Egypt (1948, 1951, 1956, 1967, and 1973). Most of them belonged to poor peasant families. They were the unknown soldiers, men and women victims who did not own an inch of the land. Successive regimes and governments did nothing for them. They were cheated and betrayed in every one of the battles. They fought and shed their blood but every time it was the rulers who shared the spoils. Every time I would remember Ahmed Helmi's words, 'We fought with arms. They became the heroes, and we became criminals to be hunted down.' Every time I remembered the stone monument erected in honour of the martyrs in the School of Medicine and which had crumbled into dust.

Om Ibrahim used to say to me, 'Our country is like a monster. It devours its own children. You cannot imagine the suffering and humiliation I went through going from Tahla to Cairo and from Cairo to Tahla like a dizzy chicken trying to find out something about my missing son. All I got from them was indifference and cruel treatment that wore me out.

'They did not give me a single piastre or pension, because my son was considered missing and not dead. Eight long years, one year after the other going and coming until I could stand it no more and gave up.'

Port Said spent forty-eight days under siege. At midnight on November 7 the United Nations announced a ceasefire. The Soviet Union had threatened to bombard London and Paris with rockets, and the United States was ready to replace the British and French colonial powers, now greatly weakened in the Arab countries. So a ceasefire was agreed, and the armed forces of the three invading states were obliged to withdraw.

I used to spend much of the night turning the dials of my radio to pick up the latest news. The station from which the Voice of the Arabs broadcast had been bombarded, and the broadcast had shifted to Damascus. The radio broadcast martial tunes and victory marches all the time, but deep down inside I had a feeling of defeat. I had been trained to use arms with a group of village youth, and we waited every day for the message that would call us to the front. Every day we asked Captain Ala'a, and every day we got the same answer, 'We are waiting for orders from Cairo.'

The war ended without orders ever coming from Cairo. I kept asking myself, was this show of preparing for popular armed resistance being used just as propaganda to try and convince our enemies that occupation would not be an easy matter? Would the regime really take the risk of arming the people, transforming the Egyptians into a liberation army as the radio broadcasts maintained it intended to do?

The revolution had not led to a change in the essential nature of the Egyptian bureaucratic state. It was the oldest centralized state in history with a long experience in the ways of oppression. For thousands of years the antagonism between rulers and ruled had remained a fact of life for the Egyptian people. No regime could have ruled without depriving the people of their essential rights, the right to knowledge, and the right to carry arms.

The government radio station had continued to hide the truth from us throughout. We never knew what was happening in the war exactly. The members of the volunteer corps, which had been trained in the use of arms or to give first aid, used to gather around the radio several times during the day and listen to the foreign broadcasts. One of the young guerrilla trainees from Kafr Tahla clashed with Captain Ala'a and decided to go to the front in Port Said without waiting for instructions. Captain Ala'a went after him, arrested him at the Benha railway station and handed him over to the police. They beat him for three successive days in the police cell where he was kept, then released him. He came back to the village with a broken arm. The youth in the camp gathered to protest. They shouted 'Down with Captain Ala'a.' Ostaz Khairallah started to threaten them and they began to shout, 'Down with all traitors.'

On the following day a brigade of policemen arrived in the village. They were headed by an officer from the Department of Security and Criminal Investigation, short of stature and wearing the usual dark glasses. They searched some of the houses for arms, arrested a number of youths, and beat up the mothers and fathers who protested, creating an atmosphere of terror. The security officer walked into my office in the health unit. 'Doctor, if you don't mind I would like to ask you one or two questions. It will take only a few minutes.'

At that time I was not familiar with the language used by the security police, did not know that two or three minutes could mean two or three hours and even much longer than that. Years later, when they came to take me from my home in Giza, they said 'just one or two questions, doctor' and that time I ended up in prison.

* * * *

The winter of 1957 in Kafr Tahla was cold and the winds carried clouds of dust. The radio kept broadcasting songs of victory but deep down inside I lived defeat. There was a wound somewhere in my heart which refused to heal. Mysterious fingers encircled my neck, and tried to throttle me as I slept. I opened my mouth to let out a scream but no sound emerged, so I curled up in bed like a child afraid of evil spirits and devils. In the village, people believed in the existence of spirits and devils as firmly as they believed in God. Before going to sleep Om Ibrahim would recite the 'Yaseen', one of the most well-known verses of the Qur'an, to chase away genies and devils. 'God mentioned them in the Qur'an,' she would say to me. The fortune-teller went round reading the future in coffee cups and shells. Barren women visited Sheikh Hamdan. He used to take them into a dark room and impregnate them. They would come out blessing his name, saying that although he was blind Allah had bestowed upon him special powers, visited him in his sleep, and revealed the future to him so that he could see what was hidden from ordinary people. Allah had made him blind, and enrolled him as a holy man, had given him the power to chase evil spirits away from their bodies and make them pregnant.

Village life was steeped in superstitions of this kind. Om Ibrahim would keep coming up to me with stories. One day she said to me, 'That girl Masouda, the daughter of Sheikh Zeidan, has become possessed by a devil.'

'You're talking nonsense, Om Ibrahim, there are no such things as devils,' I said.

She looked at me with her dark eyes, pulled open the neck of her **gallabeya** and spat into it, then she lifted her head to the heavens and said, 'May Allah have mercy on us, and not make the devils angry with what you say.' A moment later she stood up, began to brush away something invisible hovering around her, as though brushing away a fly, and resumed what she was saying. 'Haj Zeidan took his daughter Masouda to Sheikh Hamdan, but the devil refused to leave her. That Sheikh Hamdan is nothing but a charlatan, may God have mercy on me for saying that about one of His holy men.'

Not a day passed without Om Ibrahim mentioning something about Masouda, the daughter of Haj Zeidan, and how a devil had possessed her and was making her do strange things. The father of the girl kept taking her from one blind Sheikh to another. 'You see, Allah reveals what is hidden to these blind men. It is they alone who are close to Him, and know Him.'

FIVE

What is Suppressed Always Comes Back

The story of Masouda and her devil became the talk of the village. The villagers kept saying that her devil was not like other devils. It defied the holy men of Allah, so perhaps it was the Devil himself who had possessed her. 'I seek refuge in thee, Allah, from the evil Devil' was a phrase that villagers kept repeating throughout their lives. Om Ibrahim never stopped invoking God's protection from the Devil, genies and all other evil spirits, and I had to spend hours trying to chase them out of her mind and the minds of the women and men in the village. Together with Zeinat, the other nurses and the health education officer I formed a team which did the rounds of the homes regularly every Thursday to discuss these superstitious beliefs and to convince the villagers that they were not only wrong but also harmful. My grandmother kept repeating to me when I was a child, 'There are no such things as devils, the human being is the only devil that exists.'

To rid their minds of these invisible spirits was not easy. After all, they were mentioned in the Qur'an, Allah's holy book. How could the science of medicine defy the word of God? Our fiercest opponents on such issues were the landlords, the headman of the village, the Sheikh in charge of the mosque, the village barber, the village guards in charge of keeping order and Sheikh Hamdan. They formed a united front against me. For they were the people who wielded power in the village, and their power would not have survived if the devils were driven out of people's minds.

I was seized with a feeling of defiance, walked through the village in the dark of night, my eyes piercing the darkness in the hope of meeting a devil face to face. When still a child I was afraid of the darkness. Now at the age of twenty-six I had become a doctor, held a small torch in my hand and went round in the dark of night fighting against these metaphysical forces.

When the family of Masouda finally allowed me to examine her in their home I asked her: 'Tell me, Masouda, when did this devil first start riding[1] you, and where?'

'I do not know, doctor, I swear by Allah I do not know.'

She was lying on a couch in the inner courtyard of their house. Her father believed that Allah alone, and not doctors, had the power to cure the sick. Her mother, Hajja Fatma, believed her daughter had inherited a madness from her aunt. People said the devil had not left her until she had poured a tin of kerosene over herself, lighted a match and tried to burn herself. Her image began to haunt me. I could see her running along the bank of the Nile, her body in flames. Her shrieks reached me as I lay in bed, then gradually subsided into moans that reminded me of the women in my family, of all those women I had heard moaning in the night.

I felt I had to go and see her. So I said to Om Ibrahim, 'I've decided to visit Masouda in her home, and hear the story of this so-called devil that has possessed her.'

'Dr Nawal, the number of patients waiting to be examined keeps increasing every day, and now you want to go visiting them at home. It's too much for you, and all you'll get out of it is an army of fleas.'

'These stories about devils are not convincing, and I want to find out what's behind all this.'

'But doctor, don't you have enough to do examining human beings without wanting to examine devils also? God protect you from devils. Only a force more powerful than they are can deal with them.'

'I'm going to Masouda. I'm the village doctor, and I'm not going to leave her to the devils to do what they want with her.'

Something else had also made me decide to go and see her. In my memory there remained the image of the small servant-girl, Saadeya, fleeing our home after my mother had beaten her, walking along the seashore of Alexandria all alone, thinking that it was the way back to

---

[1] The popular term used to describe a woman possessed by a devil.

her village and her family. I could almost see her tiny earrings made of tin showing in the moonlight as she walked along. Somehow her image and that of Masouda became linked in my mind.

So there I stood in the courtyard looking down on her thin body as she lay on the couch.

'Tell me, Masouda, how did the devil get a hold on you?'

'I don't know, doctor.'

'Try to remember, Masouda.'

'I can't remember anything.'

Her voice reminded me of Shalabeya, the young servant-girl in my grandfather's house, of the way she pronounced her words, of her features, of her thin dark-skinned body lost in the wide *gallabeya* that she kept pulling on to cover herself, of her big black eyes looking up at me before she curled up with her face hidden between her knees. She was only fourteen years old but my aunt Fahima had taken her off to the railway station and left her there to fend for herself.

'How did the devil mount you, Masouda, from behind or from in front?'

'From behind, doctor.'

'How, Masouda?'

'I bowed down to the ground after having finished my evening prayers, and he came up from behind and mounted me.'

Her mother was squatting on the floor near the couch listening. At these words her body began to shake. She stood up and addressing her daughter in a loud voice said, 'May Allah silence you, girl. Devils fear God, and a devil would never go anywhere near a prayer carpet. God give you long life, doctor. Please prescribe something that will cure her of her illness. She's suffering from the same madness as her deceased aunt.'

Masouda sat up suddenly on the couch . She looked as though she was on the point of striking her mother. 'You are the one that's mad. May Allah take you!' she said. The last phrase, 'May Allah take you,' went through my mind like a ray of light. What had the mother done to make her daughter wish she would die? I had noticed that the girl was always silent in the presence of the mother, that the mother followed her around like her shadow, even when she went to the latrine. 'I'm afraid she might do something to herself,' she explained to me. 'Her aunt burnt herself to death.'

Masouda continued to get steadily worse. She used to get up in the middle of the night and run out to the banks of the Nile where the night guards would catch her and take her back to her parents.

One day the father brought her to me on a donkey. 'Keep her with you in the hospital for a few days, maybe God will cure her.'

I gave her a room to herself and asked Zeinat to take care of her. Every morning I went to see her before the outpatients' clinic, then again in the afternoon after I had finished examining the patients. Before going to sleep I used to drop in for a chat, hoping to find out something which would explain her state. Zeinat took an almost motherly care of her. She used to give her small doses of sedative. I had explained to her that I was opposed to the use of shock treatment, or drugs, that what was important was to discover the cause of her malady. After a while Zeinat started to sleep with her in the same room, share her meals, and stay up talking with her at night. 'Tell her about your life, Zeinat, it might encourage her to talk about hers.'

One night all three of us were sitting in the room talking. Zeinat was telling us about her childhood, how she ran away from home because her father wanted to marry her off to an old shoemaker who had a grandchild about her age. After she ran away, a relative from her mother's family took her in. She was working as a nurse in Kasr Al-Aini Hospital, was not married, and had no children. 'So I became like a daughter to her and she decided to send me to the nursing school. I'm thirty-one years old now and want to become a senior nurse in Kasr Al-Aini Hospital,' she said, 'but people keep telling me why don't you get married and have one or two children? But aren't there enough children in the world? There are thousands of them who live in orphanages. I can always adopt a child. What do you think of that, Dr Nawal?'

'Of course, but you will face difficulties with the law and with religious jurisprudence. Adoption is forbidden in Islam.'

'It shouldn't be forbidden. What would I have done if this relative of mine had not adopted me. I would have found myself living with that old maker of shoes. He was fifty years older than I was, and I had barely reached the age of fourteen, about the same age as Masouda. My body used to shake as though I was facing death every time I saw him in front of me.'

Masouda shivered as she listened. She opened her lips, murmured something inaudible, closed them tight together and was silent. Zeinat went on: 'But why is adoption forbidden in Islam. The Prophet Muhammad was always very kind to children and orphans.

Besides, you know the orphanages are terrible. You can't imagine what they are like. I lived in one of them for two months before my aunt took me into her care. One of our superintendents was a man with a huge nose and only one eye. One day he took me to his room, started to beat me with his cane and suddenly I found him on top of me.'

Masouda let out a sudden shriek, hid her head under the sheet, and began to shake violently. Zeinat went pale. I whispered to her, 'That's enough. What you were saying has touched a hidden wound in her. Give her half a tablet of valium and let her sleep. I'll go home now.'

That night before I went to bed, Om Ibrahim massaged my swollen feet. I had been sitting for three hours in an uncomfortable cane chair listening to Zeinat's stories. They filled me with an untold sadness, brought back frightening dreams. When I slept I sometimes dreamt that I was walking in the night alone, and got lost. A man whom the girls in school addressed as 'sir' would walk up to me, and take me into a room, close the door and press his body up against mine. His mouth smelt bad, and smoke used to escape from it as he pushed something like a thick hard finger between my thighs.

Om Ibrahim sat on the floor massaging my legs as these thoughts flitted through my mind. 'You're tiring yourself out with that girl Masouda. No treatment other than Al-Zar² will be of any use to her. You know these devils are afraid of dancing and tabla.³

'Shut up Om Ibrahim. What's this nonsense about zar?' I said irritably.

'Believe me, doctor, many a time have devils mounted me, and each time I was only able to get rid of them through zar. These Sheikhs know more about them than the doctors.'

Her last sentence echoed in my mind. When she massaged me her hands seemed to know by experience exactly where the pain was. Her fingers would travel down my spinal column, and stop at one particular vertebra. Then she would put pressure with her finger on one particular spot and say, 'Is that where it hurts you, doctor?' I would gasp out in relief, 'Yes, exactly there.'

After she had finished with my back she would move over to my head, my shoulders, my neck, my arms and legs and feet, pressing in

² Exorcism.
³ Beating on a hollow long-necked drum with the hands. Used in sessions for exorcising spirits in music and dancing.

a special way over the heels and soles and joints of my feet. 'You have a lot of pain in your body,' she kept saying.

I heard exactly the same phrase spoken in English thirty-eight years later in the American city of Seattle on the north-west coast of the United States. In the year 1994 I spent six months as a visiting professor at Washington State University. I had a Chinese colleague who, like me, was over sixty. She heard me complaining of back pain, caused by a prolapsed disc. So one day she came to my house carrying a small box in which there were a number of needles. She moved her slender pointed fingers over my body, defined a number of painful spots, and over each of them she sunk a needle. The points she chose were exactly the same ones that Om Ibrahim used to press on with her fingers when I was in Kafr Tahla. The words she pronounced to describe my condition were exactly the same words that Om Ibrahim had pronounced thirty-eight years ago: 'You have a lot of pain in your body, Nawal.' I looked out of the window from my house in Queen Anne. The calm waters stretched over the bay down below. They reminded me of the Nile in Kafr Tahla.

When I was still a child I had accompanied my grandmother and my aunts to sessions of exorcism (*zar*), but since the age of six I had not been to any of these sessions again. I wanted to renew this experience, so when the parents of Masouda began to organize a session for her in the hope that it would lead to a cure, I decided to attend.

Present were a number of women including Om Ibrahim, the mother and the aunts of Masouda, Masouda herself and a number of other women relatives and neighbours I did not know. We all gathered in an empty inner courtyard, and the dance began, slow and rythmic at first then becoming gradually faster and more frenzied. The drumming of the *tablas* made everything shake, the walls, the bodies of the dancers, the earth and the sky, the ground under the pounding feet. As we danced everything seemed to fuse into the rhythm of the beat, body and soul, heaven and earth. The dancing bodies seemed to become a single body so that after some time I could no longer distinguish between Masouda's mother and Om Ibrahim, or between Masouda and any of the other women present. The present, too, seemed to fuse with the past, and the images of other women I had met years before kept flitting through the courtyard as though they had joined in the dance, so that at moments, I glimpsed one of my aunts, or my maternal grandmother, or Shalabeya, or Saadeya, enveloped in the rising clouds of burning incense and alum. Little by little the clouds of smoke took different shapes, became devils or evil spirits mingling with the dancing bodies as they leapt to the drumming *tablas* and the rising sound of shrieks, to the voices crying out, 'Thou Sheikh who hast power over spirits, join us and let the body mounted by a devil come.'

The swaying, dancing, shaking, shivering bodies were freeing themselves of all constraint. They writhed and twirled around the flames, which kept leaping higher and higher like fiery snakes. The breasts and buttocks of the women jerked up and down to the beat of *tablas*. The long tresses of their loosened hair flew up and down and round and round, their mouths gaped open as they screamed out loudly, 'Thou Sheikh who hast power over spirits, join us and let the body mounted by a devil come.' Sweat poured down their faces and their bodies, their shrieks and cries rose in the air with the gasps of breath and the beat of the *tablas*. Sweat mingled with the red blood flowing from slaughtered cocks and chickens, or from the dancers' flesh torn open by their nails as they dug them into their own bodies or into someone else, as though in this frenzied dance they had become a single mass of quivering flesh. Heads threw the dark tresses of their long hair back and bared their naked breasts, or bent forwards and threw the tresses forwards over their chests in an ecstatic agony. Their hands split the long robes from top to bottom and exposed the writhing bodies and the twisting thighs. Their legs rose up in the air, their breasts shook up and down over shivering bellies, their heads tossed their mad hair around, their bodies bent down lower and lower, until their heads touched the ground as though licking the dust, then rose up again, and the voices screamed out 'Thou Sheikh who hast power over spirits, join us and let the body mounted by a devil come.' Their minds no longer had control over their bodies, and their bodies no longer enveloped their minds. It was the shock of an absolute innocence facing an evil no longer by the clash between Satan and God, or between freedom and constraint. It was high-powered electricity, the shock of irons heated red on flesh, of extreme pleasure coupled with extreme pain, of joy in eternal salvation, and the sadness of eternal suffering, of the razor blade when it cut into flesh, and the stick when it beat down on wedding nights. It was the blood of a hymen torn out, the singeing of hot earth under bare feet, the salt of salted food burning into their bellies, the bitter gall in their livers and the worms eating their guts.

It was their sons dead in the war, and their children, early victims of death.

'Scream at the top of your voice, Masouda! Let the devil out of your body. Come on, Masouda, scream at the top of your voice.'

Om Ibrahim's voice was louder than that of any other woman in this frenzied dance, as though she wanted to go all the way to the seventh heaven, to pierce the ears of the devils and the angels, to reach the Creator of the universe on high. She invoked the name of Allah, the One and Eternal, of the prophets starting with Abraham, down the line, from one to the other until she reached Muhammad, the last of all prophets sent by God. She invoked the name of our Sayeda Khadija, wife of Muhammad, Sayeda Zeinab, and the Virgin Mary, mother of Christ. She called upon them all to restore her son who had been reported missing in the war eight long years ago. She opened her arms to the heavens as though to embrace the son she saw descending from above. He came down hanging from a parachute, his feet standing firmly on a magic carpet and her screams suddenly changed into 'yooyoos' of joy that rose up higher than any other voice. She shouted with ecstasy, 'The doors of heaven have opened wide and I can see my son Ibrahim descending by parachute. Come my darling son, come into the arms of your mother.' The tears flowed from her eyes shining with joy. She embraced her son, held him to her breast, embracing truth and illusion, spirit and body, Allah and Satan, her subconscious and her conscious, all at once.

I kept asking myself a question. Had Om Ibrahim lost her mind, or was her reason superior to that of any one else's? I opened my secret diary and in the middle of the night wrote, 'Is the highest degree of reason, a capacity to lose the reason we have?'

On that night when the zar was over, Masouda lay down to sleep before dawn. Every one else was fast asleep. I listened to her as she lay there whispering in the dark, in a kind of delirium. Her face was bathed in sweat. The birds had not yet risen from their nests. The tree leaves were shining in the moonlight with early dew. Her voice came to me as though in a dream, without time, without place.

'I was twelve years old, and very clever at school when my father and mother forced me to marry the cousin of the village headman. He was an old man, even older than my respected father's father. Everybody was scared of him. He had been a brigand and a killer, and was known to have murdered his wife, had grown-up sons and daughters living in Cairo who were themselves married with children. He used to call out to me in the middle of the night in a loud voice, "Get up girl and come here". I used to run out of the house into the fields, but he would come after me, and I do not know how he was always able to find where I was hiding. He used to drag me out by the arm and say, "Listen to me, girl, when your master summons you to him you are to obey at once. Here, that's for you!" And he would land his hand on my face with all his force. Then he would mount me in the same way as he mounted his donkey, clap both his hands over my mouth so that nobody would hear me cry out. I could hardly breathe under his weight, felt I was dying, that my spirit would leave my body at any moment.

'Before going to bed every night he would insist on my massaging him all over. He would lie on his back and make me squat at his feet, then ask me to massage them, toe by toe, then up under the sole to his calves. Every now and then he gave me a kick in my belly and said, "Massage properly, you hussy. What's the matter with you. Where has all the food I give you gone? Push harder can't you! Where does all that food go out from, you bitch? Open your legs so that I can take a look."

'He'd lift my *gallabaya* over my head so that I couldn't see and repeat, "Come on where does all that food go to, you hussy, tell me." "I don't know master, I swear by the Prophet that I don't know. Have mercy on me, and may God preserve your life, something is burning me like fire." "Where is it burning you, you bitch, where?" "I don't know master, I swear by the Prophet that I don't know where."

'You know, doctor, I used to feel a terrible burning pain inside my body. He used to hold something in his hand, I don't know what, something like a rod, or the leg of a chair, and keep pushing it, and when I screamed he would put his hand over my mouth to stifle my voice, hit me on my belly, or on my mouth or anywhere else and say, "You don't want to tell me where all that food ends up? I'll find out for myself where the hell it all goes. I'll go on reaching for that part of you that's lost until I find it. Do you know where it is, you bitch? I'm going to show you."'

I heard this story from Masouda several times. Every time she got to this point she would go into a kind of faint, lose her voice and start turning her face up towards the heavens then down to the ground again and again with a terrible look of fear in her eyes, then she would gasp, 'Keep the Devil away from me.' Her face would contract as in an epileptic fit. After a little while she would calm down and fall into a deep sleep, her body bathed in sweat.

In my medical report I wrote: 'The patient Masouda Zeidan is suffering from a psychological disorder, in which she goes through fits similar in some ways to epilepsy, and in which she loses consciousness. She should be kept under supervision in hospital for some time until her condition improves. I recommend that she be separated from her husband. He is the cause of her malady. He is fifty years older than she is, beats her viciously every night, and violates her sexually by forcing her to undergo anal intercourse when she bows down to do her prayers.

'Her father obliged her to marry him when she was only twelve years old. She was under the illusion that it was God who was violating her since the intercourse only took place when she bowed down in prayer. When she grew older she rejected the idea that it was God, and began to imagine that it was the Devil, or the evil spirits that mounted (possessed) other women in the village.

'When examined, the patient showed signs of severe chronic inflammation with multiple ulcers around the anal orifice, resulting from the force used by a grown man to introduce his male organ into the anus of a small girl, and the almost nightly repetition of such violence for a period of almost five years. The girl found no other way of escape except through mental disease. The fear suppressed within her manifested itself in the form of a devil which mounted her.'

When she became normal again Masouda said to me, 'Please, for the Prophet's sake, doctor, keep me here with you. I don't want to go home. May Allah give you many years to live.'

She had slipped into the life of the hospital, and her mind was now perfectly clear. The inflammations and ulcers which had given her so much pain were completely healed. Now she talked with the patients, smiled and even laughed. Her face radiated with a new hope.

When her husband came to the hospital to take her home, she locked the door of her room and threatened to set fire to herself. Her husband came to see me. I found a huge corpulent body dressed in a silk *jibba*, with a red turban wound around his head. He stood in front of me slipping the yellow rosary beads through his fingers, muttering prayers under his breath, coughing with the wheezing sound of an asthmatic. Every now and then he pulled out a small bottle, put it to his nose and sprayed.

'Masouda is my wife, and I must take her back home,' he said.

Next day the father came along and insisted on having a talk with Masouda. 'Be reasonable,' he said 'and go back to your husband. I am your father and I want what is best for you.'

But Masouda was adamant, refusing to go home, so I said to the father, 'The girl does not want to go back. Why don't you let her do what will set her mind at rest?'

'Set her mind at rest, doctor! How can that be? She is the man's wife according to the laws of Allah and His Prophet, and if she does not go back to him of her own free will he can take her back by force. He is a man, knows what is right, and follows what God tells him to do.'

Religious jurisprudence did not allow a woman to leave the marital home without the permission of her husband, and Masouda's husband knew that very well. If she left home without permission he could insist that she return, and if she refused he could make the police take her back home by force. This was known as the law of obedience.

I was using my medical authority to keep Masouda away from her husband, but the law was more powerful than medicine. It drew its authority from God's divine jurisprudence. I was putting myself in the position of someone opposed to God and His laws. Nevertheless I could not let Masouda down. I had done that with Saadeya and Shalabeya, but that was years ago when I was still young and had no weapons with which to fight, but the memory of those moments in my life was still vivid in my mind. Now I was the medical doctor in charge of the health unit, so how could I abandon the responsibility that was mine?

Masouda remained in the health unit. But one day the police came for her and forcibly took her home to her husband. Accompanying them was Ostaz Khairallah. He had sent a report against me to the Supreme Council of Combined Health Units in Cairo. It was composed of three typewritten pages and he had made three copies of it. He sent one copy to Fouad Galal, the President of the Supreme Council, the second to Dr Abdou Sallam, the Secretary-General of the Council and the third to the President of the Republic. I did not read the report until a year later, after I had moved to Cairo. Dr Abdou Sallam showed it to me. The gist of the report was that Dr Nawal El Saadawi, the medical doctor in charge of the health unit of Kafr Tahla, had exhibited a signal disrespect for the moral values and customs of our society and had incited women to rebel against the divine laws of Islam.

* * * *

'Inciting women to rebel against the divine laws of Islam.' This became the accusation that was levelled against me whenever I wrote or did anything to defend the rights of women against the injustices widespread in society. It followed me wherever I went, step by step, moved through the corridors of government administrations year after year, irrespective of who came to power, or of the regime that presided over the destinies of our people. It was only years later that I began to realize that the men and women who posed as the defenders of Islamic morality and values were most often the ones who were undermining the real ethics and moral principles of society.

Masouda lived for a week in the house of her husband. At the beginning of the second week she disappeared. The police looked for her everywhere: in the surrounding villages and fields, in the railway stations, in the hospitals and orphanages, in the bordellos of country 'madams' and dancers. They even came to the health unit, searched every corner in it, including my house.

After a week they found her body floating on the waters of the Nile, somewhere between the village of Ramla and the provincial city of Benha.

It was a very murky humid day, heavy with dust. I stood helpless on the bank of the river wearing my white coat, my arms hanging uselessly at my side amidst a crowd of helpless women who, dressed in their black *gallabeyas*, watched as Masouda was pulled out of the water. Seeing her small, child-like body carried by the rough brown hands of the men reminded me of the days when a young virgin was sacrificed to the ancient god of the Nile. He was ten thousand years old with an appetite that could only be satisfied by young virgin girls. So they used to choose one of them, whom they called 'The Bride of the Nile', and throw her to him to be swallowed up by his waters. He had travelled 6,825 kilometres from the heart of Africa, through rock, desert and wasteland, to reach Egypt. His waters swelled to the maximum on the twelfth night of the Coptic month *Ba'ouna* (June). On that night a drop of rain would fall from the heavens. It made the Nile overflow its banks and flood the land on either side. They called it 'The Night of the Drop'. The name was carved on walls five thousand years ago. Next to it they wrote in hieroglyphics, 'This is the God who emerges from the waters of the Nile, and no-one can say anything against him'. They called him Osiris, the totem King of the Dead, and prostrated themselves before him. They built a dwelling for him, called it the House of Worship, offered food to him and slaughtered geese, ducks and pigeons. On The Night of the Drop they sacrificed the young Bride of the Nile by throwing her into his waters.

The men pulled Masouda out of the waters, carried her in their arms, and climbed up the bank. Her wet *gallabeya* stuck to her body, and it showed like a slender stick of cane through the clothes as they carried her under the gaze of her mother, her father, her husband and all the village people standing around. I asked myself where all these people had come from as I stood there in my white coat with Zeinat and the other nurses, surrounded by men and women sitting on the bank of the Nile as though waiting for something. Grey wisps of cloud floated in a dead sky, and dust filled my nose and mouth with every breath. In the distance I could hear the gasping noise of the flour mill, the occasional desolate barking of a dog and sounds which seemed like voices wailing. Everything moved slowly as though we were all in a daze. Women kept arriving from the houses and fields, their rough cracked heels showing from under the hem of their black *gallabeyas*. An old woman hobbled up on her crutches, her feet black with charcoal dust, her wide skirt held up by a piece of rope tied around her waist. A woman who lived alone in a straw hut on the outskirts of the village came walking through the fields, stopped next to us, tied her kerchief tightly around her head, and pressed her fingers over her tired colourless eyes, then sat down on the ground and stretched out her legs which were covered in mud. A lone fisherman pulled in his net from the water, folded it and squatted on his haunches with his back to a tree.

People were arriving all the time. Young village boys and girls, who had left their games and come running as fast as they could out of the alleys and lanes to witness what was happening, stood in groups watching with a mixture of wonder and fright, side by side with labourers who had been working in the brick kiln and women whose clothes were covered in white flour from the dough they had been kneading for bread. Last of all came the village dignitaries, wearing long *gallabeyas* made of fine cotton and waistcoats of silk, walking with their hands behind their backs as they approached with slow steps and solemn faces.

Everyone stood there motionless as her body was brought out, as though they were expecting the appearance of the Virgin Mary on the dome of the church,[4] or the long-awaited Mahdi who would come at last to save mankind.[5]

It was as though the whole village were there. I stood without moving too, dressed in my white doctor's coat, my heart heavy with grief. I had failed to save Masouda from her fate, abandoned her when she needed me most, just as I had abandoned Shalabeya many years ago without knowing to this day what had happened to her, or where she had gone.

In my memory Masouda and Shalabeya remained linked. They resembled one another so closely they could have been twins. I could see their faces looking down on me from somewhere above, from an opening in the clouds. Their features were sharp and thin, their skin brown like the silt of the Nile but with a strange pallor, their big dark eyes full of a childlike sadness, their emaciated bodies lost in their clothes. Shalabeya the victim of an 'illegal violation' and Masouda the victim of a 'legal violation' within the marriage law.

At the age of ten when I was still in primary school I had acted in a play. My role was that of the goddess Isis. She was the goddess of Wisdom and Knowledge, and she was able to restore life to her dead brother, the god Osiris. Her mother was Noot, the goddess of heaven. Before she died Noot wrote a testament to her daughter Isis in which she said: 'My daughter, my advice to you is that when you inherit my place on the throne do not be a god to your people, do not draw your authority from the divine and sacred position that is yours, but from being a just and merciful ruler.'

This sentence was carved in stone seven thousand years ago in the year 4,988 BC. Later, things changed completely, for in the Old Testament Jehovah's authority is drawn from the fact that he is the one and only sacred and divine god, rather than from his following the principles of justice and mercy. The Qur'an explains that God does not forgive those who worship other gods, for that is the greatest sin of all. Yet He is prepared to forgive any other sin.

---

[4] In the late seventies a rumour arose that the Virgin Mary had appeared on the dome of a church in Shoubra (Cairo) and people flocked in great numbers to see her.

[5] The Shiites believe that Allah will send a new prophet to mankind. They call this prophet 'Al-Mahdi al-Montazar', and he has become one of the folkloric beliefs.

Thus, after a period of about two thousand years the greatest crime became to worship a god other than the God of Moses, whereas injustice became a minor sin. I began to ask myself how this change had come about. Was it linked to a new order in which the female goddesses had been replaced by one male god?

A few days after Masouda's body was pulled out of the Nile, instructions arrived from the Supreme Council for Combined Health Units in Cairo transferring Dr Nawal El Saadawi from the health unit in Kafr Tahla to the Department of Chest Diseases in the Ministry of Health. The instructions made no mention of the reasons for this transfer, and included a request that she travel immediately to Cairo.

I left the village carrying my bag in my hand, with Mona on my arm. Om Ibrahim refused to say goodbye. She put all her belongings together in one bundle and said, 'I'm coming with you, doctor.'

My mother was radiant with happiness when I returned to the family home. She had been sick in bed for some time. 'I'm glad you've come back. Stay with us. You'll be able to treat me,' she said. My father too was very happy. 'You should open a clinic in Giza. Your future is not in rural health units,' he said to me as we sat talking on the balcony. My friends were delighted when I went to see them. Safeya embraced me warmly and said, 'Now, Nawal, we can go to the courts and play tennis together again.'

Batta kept hugging me, and gurgling with laughter. 'Working amongst villagers. Bullshit!' she said, 'Stay with us. Here we can go to films and the theatre.' Samia visited me at home. 'You know, Nawal, all the time you were away I felt so lonely. Rifa'a[6] is in hiding. His party clashed with Abd Al-Nasser over unity with Iraq. Abd Al-Nasser wants unity to be a complete fusion under one central government, but Rifa'a's party says it should be a federation,' she explained to me. 'I'm now working on my own in the drug store,' she added.

---

[6] Her husband.

SIX

Love and Despair

In my deepest being there is this yearning for something that has no name. The word 'love' which we use to describe it is inadequate. It is all mixed up with taboos and licence, with forbidden and contradictory values.

At night I dreamt of love. During the day I searched for it, for him, for her, for them in the singular and the plural, in the masculine and the feminine. But love went beyond these categories. For me it was made of a substance which is neither body, spirit, nor mind, but a combination of the three, a combination which did not resemble any human being. It had no beard or whiskers, no breasts or buttocks, no vagina or penis. It had the features of a human being but in its eyes I saw nothing but light, in its arms I felt nothing but tenderness, on its fingers I did not see rings, on its arms there were no bracelets, and around its neck or body no chains. When it stretched its hands out to me they carried no gifts other than that of love.

Sometimes when I walked through the streets I glimpsed a face that was his. I stopped all of a sudden as though coming out of a dream. The look in his eyes reminded me of love, the way he moved, the way he walked and held up his head, his tread on the ground. The ring in his voice was different from the ring of any other voice. It was a ring which I had never heard before, or which I had heard many times before I was born, a ring that seemed familiar. All these things reminded me of love. His voice whispered in my ear every night, 'Nawal'. It knew who I was, picked me out of the billions of bodies that floated in space, embraced me. For me he was nothing but that embrace. It flooded over me in waves of pleasure, drowned me in warm water like the summer sea in Alexandria.

Since I was a child, throughout the sixty years I have lived, whether in waking or in sleep, this dream has kept coming back to me. Of all the living creatures on earth, it alone knows how to embrace me, how to become one with my body without causing pain or regret, or feelings of sin or guilt, without the need to seek permission from church or mosque, parent or state.

I respond to it like earth responds to sky, God to Satan, desert to rain, gulls to the sea, like moths are attracted to fire, burnt to ashes by it again and again in a cycle of life and death which goes on unceasingly.

Was 'love' this unattainable pleasure, possible only in dreams? When I was a child I used to hear women whisper to one another about it. Their heads would move close together and their voices, hoarse with desire, would whisper words I could not understand. Their eyes would glimmer with a burning lust, suppressed deep inside their bodies, their minds and their spirits. They married, had children, reached the age of menopause but the lust would still be there, suppressed deep down in their flesh. They lived, died and were buried virgins. Why were all the men in this world incapable of deflowering the hymen of their virginity? Had it do with history, with the separation of body from spirit, earth from sky? Is it why men will have no role to play in paradise other than to deflower the hymens of virgin women? For each man will be allowed ninety-two virgins for his pleasure, and each time he deflowers a virgin the hymen will heal again[1] so that his pleasure will be without end.

*   *   *   *

I spent the year of 1958 working at the Hospital for Chest Diseases in Abbaseya.[2] I used to take the bus from Giza to Tahrir Square, then a tram to Abbaseya that took me to the end of the line, after which I walked for almost an hour at a quick pace through desert sands to reach the hospital. On my way I used to pass by the walls of the Hospital for Mental Diseases, look up at the tall trees carrying a thick

---

[1] According to the Qur'an.
[2] A suburb of Cairo.

green foliage and glimpse patients walking around with dishevelled hair and dirty white clothes. Sometimes one of them would climb over the fence and come towards me shouting, 'Are you mad, or what?'

My mother's condition was getting steadily worse. At night I could hear her moaning. My father was like a camel, exhausted by the load he was carrying. My elder brother had graduated and was working in Tahrir Province.[3] This was a project started by the new regime which aimed at cultivating the desert to expand the agricultural area. My other sisters and brothers were either in school or at the university. I had lost weight and began to feel weak. Every morning I left home at six o'clock to be at the hospital at eight. It took me two hours to get there, an hour in the bus and the tram, and an hour on foot, walking in the desert. Sometimes I suffered from sunstroke, or a sandstorm arose and the sand got into my eyes, my nose, my mouth, my ears, under my clothes and into my shoes. When it was hot, sweat poured down my body as I walked with my bag held over my head to protect it from the sun. My toes developed small ulcers and my feet burnt. My eyes were inflamed and red.

By the time I got to the hospital I was exhausted. Inside the hospital I felt even worse. The patients were no more than human skeletons sitting on the beds, or moving around like phantoms suspended between life and death. They kept coughing all the time, spitting into the rusty tin mugs with which they were provided until they became full of a yellowish spit threaded with blood. Some of them had neither bed nor mattress, nor even a mug in which to spit. They slept in rows on the floors of the corridors outside the wards, and spat on the floor leaving red blobs scattered on the tiles. The air was heavy, suffocating, with a fetid smell. I could hardly breathe as I walked from one ward to the other treading on red sticky blobs which covered the floor.

My face had changed. It became long and thin. My eyes seemed to have grown bigger and blacker and there was a feverish shine in them that had not been there before. Tuberculosis patients have big shining eyes, as though the proximity of death endows them with a burning desire for life. The hair on their heads becomes smooth and silky, their eyelashes grow thick and dark, they develop a strong attraction, a kind of spirituality, a transparency of the flesh, a delicate pallor of

---

[3] An agricultural province reclaimed from the desert about 60kms from Cairo.

the skin, their feelings are made finer by pain and despair, by living on the border line between illusion and truth.

Writing was my refuge. Life for me became the words written on paper, words expressing sickness and death, and love to which I could succumb. They were infection from a whiff of breath, the silent bleeding to death, the heart ready for love.

I wrote a short story called 'Love and the Lizard', but Ahmed Baha'a Al-Dine, chief editor of the weekly magazine *Sabah Al-Kheir*, refused to publish it. 'Please keep away from sensitive matters, Nawal,' he said to me. 'What do you consider to be sensitive matters?' I asked him. 'Don't you know? The triad,' he answered. 'I know only two of them,' I said: 'God and Abd Al-Nasser. What is the third?' 'Sex,' he said. 'But there's no sex in my story at all,' I said.

The story was about a lizard I used to come across every day in the desert on my way to work. It was yellow, like the sand in which it hid. In the story I ask myself why God created an antagonism between Eve and the serpent, and between Eve and Adam? Was it because they ate from the tree of knowledge? Was God able to exercise his will only over people who were ignorant. Did he want them to remain ignorant so that he could continue to rule over them?

The lizard was my serpent. Every morning she used to look at me and smile. I smiled back, then continued on my way. If I did not find her waiting for me on a sand-dune I used to be seized with anxiety. Had some misfortune befallen her? Had someone hit her with a stick and killed her? When she heard my footsteps she would come out from under the sand, twirl around in a dance and lift her tail in the air as though she were waving to me.

When I continued on my way to the hospital my heart would be light. I had no feeling of enmity for the serpent. I knew I had disobeyed the commands of God by allowing myself to love the serpent and sometimes I would be siezed with feelings of guilt. Old fears would come back, for perhaps God would punish me for this sinful love!

*   *   *   *

A month before he died my father said to me, 'Write a letter to the Minister of Health asking him to transfer you from the Hospital for Chest Diseases in Abbaseya. It's much too far away.' I was coughing all the time as though I had developed tuberculosis myself. My father used to wake up in the middle of the night, make me swallow some cough medicine, cover me up, and go back to bed. But I refused to go to a doctor and be examined. I disliked doctors, preferred to die rather than to go to one of them. My father used to force me to swallow spoonfulls of medicine as though I were still a small child. 'How can you be a doctor and not know how to treat yourself?' he kept saying. Then he would cite an old proverb: 'The carpenter's door is unhinged.'[4]

I used to suppress the cough as I lay in bed to prevent him from hearing me. Om Ibrahim would wake up at dawn and bring me a big cup of steaming liquid to drink. 'The best thing for cough is boiled raw gum. Drink it all up,' she would say. On Fridays she accompanied me on a long walk in the open air. The stream of Tiri't Al-Zoumour, in the district of Omraneya where we lived, flowed along as far as the green fields that extended to the Pyramids.

She used to hold my hand and walk with me through the fields. The scent of budding fava bean flowers in the early morning air took me back to my childhood days. I would pull my hand out of her grasp and run far into the fields then stop. My eyes would drink in the wide expanses of green as though my soul thirsted for the colours of nature. The pores of my body opened up to draw in the warm rays of the sun. My arms embraced the green spaces as I waved them up and down like the wings of a bird or a butterfly. I was reliving the dream of flying that returned to me again and again in my sleep. 'How beautiful the world is,' I would say to Om Ibrahim. 'That's right, doctor. I want to hear your laugh again. When you laugh the sun becomes all golden.'

In response to my letter the minister transferred me to the Hospital for Chest Diseases in Giza. It was much closer to our house and stood at the confines of Omraneya district, right in the middle of green fields. I no longer wasted four hours going and coming every day. Instead I went on foot from home to the hospital. It took me one hour walking at a good pace along the stream. The exercise was excellent, the fresh air carried with it the smell of water and green fields. But my father was still anxious about my health, for I was still working with tuberculosous patients. Every time he heard me cough he would say, 'Write to the minister again and ask him to transfer you somewhere else. Then you can open a clinic in Giza.'

---

[4] The carpenter should be able to repair his own door.

My own clinic had always been my mother's and my father's dream for me. My mother died before her dream came true. Would I be able to open a clinic and fulfil my father's dream before he died? I did not have the money at that time. My monthly salary was only fourteen pounds. My father had reached the age of sixty and was now living on his pension which was only half the salary he used to earn. After my mother's death we had become ten people in the family: my father, two brothers, four sisters, Om Ibrahim, myself and my daughter. My sister Leila had married and left our home. My brother Talaat had gone to Tahrir Province and no longer lived with us. How could I possibly open a clinic when I was contributing to the expenses of this large family?!

*   *   *   *

The first time I earned money for my writing was during this period. I was given three pounds for a short story I had written.

I held the three pounds tightly in my hand. Their paper crackled in my palm. For the first time in my life I was beginning to understand the relation between matter and spirit, to realize that money had a value. Ever since I was a child I had heard my father pronounce the word 'money' with scorn. He would spit it out of his mouth in disgust. 'The only people who love money are traders, and traders are people with no conscience, no feeling. They don't read books, they don't participate in demonstrations against the British, they care about nothing except piling one millime[5] on top of the other until they've accumulated millions.' I had become immunized against wealth, and the word 'trader' was repugnant to me.

I went home holding the three pounds in my hand. My father was sitting alone on the balcony. I put the three pounds in his hand, looked into his eyes and saw the old glimmer which had disappeared from them shine out again, as though the tears in them were being held back. Success in anything I did had never had any meaning to me unless I sought this glimmer in his eyes. When I was a schoolgirl I used to bring my grades home to him and look into his eyes, waiting for the glimmer to show. If I did not see it, my success became a failure.

---

[5] One millime is one tenth of a piastre and one piastre is one hundredth of a pound. Neither the millime nor the piastre exist any more.

'These three pounds are for the short story I published in the magazine,' I explained to him.

'Congratulations, Nawal,' he said. 'Now I'm looking forward to the opening of your clinic in Giza.'

My happiness was cut short when he pronounced the last sentence. He loved literature and poetry. He had taught me to love the Arabic language, and when I was still a small child he was in the habit of reading the poetry of Al-Moutanabi, Abou Al-Ala'a Al-Ma'ari, Bashar Ibn Bourd, Akkad, Hafez and Shawki to me. Yet in his dreams he still saw me as a doctor in a clinic.

'Literature is closer to my heart, more important in my life than medicine,' I replied.

'In our country writers die of hunger and go to prison. Stay with medicine,' he said, 'and open a clinic.'

My father kept urging me to open a clinic. 'Free yourself from the bondage of being a government civil servant. Do not bury yourself in a government job, even if you are to become a minister. Ministers become ministers by decree, and are demoted or fired by decree. But in your clinic you are your own master, no-one puts you there, and no-one can remove you from it.'

But opening a clinic was not what I had dreamt of doing. Besides, I did not have the means. I needed at least seventy pounds for the cost of the equipment, the instruments, the furnishings and the rent of the flat which I was to find in the tall building overlooking Giza Square.

When I went to see the flat the owner said to me, 'If you cannot afford the expenses, there is a flat occupied by a dentist and he's looking for someone to share it with him.'

I wanted to be alone in my own clinic, but the money I had was not enough, so I decided to take a look at the dentist's flat. When I went in I found much more sunlight there than on the ground floor where I had been looking. There was a spacious hall used as a waiting-room with coloured chairs in it, the walls were freshly painted, the toilets were spotless, the male nurse wore a snow-white apron, and the eyes of the dentist who owned the clinic looked straight at me. He was lean, quite good-looking with sharp features, and his movements were quick and full of energy.

'Dr Nawal, you are most welcome. You can occupy the inner room. It's bigger than my room and further away from the noise of the patients who sit in the waiting-room,' he said.

By sharing the clinic I was halving the rent, as well as the salary of the male nurse. My room required simple furnishings, no more than a desk and chair, a small library for books, an examination table which could also be used for simple operations, sterilizing drums, and a few instruments which I could buy on instalments through the medical syndicate.

I inaugurated the opening of my clinic with a small celebration. It was attended by my father, by a few medical colleagues, new friends who belonged to young literary circles, the dentist owner of the clinic and his wife, and a couple of doctors with clinics in the same building. The owner of the building also attended, and for the first time in my life I saw my father throw back his head and laugh out loudly as he stood listening to Batta telling one of her jokes.

SEVEN

My Mother has no Place in Paradise

The sadness I felt for my mother was greater than any sadness I had ever known in my life. It increased as the days went by, refused to fade away like other feelings of sadness had done before.

I walk into the house, go into her room. My eyes wander over her empty bed. I ask myself, 'Why is the mind incapable of assimilating the reality of death at the moment when it happens? Does the spirit remain behind after the body has gone away?' I do not believe in the separation of body and spirit, yet I walk around the house as though expecting to find her somewhere, go into the rooms and come out, open the door of the kitchen, look into the toilets, the bathroom, everywhere. Her absence is a continuing shock, although I know she is dead. Her clothes still hang in the cupboard. I can see the yellow dress with shoulder straps she used to wear on occasions, her powder box, lipstick, small mascara bottle with the fine brush, the square comb made of ivory with which she used to comb her hair as she sat in front of the mirror. I stretch out my arm to where she sits with her back to me, and suddenly she is no longer there.

On the wall hangs a picture of her in a black frame. Her eyes look straight at me, her nose is tilted up in the air, her front teeth are slightly protruding, her forehead broad, the features of her face clear-cut, untouched by time.

She dreamt of playing the piano, of travelling in planes and discovering the world. She was married at the age of fifteen, died at the age of forty-five without fulfilling any of her dreams. She used to fast the month of Ramadan,[1] prayed when it was examination time for us, believed that God existed, but when she fell sick she forgot God and turned her hopes to the doctors.

Her voice calls out to me in the dark of night. 'Nawaaal. Can't you do something to cure me?' I wake up, walk on my bare feet so as not to awaken my father who has left the big bed and the room he used to share with her, and now sleeps on a couch in the hall. Her face looks out at me as white as the sheets. The cancer has eaten its way into her bones, slowly devoured them one after the other, day after day, month after month. She is no longer able to move her arms or her legs.

I lift up her helpless body to change the sheet from under it.

'Death would be more merciful than this. If only I could go to the toilet!'

'I am your daughter, mother. What does it matter?'

She had become like a child, urinated in her bed, hated the feeling of wetness under her, the odour of sickness. She had been a beautiful young woman, wore make-up, and perfumed herself. When she looked in the mirror she saw a princess. If she sneezed she covered her nose to hold the sneeze back. She never burped, and no-one had ever heard a sound from her intestines. Her body did not sweat, and if a small drop showed somewhere she would wipe it off quickly with a silk handkerchief. Her skin was soft and smooth, and no hair showed on it. If it grew she removed it before anybody had a chance to see it.

'Nawaaal, if you have any mercy in your heart bring me a poison that I can take. I want to die.'

My heart was full of love, full of tenderness for her, so how could I kill her? Could the love I had for her become great enough for me to end her life and save her from this terrible suffering?

In my dreams I used to search for a painless way to end her life. Why not increase the morphine enough for it to stop her heart? At least with morphine she would feel nothing.

'Nawaal, please have mercy on me and end my suffering!'

Her voice followed me day and night calling for mercy, for an end to her life. Death had become her only hope. Like an unattainable dream it occupied her thoughts. Would her daughter's heart ever love her enough, be kind enough to end her life?

---

[1] The Muslim month of fasting from dawn to dusk.

I was torn between love for my mother, and love for myself. I hesitated at the idea of giving her an overdose of morphine. Since I was a doctor it was very simple. All I had to do was to fill the syringe with the transparent, colourless liquid, push the needle into her vein and press on the piston. In one or two or maybe three minutes it would be over. Yet my fingers trembled at the idea, and my hand seemed paralysed. Was it right for a doctor to end the life of a patient after all hope of a cure was lost, and after suffering had become unbearable? What use was it for a body torn by endless pain and despair to continue living? My reason, my heart, kept telling me that there was nothing endless, nothing absolute. There was always a shred of doubt in what seemed certainty. Only the mercy of God, or miracles, were absolute and even here doubt crept in.

One night her suffering became worse than it had ever been before. I decided to do what had seemed impossible to me throughout the long months of struggle between my heart and mind. My love for her welled up in my heart and overflowed. It was a decision that required me to sacrifice myself for my mother. It was the desire of a daughter to try and return just a part of what her mother had done for her. It was the repayment of a debt owed to motherhood.

I boiled the syringe, filled it with morphine, walked into her room, holding it in my hand. She stretched out her pallid white arm. Through her skin I could see the blue vein thickened by injections. I cleaned the skin with alcohol, pushed the needle down, pressed on the piston, watched it move slowly in but before it went further, the syringe slipped out of my trembling hand, and I sat there, my heart pounding violently under my ribs, my mouth dry as a stick.

I had failed.

My mother lived with her pain for another month or so. She died on September 28, 1958 and the city, the whole world seemed to end with her. In the holy books mothers are described as being either sacred or accursed, the embodiment of evil or the essence of purity and love. Is that why on that day the city where she had lived and the world she had filled with her presence ended with her. In my secret diary I wrote, 'It's as though when my mother died, Cairo died with her. How can a woman become a whole city? Is it the first time this has happened in history?'

*   *   *   *

Years after the death of my mother when I was preparing to write my book, *The Naked Face of the Arab Woman*,[2] I reread the Old Testament and came across the story of Babel. The story says that in the old city of Babel there lived a woman who decided to defy the male God, to build a tower which would reach high up in the sky. She gathered all the inhabitants of Babel around her, convinced them to unite their efforts, to have a single will, to speak in a single tongue, and to construct the new city together. But God felt threatened. He stood against the united efforts of the inhabitants, transformed the city from a mother who embraced all her children with love into a scheming and corrupt adulteress. He looked down on the city and on the tower they had built and said to himself, 'Now these people are united, and speak with one tongue. This could be the beginning. From now on they will be able to accomplish whatever they may wish to do. So let us descend upon them, make them speak with many tongues, thus they will no longer be able to understand one another.' After that He scattered them over the face of the earth, so they ceased building their city. It became known as Babel because He made the people there babble[3] in all the tongues of the earth.

I first read about Babel in primary school. This story has remained vivid in my mind ever since. It evoked an image of the city, of the woman who was an adulteress. The Old Testament paints a description of her that is unforgettable. So one day I made a drawing of her during the class on religion. The drawing showed her as a tall graceful woman, sitting on a throne in heaven, on the back of a fiery red monster. For it was said of her that all the kings on earth had fornicated with her, and that all its inhabitants had become drunk with the wine of her fornications. She described herself as a queen, refused to be described as a widow, said that she would never know sadness. But the God on high ordained that she be punished with suffering and sadness, be beaten and starved to death, and be burnt in fire, for He is the greatest of gods, His eyes are like tongues of fire, on His head He wears many crowns, His body is enveloped in a splendid robe bathed in blood, and His name is called Jehovah (Allah). Out of his mouth protrudes a mighty sword with which he

---

[2] The title in the English translation is *The Hidden Face of Eve*, Zed Books 1980; 19th impression 2001.

[3] 'Balbala' – Babel in Arabic means 'to confuse'.

smites all nations, and on His robe and thighs is written his name, King of kings, God of all gods.

* * * *

When my mother died I did not put on black clothes nor did I go into mourning. I was too sad to find time for mourning, or to go out and look for a black dress. Besides, why black? Sadness goes beyond all colours. No colour can express it. I wore my ordinary clothes. I did not know what colour they were because I never stood in front of the mirror to see what I was wearing. Sadness abolished the sense of time, and the use of words. Silence was more eloquent than any words, and those who wept and shrieked were the least sad of all.

The person who shrieked louder than any one else was my Aunt Hanem Shoukry. Gathered around her were my aunts Fahima and Ni'mat and other women from my mother's family, all of them screaming. Aunt Hanem led the procession, advanced towards me shrieking. Her soft fat body was squeezed inside a new black dress made of shining silk, tight around the buttocks, and open at the neck to show the furrow between her breasts. Her eyelashes were thickly mascared, and on her lids was a faint dark shadowing under eyebrows which had been plucked and drawn in a pencil line. Her lips were painted 'naturel', her hair covered in a fine black **tarha** which dropped down over her forehead leaving exposed a lock of hair which the hairdresser had ironed and snipped, her diamond earrings flashed through the open folds of the **tarha** hanging on either side of her head, and her neck was encircled by a diamond necklace to match the earrings. In her hand she carried a bag made of snakeskin, and she wore fine dark stockings around her bandy legs. Her body swayed as she walked on the thin high heels of her shoes.

'My darling Zaynab, it was much too early for you,'[4] she shrieked out loudly. Although she shrieked there were no tears in her eyes, for tears were liable to wet her mascara and spread it over her face. She kept repeating the same shrieking sentence again and again, stopping every now and then to take a few gasping breaths, stretching her neck upwards with every gasp as though she would suffocate at any moment. In her eyes I could see a glimmer of happiness shining

---

[4] Meaning an early death.

through, for after all Allah had been merciful enough to spare her and take her younger sister away instead.

She made a move to enter the room where the body of my mother lay, but I blocked her way and closed the door. Om Ibrahim was washing my mother's body before wrapping the fine shroud around it and lifting her into the wooden coffin. I did not want any of the women to feast their eyes on my mother's naked body, for in their eyes I could read what they were unable to conceal, a gloating happiness, an unwholesome curiosity to see what normally is not seen, and a burning desire to examine my mother's private parts.

My mother had always tried to hide the fact that one of her breasts had been removed in an operation. To me she had remained the goddess with a single breast, but she did not feel the way I felt. It was as though she felt responsible for the loss of her breast, and so she continued to do everything she could to hide it. She used to fill up the empty space in her bodice with cotton. It reminded me of the dolls she made for us with her skilful fingers when I and my sisters were still small. She felt that this way she could still show two breasts like all other women, walk with the pride of her full femininity as a woman. What worried her most was her appearance, what she was on the outside. No-one could see what was missing, and so for her what had happened was only a dream, and there was no reason for her to believe it. She refused to open her eyes lest she discover that it was not a dream but real.

I bought a shroud for my mother, ten metres of green silk from the store of Islam Pasha in Giza Square. The colour green was a symbol of death at a young age. As Om Ibrahim wrapped it around her body she held back her tears, and smiled at me. 'All blessings come from you and from Sayed Bey, your father. May God help him to bear this separation,' she sighed.

I sat in the black funeral hearse next to the wooden coffin. I wanted to stay with my mother until the moment she was buried. I had to make sure that she would be lying on a surface that was smooth and clean, so I climbed down into the pit in which she was to be buried, removed all the pebbles and pieces of stone, smoothed over the bottom with the palm of my hand, sprinkled soft earth over it and then allowed them to lower her into it. She lay on her back looking up at a patch of blue sky. I put my ear over her breast and listened as though I might hear the sound of heartbeats or of breathing. But there was nothing there, nothing but her body enveloped in the green shroud, no movement, no heartbeat, no sound of breathing. Perhaps she would wake up after a short while? The pit was enveloped in darkness except for a faint light coming in from the opening above. My Aunt Fahima kept peering through it. She held a pair of big scissors in her hand, and I saw them dropping towards me through the opening. She said, 'You must cut up the shroud around her body, otherwise it might be stolen by graveyard thieves,' and her voice seemed to reach me from another world.

Graveyard thieves commonly engaged in stripping bodies of the shroud if it remained intact, because then they could sell what was usually quite costly material. They also pulled out gold teeth from the mouths of the dead and sometimes visited the graveyards to pick up the bones of the skeleton since they could sell them to medical students.

I moved the body of my mother carefully first to one side, then to the other so that I could cut through the material with the scissors. Sweat streamed down my body as I worked in the small dark suffocating space. At one point the scissors cut into my mother's flesh and I shivered. I had barely finished when I heard my father's voice call down to me.

'That's enough, Nawal. Hold on to my hand and I will lift you out.'

I saw my father's long arm come down through the opening. I grasped his hand feeling like someone who had fallen into a well, had almost drowned and was now being pulled out. At last I came out into the sunshine, breathing freely, dusting my clothes, sweeping it off my face and hair, removing it from my eyes and ears as though I myself had been a corpse buried under the ground.

When I got home Om Ibrahim took me to the bathroom, swished me with hot water, rubbed me down, all the time keeping up a running conversation. 'My child, you're still too young for all this. Your Aunt Fahima should have been the one to go down into the pit and cut the shroud. She's your mother's sister, hefty and strong and with a heart made for this kind of thing, smooth as a snake on the outside and like a dagger on the inside.'

That night I ran a high fever, and as the hours went by became delirious. I kept looking out from under the cover as though I had been buried with my mother and was searching for a hole through which I could climb out from the pit in which we lay. She and I were one body, enveloped in the shroud. Her arms held me tight, then all of a sudden she let me go and a moment later she was dead. Her body became separated from mine, and I was left sad and alone. Then I felt her come close and embrace me in her arms again, and we continued to play this game of becoming one body then separating, over and over again, just as we used to do years ago in the sea of Alexandria, when I was only five years old.

After she died I used to hear her calling to me in the middle of the night. I would get out of bed and walk to her room on tiptoe to avoid waking her up, only to discover that my father was asleep in the big bed, that he no longer slept on a couch in the hall. He would wake up and say: 'Why are you not asleep, Nawal?' 'What time is it, father?' I would ask. 'It's half past four in the morning, just after dawn,' he would answer. 'Let's go and see my mother. I have a feeling the shroud has been stolen off her body and that she's lying naked in the earth.'

I spent sleepless nights before my father said that we would go on a Thursday to visit her grave in the cemetery of Al-Ghafeer located near the Mokattam Hills. The family tomb[5] had been built there out of red stone by my grandfather Shoukry Bey. It looked like a small house, and was surrounded by a stone-walled courtyard which one entered through a small iron gate. The key of the iron gate was kept with the cemetery guard. He was a tall, lean man wearing a dirty tattered *gallabeya*, and the skin covering his hands was all cracked. He looked like the janitor in the anatomy hall of the School of Medicine, or like an undertaker.

Thursday was the visiting day when people went to the cemetery. The big courtyard was crowded with cane chairs on which the women of the family were seated. They were all smartly dressed in black silk, with lots of make-up on their faces, and jewellery. The smell of powder and perfume filled the air. They kept talking all the time in an insipid way, mixing Arabic with French words, saying stupid meaningless things, exchanging gossip about friends and members of the family, lowering their voices and shooting side glances if one of the people they were talking about was there. Every now and then one of them would stop talking suddenly and scream. 'It was too early for you, darling Zaynab,' then lean back in her chair and let out a deep sigh as though she were drawing the air upwards from somewhere down in her belly.

---

[5] In Egypt people of one family are buried in a single big grave with a dome-like tomb built over it. However, the men are buried separately from the women.

After some time they stopped screaming, as though they had done their bit, sunk their fleshy bodies deep in their chairs, took off their shoes, stretched out their short fat legs and basked in the sun, their eyes shining at the thought that they were still alive. After a while they began sinking their teeth into the pastry that had been brought as an offering[6] by my father.

I was the last to leave the graveyard, walked several times around it to make sure that everything was all right. The guard watched me through his narrow eyes. One of them was almost closed, the other blinked rapidly. I wanted to be certain that the tomb was properly closed, that the shroud had not been stolen, and that the body of my mother had not disappeared.

'Open up, Uncle Muhammad. I want to see my mother,' I said to him.

'I cannot open the tomb. That's not allowed.'

'Why not?'

'It's a sacrilege to open the tomb. God said in His holy book...'

'What has that got to do with God?'

My father intervened between us. 'Don't worry, Nawal,' he said 'Uncle Muhammad is a good man, and would never allow anybody near your mother's grave.'

So I gave in, left the courtyard with my father and waited until the iron door was locked. The guard threw unpleasant looks in my direction, and I noticed this time that the eye that had been closed earlier was now wide open. My doubts invaded me again and before we had gone far I kept turning round to look at the small iron gate, stopped for a long moment, and only started moving again when my father told me not to dawdle. I walked along by his side down the narrow lane, then stopped once more, turned round to look at the iron gate and at that precise moment it seemed to me as though my mother's naked body walked out of it. As a matter of fact, I was sure that it did. I continued to walk beside my father with a heavy heart and dragging step, for the image of my mother emerging from the gate refused to go away.

At night in my dreams I used to open the iron gate, walk into the yard, dig the ground over her grave, and jump into the pit like a cat.

---

[6] Pastry cakes are distributed to the poor when relatives visit the deceased in the cemetery and visitors may partake of them – one of the traditions related to mourning the dead.

The grave in my dreams was much deeper and very dark, and had a very low ceiling, so I had to stoop as I walked, holding my arms stretched out in front of me so that I did not collide against anything. But after a little while I discovered a torchlight in my pocket, and with it began to search for my mother's body. There was a large number of bodies enveloped in old shrouds. I was able to recognize my grandfather Shoukry Bey, my grandmother and all the men and women in my mother's family who had died. At one moment my foot hit against a skull that resembled the one I had on my desk, but it had long whiskers like those of my grandfather. I almost fell on my face from the shock, but regained my balance and walked on. I was able to discern the green silk shroud in which my mother's body was enveloped, and to distinguish the configurations of her body. I knew all its details so well, the characteristic curve of her shoulders, and her buttocks, the breast missing on the left. I knelt over her, brushed away the dust which had settled on her right breast, wrapped the green shroud more tightly around her body, closed the window and the door to make sure that she did not catch cold, put off the lights and left her sleeping.

*   *   *   *

I can hear my father's voice saying to me, 'Your mother will go to Paradise, Nawal. Paradise lies beneath the feet of all mothers.' Whenever I wondered about the fate of my mother that is what he used to say to me. I believed everything my father said to me. I was twenty-seven years old and a medical doctor. I treated sickness, knew that death was as real as the body, that when the body left this world the spirit left with it, yet I still believed the things he said to me.

But where did the spirit go when the body departed from our world?

This question was the beginning of a long journey through the vast domain of what is considered sacred, and protected by Almighty God. The first step in this journey was the phrase often repeated by my father, and other authoritative people: 'Paradise lies beneath the feet of all mothers,' a phrase my father explained to me was one of the sayings of the holy Prophet.

I started to search for the rights of mothers in the teachings of the Prophet. All I wanted was to be reassured of the fate that my mother would meet after death. I could not imagine her in hell. She had lived and died for her husband and her nine children. She worked and cared for them day and night, got nothing in return except a roof over her head, and food. She was a child when she left the family home and went to live with her husband. She was still a young woman when she died. She remained faithful to him throughout her married life from the moment she started to share a bed with him on the wedding night, until the moment she died in the same bed thirty years later. She never gambled, or drank, never smoked even a single cigarette, had no friends whether men or women. She spent her whole life between the bedroom and the kitchen. After all that, surely she deserved to go to Paradise?

I looked through my father's library until I found a collection of the sayings of the Prophet. The sayings in this collection were considered authentic since they consisted of what his wife Al-Sayeda Aisha[7] and his immediate disciples had heard directly from him. Only a small number were looked upon as being doubtful, but these my father had marked with his comments.

The idea of a life after death originated with the ancient Egyptians. They believed that when the body died, the spirit left it, and if the spirit had been obedient and good it went to the dwelling place of happiness to live with angels, princes and kings, but disobedient, rebellious spirits went to Hell together with the devils and slaves. The ancient Egyptians believed that the Pharaohs ruled on earth, but also ruled after death and decided who should be sent to heaven and who deserved to end up in Hell.

Many of the ancient descriptions of Paradise and Hell have been lost but those that remain do not differ much from what is in the holy books. Paradise is a place where there are succulent fruits, rivers of pure water or honey, or milk, or wine, and virgins with whom men satisfy their sexual appetites.

Among the numerous sayings of the Prophet I came across a description of life in Paradise. What surprised me most were the details related to sexual pleasure. Sexual pleasure was strictly confined to men, and included the relations a man could have with numerous young virgins, since each man was allotted seventy-two virgins. When he deflorated one of them, her hymen was repaired all by itself. Every time a man had intercourse with one of these virgins

---

[7] Lady or Mistress Aisha, the wife of the Prophet Muhammad.

she would say to him: 'In Paradise there is nothing better than you, nothing that I like more than being with you.'

*   *   *   *

I tossed and turned in my bed, unable to sleep. I could see my mother walking through Paradise all alone. She had died at the age of forty-five, a mother of nine children. She was not a young virgin, and at her age certainly had no desire to become a stupid naïve young girl standing in a queue of seventy-two virgins waiting for her turn to be deflorated. No sooner over with this painful ordeal than she had to begin all over again, since her hymen would heal, and she would once more stand in the queue waiting for her turn. Paradise for women was Hell since it meant either eternal loneliness, or an endless cycle of pain and humiliation to ensure that men could satisfy their insatiable lust.

One day I asked my father, 'Didn't Prophet Muhammad say that Paradise lies beneath the feet of all mothers? Then why is there not a single saying of his concerning the rights of mothers in Paradise? Why is there nothing at all about the rights of women in the Qur'an, or the Old Testament or the New Testament?'

I kept searching in the holy books and sayings for mention of the rights of women. There was nothing, absolutely nothing. All I could find was a saying enunciated by one of the Muslim scholars in which he maintains that 'in Paradise a woman will have no-one else but her husband'.

My mother therefore had no alternative but to wait until my father died. My father was still strong and healthy. He walked upright, his tread on the ground was steady. True, he was sad when my mother died and wore a black tie. But after the forty days of mourning were over, he took it off, started to pay attention to his clothes, to rub his neck and arm pits with eau-de-Cologne. In the meantime my mother lay in her grave, or sat on green grass in Paradise all alone, waiting for him.

My father did not live long after her. He died four months later. In my imagination I could see her stand up to embrace him when he walked in through the gates of Paradise, could hear her say in a ringing voice, 'Sayed, it's good to be together again, here in Paradise.'

My father had remained faithful to his wife ever since they were married. In Paradise, according to the religion in which he believed, he had a right to seventy-two virgins. So I wondered whether he would continue to cherish my mother as he had done when they were together on earth, or whether he would succumb to God's temptations!

* * * *

During those days I wrote a short story entitled *My Mother has no Place in Paradise*. It lay in the bottom drawer of my desk for almost a quarter of a century. I could not find a single magazine in Egypt that was prepared to publish it. One morning at the beginning of 1982, I came across it lying at the bottom of the drawer. At that time I was going through some of the things I had written prior to embarking on a new book called *Memoirs from the Women's Prison*. It could have been lost forever, been turned to dust, but I reread it, deleted a few things that could be considered particularly sacrilegious. Instead of my mother I chose a woman very different from her as the heroine. She was poor, and had a dark skin like my grandmother. She worked in the fields, under the burning sun if it was summer, and in the bitter morning cold if it was winter, and was still a young woman when her husband died, but after he died she remained faithful to him, and refused to remarry. Her dream was to be with him again in Paradise, so she died and went up to Paradise. She kept looking for him but he was nowhere to be found. One day, while searching, she came across a closed door and heard something like moans of pleasure coming from behind it. She pushed the door open and looked in. There was her husband naked in bed with one of the young virgins. At the back of the room stood a long line of virgins waiting for their turn. She closed the door silently and went back to earth, and that is how the story ends.

* * * *

'To work as a civil servant in the government is to bury yourself, Nawal.' This is what my father kept repeating to me days before he died. When he had reached the age of sixty he was obliged to retire from government service. That day he came home, stretched his arms out as though they had been in chains all the time and were now free and said, 'After thirty three years in a prison I have been freed. At last I will have the time to read and write.'

He sat in the hall wearing the dressing-gown I had bought for him. It was made of soft grey wool and I had paid fourteen pounds in the department store of Omar Effendi to buy it. This was the first sum of money that had accumulated in the drawer of my desk from the proceeds of my clinic. So on a cold winter's day in the month of February 1959 I walked out of my clinic with the fourteen pounds in my pocket, and with mixed feelings in my heart. The sum I was using to buy the dressing-gown for my father had come from the suffering of sick people. I found it difficult to accept the fact that I was selling health to people for money. But at the same time I could not forget the sight of my father shivering in his summer pyjamas. He used to save money on his clothes to keep us warm.

When I got back that day, he was sitting in the hall. There was something majestical about him as he sat there looking at me when I came in. Was it his hair that had now turned all white? The look in his eyes? Something deep in the spirit that was not visible, but could be felt. He had a presence. When he came into a room he never went unnoticed, and when he left his absence was always felt.

There was a dignity about him which was difficult to define. It did not come from a position of power. It could not be attributed to some noble descent, since he had come from a poor family. He seemed to be able to see right into people. He never used his physical strength against anyone weaker than him. His broad chest sheltered a big heart and he had the fortitude of a camel, bowing slightly beneath its load but determined to carry it to its final destination.

He opened the package on which was printed 'Omar Effendi', and took out the dressing-gown.

'I bought this with the first sum of money earned in the clinic, father.' When I said that I saw his eyes light up with the shine of the tears he was holding back.

'Congratulations, Nawal, for I'm glad you're doing well in your clinic. But you shouldn't have bought this for me. I am just a simple villager and this is a luxury. You should have bought a jacket and skirt for yourself.'

'No, father, this will keep you warm in the winter.'

'What's more important is you, your future, that of your daughter Mona and your brother and sisters.'

'Don't worry, father. I can take care of them.'

'I know I have no reason to worry as long as you are with them, but I do not know how long I'm going to live. One or two years, or one or two days, God only knows.'

It was ten o'clock on Thursday night and my father had just come home from the coffee-house where he used to spend time with colleagues who had retired like him, talking and playing backgammon. I had finished my work earlier than usual to go to a party organized by the Medical Syndicate in a cabaret restaurant called 'Auberge'. We were supposed to have dinner, watch a few dances and listen to a few songs. I was not very fond of parties, but my friend Batta had insisted that I go for a change, and we had arranged that she pass by me with her car to take me there. So after buying the dressing-gown I took a short cut home to be on time.

After my father had tried it on I told him I was going out. My friend Batta would come to pick me up, although I hated parties and did not really feel like going. He closed the book he had been reading, took off his spectacles and said: 'Why, Nawal, you need to relax? You can't spend all your time working in the hospital and the clinic, or at home reading and writing.'

I agreed with a heavy heart. Since I had started working I almost never saw him, except sometimes in the morning before I left for the hospital. I would have preferred to stay at home and spend time with him. Besides I had noticed that the book in his hand contained some of Al-Gahiz's writings, and I wanted to discuss Al-Gahiz's theory of knowledge with him. I was sure that this would be much more interesting than going to a party, but as I stood there hesitating, I heard the sound of a horn outside the door of our house. Batta had come a long way, and I could not let her down.

My younger brother was studying in his room so I left the telephone number of the Auberge on a slip of paper addressed to him. As I opened the front door to leave my father looked up from his book and our eyes met. Was he trying to say something to me? 'Don't go to bed before I come back, father. I shan't be late,' I said. 'All right, Nawal, I will wait for you. Don't worry, I'm in good company with my friend Al-Gahiz.'

I was wearing ordinary everyday clothes: a blouse, a shirt, a black pullover and flat-heeled shoes. Batta was wearing an evening dress made of satin, and was accompanied by her husband in a shining black suit and a butterfly necktie. As soon as we reached the Auberge we parted company. She went off with friends but I chose a table away from the bustle and noise, sat at the far end. I felt estranged from everything that was going on, from the men and women doctors busy eating, drinking, talking and laughing. The dancer was whirling around on the floor clicking her castanets to the beat of the drums. In front of me was a plate of food and a glass of beer that I had not touched. At one moment a photographer came up to take a picture of me, but all I noticed was the sudden flash. Immediately after I heard a voice call out.

'Dr Nawal El Saadawi, there is a telephone call for you.'

It was my younger brother calling from home. All he said was, 'Come quickly.' In a second I found myself outside the Auberge running in the street. I did not stop to call a taxi. It seemed as though my flying feet could get me there quicker. But one of my colleagues must have noticed my hasty departure from the table. He came after me with his car and took me home, and to this day I do not know who he was. When we arrived I found my brother waiting on the steps. The door was open, the lights were on. I walked into the hall, noticed my father's eyeglasses lying on a small table next to an open book, and an empty chair. I felt my body sway under me as though I were a small boat far out at sea. I found my father lying on his back in the small corridor, his face towards the ceiling and his eyes open. I bent over him, held his wrist, felt for his pulse, laid my head on his chest. I heard my colleague say, 'May the rest of his days be yours.[8] It's better if we carry him to the bed.' We lifted his tall, heavy body with difficulty as far as the bed. Our breathing came and went in gasps but we managed to stretch him out on it full length. I nestled his head in my arms to prevent it from colliding with something else and my colleague lowered the lids over his staring eyes.

The house was plunged in a deep silence as we sat in the hall. My sisters were asleep in an inner room, my daughter in our bedroom, and Om Ibrahim was on a visit to her sick daughter in the village. My brother said, 'I was studying in my room when I heard the noise of something heavy fall down suddenly. It was like the noise of a tree falling to the ground. Then there was a silence, a silence that I will never forget, because in my heart I knew it was death.'

* * * *

---

[8] The popular way of expressing condolences, i.e. if there were a chance for him to live longer may the difference in years be added to your life.

My colleague left us after a while and my brother went back to his room. I got up and tiptoed to where my father lay on the bed, and looked at his face. He seemed half-asleep half-awake, his features looked carved in rock, calm with a quiet smile around the lips, as though he had found eternal rest, or at least a heavenly silence which nothing could break.

I spent the night sitting next to him. His body was there, but he had left for ever. From now on I would face the storms of life alone, like a tree in a forest swept by mighty winds left standing on its own, leafless in the bitter cold, shivering in the storm blowing from the north.

Next morning I awakened my younger sisters with a smiling face. 'Today is Friday and you're on holiday. Where would you like to go?' The youngest one said, 'To the zoo, to the zoo.'

I did not want to live with the dead. It was better if I cared for the living. So I prepared breakfast and lunch and we went off to the zoo. I left them to play in the sunshine, ran quickly to the nearest health bureau for the death certificate, then to the department store of Islam Pasha where I bought a white silk shroud and finally to the undertakers in Saad Zaghloul Street to arrange for the hearse that would carry my father to Kafr Tahla. The undertaker looked me up and down, then asked for double the normal price, but since my mother's death I had become canny about undertaker's prices. He thought that with a woman who had just lost her father he could have his way, but I said to him:

'Don't try to take advantage of me or else I'll go to someone else.'

He gave in and agreed to rent me the hearse for half the price. I had to do a lot of things before five o'clock in the afternoon, closing time for the zoo. The death certificate, buying the shroud, renting the hearse had all been done, but there still remained the one-hour journey to our village Kafr Tahla, the prayer for the deceased in the mosque, the funeral procession to the cemetery, and the burial. There was no time to think, no time to feel sad.

I sent a telegram to my elder brother in Tahrir Province, and telephoned my aunts in Kafr Tahla to tell them that my father had died, and that his funeral hearse would arrive in the village at twelve noon, and that after the prayer in the mosque the funeral procession should go to the cemetery, but there would be no marquee to receive mourners. Whoever wanted to express condolences could do so by telegram.

* * * *

My heart dropped as the coffin was carried down from the house on the shoulders of relatives. I helped to carry it with them. Every day my father had walked down these steps on his own two feet. Now he was being carried down in a wooden coffin. With every step my heart sank lower like a heavy stone behind my ribs. Now the coffin was in the street, and my father was leaving our house for the last time.

I sat in the black funeral van. I wanted to be with him until the very last moment. When we arrived in the village there was a big crowd of men waiting. They had come from Tahla, Kafr Tahla and the surrounding villages.

At the cemetery I went down into the deep pit with the body of my father enveloped in the silk shroud. My Aunt Fatma whispered in my ear as I went down, 'Nobody will steal the shroud here in the village, doctor,' so I came out again, leaving my father behind to be buried under the earth. The sky looked grey despite a bright sunshine. The world without my father was grey and empty. I kept searching among the faces for him, felt the cold winds buffet my shivering body.

The long procession headed by my uncle Sheikh Muhammad walked slowly back to our small house in the village. My father disliked his brother, Sheikh Muhammad, said he was a liar, had stolen his share of the land, then gone off to Mecca to wash away his sins and returned with the title of Haj.

Sheikh Muhammad moved pompously, deep in thought, as though his sadness had overcome him. Around his head he wore a huge turban, and in his hand he moved the long rosary, repeating the ninety-nine names of Allah. He had small narrow eyes that shone with a strange yellow light, like those of a hawk, and on his forehead was a dark blue bump from repeated prostration in prayer.

After we reached the house he said to me, 'Sayed Bey deserves to have a big marquee where people can gather to give condolences. I know they will flock to our village from Cairo and from all around. We must have a mourning which befits him.'

'Uncle, my father said to me that when he dies we should not bother about appearances. The money needed to do what you want is better spent on his children.'

'But Sayed Bey is not just anybody.'

'Then why don't you shoulder the expenses from the land which you stole from him?' I said, and that ended the exchange we were having.

My father belonged to the generation of young men who participated in the revolution of 1919. It was a generation that wanted to prove itself. Through education he moved up to the middle class, lived through the corrupt rule of the King supported by the British, witnessed the gap between rich and poor, was a Muslim believer who felt that religion was the justice of God and tended towards Sufism. He read the Qur'an with an open mind, the way he read many Egyptian and Arab writers, poets, historians and philosophers, dreamt of living in a country freed from colonialism, of becoming a writer or a poet like Hafiz and Shawky. But the oppression under which he had to live, his lifelong struggle as a civil servant in the state bureaucracy destroyed all his hopes, made him live a life of frustration.

His solace was the Qur'an, which lifted him above worldly desires and ambitions, helped him to struggle against them, to experience the melancholy, the sadness, the happiness of rising above them, to yearn after the pleasures of the world and yet sacrifice them for everlasting bliss in the afterworld, to make this painful choice, which nevertheless gave him comfort.

My father was not an ordinary man. He was conscious of his worth. He walked on the earth, tall, upright, his stride long, his spirit strong, in control, wise to the Devil and his lures. He held his desires well in hand, despite a body full of life. He watched himself with sadness, a giant riding in a bus, crushed into it like a sardine in a box or standing in a long queue waiting to buy bread. He knew what it was to endure humiliation, to work in a government job that destroyed initiative, originality and freedom of thought, to come back at the end of the day feeling that his spirit had been crushed, that he had no more energy left.

His death was different from that of my mother. Only four and a half months separated them from one another. I was present at her death. She insisted on waiting for me, on holding on to my hand as her spirit left. She wanted to lean on me when the time came for her to depart from this world to the next, in just the same way as she leant on my arm when we walked on the river bank.

I used to carry her in my arms like a child, feed her with a spoon, rub her back with talcum powder, change the sheets from under her body when she wet herself, bathe her naked body with a sponge. Pain left my body when she died. Her ailing body occupied mine and when she died it left. I was able to stand upright, to stretch my arms, breathe the air in freely, no longer feel her weight pressing down on me.

But when my father died it was different. I was not there. He took advantage of my absence at that party and went off all alone, did not want to hold my hand, did not warn us before he left. He came back from the coffee-house where he had played a few games of backgammon and exchanged a few jokes about the Ministry of Education where he and his colleagues used to work, had wended his way home, stopping at the fruiterers to buy three kilograms of oranges and two of spotted Maghrabi bananas, then walked on, taking big strides with a parcel in each arm, his lust for life intact, his mind eager to explore the book he had borrowed from a friend.

Once at home he took off his clothes, put on his pyjamas and, after I came back, tried on the dressing-gown, felt its soft wool gradually warm his skin, then settled down to read the book written by Al-Gahiz about the essential meaning of life. After some time he stood up and went to the bathroom to wash before he went to bed. He came out of the bathroom, took two steps in the corridor and then collapsed, the way a tree collapses, standing up.

Sudden death is not like slow death and when a big body collapses the sound of its fall echoes far and wide because it falls from a height like a mountain. That night as I sat in the Auberge I heard his body fall, felt the tremor where I sat, for there are waves and rays in space that carry knowledge to us in invisible ways, and we become like a sensitive radar that picks them up.

Between my father and me there remained a distance that we were never able to cross. He belonged to another sex, was not like my mother and me, was different. When he died I felt the pain enter my body. The distance between us had vanished and his dead body became a part of me. His body was now my body. It fell in the corridor with its back to the floor and its eyes open. And whenever I tried to get up pain assailed me, and cold winds went through me as though I were still lying on the stone floor, or had fallen half asleep in the open.

When my father died I did not weep. Deep down inside I did not feel sadness, but something else that was more a mysterious happiness, like a prisoner who has been told that he will be set free as soon as the morning bell rings.

EIGHT

Moments that Belong Nowhere

The sheet of paper in front of me is blank. I move my pen over its surface but it stays blank. Its pure white surface taunts me, sneers at me as though I have never written a single line in my life, and never will. The Arabic language was not made for me, does not speak to me. It was made for men, uses divine words and expressions that deny my existence. God and Satan are masculine. Death is masculine.

The sheet of paper stares back at me, the colour of death. For white is the colour of death. The shrouds in which dead bodies are wrapped, the hospital beds, the coats of doctors, the uniforms of nurses are all white. My eyes are open. I do not know who I am, the patient or the doctor, the writer or the white page with no words on it, the empty spaces between the lines or the lost moments in my life, the years flying by so fast, the spirit abandoning my body, or the mind now totally blank.

Had I lost the ability to write or was I now close to death? There is always an intimate relationship between death and the moments when I cannot write. Over my mouth they have put a mask. A smell of ether hangs in the air. They are always using anaesthetics to blot out my consciousness. Now my body lies crucified on a surgical table in the operating theatre. Or perhaps it is lying on a dissecting table in the School of Medicine. My arms and legs are tied down by rubber tubes. I can hear them talking about me in the third person, as though I am not there. Their voices sound the same, their clothing is the same white colour, they have the same smell: a mixture of ether, iodine and cigarette smoke. A voice pronounces my name, and my father's name. But is he my father? There was always more than one man, and one never knew who was the father. A father's name was no more than a myth. In history our descent was concealed behind the image of a symbolic patriarch. Language made us males and women did not exist. The sacred image could live only by suppressing the truth. But the truth kept peering through the mists of anaesthesia like an iceberg showing its tip above the water.

But where is my mother? I asked.

I tried to see my mother's face among the faces that were gathered around me, but steely fingers held my head down on the table, then crept towards my neck and pressed into its flesh. Were they trying to choke me because I had called out to my mother? Where had she disappeared? Had they killed her? Burned her, and buried her name under the ground? Erased it for ever? Rubbed its letters away from where it was inscribed? Said to themselves that I am dead? And that after death I can carry my mother's name, since it is only after death that the truth will come to light, and the false father's name will no longer be linked to me?

Once more the voice pronounces my name. It has a familiar sound to my ears. I had heard it pronounced so often before, I had read it so often on the covers of my books and novels. The voice I heard was harsh, masculine. It was the voice of a man whose features were strange to me, yet he was holding my hand as it lay tied to the table. The men and women doctors said he was my husband.

When did I marry that man? I asked myself. I tried to lift my hand and hold up my head, but it did not move. I had a splitting headache. My memory was failing me. Moments of my life seemed to drop out of it, to fall away. I tried to bring them back, but in vain. This ether was drugging my brain. They used drugs to kill one's memory. I struggled, opened my mouth to protest, but my voice refused to come out.

* * * *

Her arms and legs tied down, her mouth covered by a mask, she nevertheless struggled to open it and say, 'I do not want an anaesthetic! I do not want to lose consciousness! I am a doctor, I am not a patient. My name is Nawal and my mother's name is Zaynab. Saadawi is my grandfather's name and I never saw him, for he died before I was born.'

The voice kept repeating her name but she did not answer. Her husband kept telling them that she was not asleep, was not unconscious, that she was just writing, that when she was writing the world no longer existed for her. It was as though she had left it behind. She heard nobody, answered nobody.

After the painful experiences of her wedding night she told her husband that now she must write the unwritable. Every day she sat at her desk from the beginning of the day until late into the night, held the pen between her fingers and moved it over the white sheet of paper. She kept tearing up sheet after sheet of paper, pulled out locks of her hair, opened her mouth wide as though gasping for air, pulled the mask off from over her face, and clamped down with her teeth on the fingers encircling her neck.

Her body seated on the chair became a part of it as though she were tied down to it with a rope. The lower part of her body did not move, the upper part was no more than a head bent over the desk.

The pen held between her long brown fingers moves over the sheet of paper. Its tip makes a faint, scratchy sound, leaves behind dark twisted, unfinished words. The sound is audible to her ears in the silence of the room. She lifts her head, looks out of her half-closed eyes.

*   *   *   *

I feel as though I have never written a single word, never held the pen between my fingers, as though language and I are total strangers. The words on the sheet of paper are not mine. I did not hear them from my mother though they are described as my maternal language. Yet they are the words of a language that belongs to a man unknown to me, a man who died years before I was born.

I try to get up from the chair on which I am sitting behind the desk, but my arms and legs are tied by ropes to the chair. I walk to the bed with the ropes around my body, cry out for help in my sleep, but my cries are no more than muted shrieks. Sherif is lying by my side sound asleep. I look at him with envy. We married in 1964 and he always finds it easy to fall asleep. He only has to rest his head on the pillow and after a second he is fast asleep. Faint rays of light pass through the shutter slits and reach the wall. A whiff of air moves the calendar hanging on it. The year printed on it in black letters says '2000'. It looks strange to me.

Sherif opens his eyes and stares at it in surprise. 'My God,' he says we're already in the year 2000?' My body floats up on the bed. I feel as though I am swimming in space and time.

* * * *

Time is passing and here I am lying under the bed covers, trying in vain to sleep. It is as though I have forgotten how to sleep. I try in vain to write. It is as though I have forgotten how to write. Sherif is sleeping by my side. He left his bed in the other room and came to me. We talked with one another for a while. He is writing a new novel, but I am unable to write. He sleeps, but I spend the night with wide open eyes. It is as though I had never written, never slept, never done anything. He opens his eyes, sees me awake staring up at the ceiling and asks: 'What's the matter, Nawal?'

'I am unable to write, Sherif. I will never be able to write again.'

'You say that every time, Nawal, but after that you write another book.' he says with a laugh.

'But this is the last time that will happen. It is really over.'

'Every time you say it's the last time.'

'No, this is really the last time, and I'll never be able to write again. It's finished. I've lost the ability to write.'

'Try and get some sleep, Nawal.'

'I can't sleep, Sherif. I can't sleep any more.'

* * * *

I get out of bed and walk in the dark on tiptoe so as not to wake him. I stand at the windows. We are up on the twenty-sixth floor and we are now in the twenty-first century. I climb up onto the sill and jump over into space, but when I open my eyes my body is stretched out on the bed. By my side lie sheets of white paper covered in crooked letters, with words that have no meaning.

Sherif opens his eyes, sees me gazing at the ceiling. He caresses my shoulder. 'Try to get some sleep, Nawal.' I whisper back, 'Sherif, do you think that marriage destroys creativity?' He laughs. 'Maybe, Nawal,' he says, 'but what can we do after thirty-five years of life together!'

* * * *

Writing for me meant burrowing into a deep tunnel in the earth and living in it, into a place where there was no-one apart from me, into a space not shared by anyone else, a space where nothing moved, where nothing could be heard but a complete silence like that of death.

I used to carry pen and paper and leave the house. Out in the street I walked on and on without a halt, my eyes looking here and there searching for something, sweeping over the earth, the sky, the houses, the buildings, the streets and the lanes, trying to find a hole into which I could escape, then close the gap behind me with one layer after the other of stone and mud, for one layer would never be enough to prevent sounds from filtering through. I was searching for a silence wrapped in silence.

I kept going round and round, not knowing where to go, and ended up walking along the Nile. There I would stop, stare at the water, climb onto the parapet and jump.

I woke up from sleep bathed in sweat. My papers are scattered over the bed but my hand still holds the pen. By my side there is a man lying in my bed asleep. The calendar hanging on the wall bears another date, another day and month and year. The number of the year on it says 1956. I stare at it. Could the clock of time have been turned back forty years while I slept? The man sleeping by my side opens his eyes. It is very dark and I can see only his eyes, cannot distinguish the features of his face. But after some time his nose emerges from the dark. It is big and slightly hooked. Under the nose he has thick black whiskers.

Nothing in men drives me away from them more than the hair on their faces. It reminds me of the hairy ancestors of our human species. He was lying on his left side with his face towards me. The calendar on the wall says 1956. A cold shiver steals through my body. My memory floats up to the surface gradually. I rise up from the depths in stages, come to lying on something that shakes. My eyelids are heavy and I open them with an effort. The date on the wall has not changed. It is still 1956. The window is open. There are no glass panes or shutters and the cold air goes through my body as I lie there on my back. Something is choking my throat, and there is an odour of blood in my nose. My eyes travel over the walls. The place seems strange to me as though I had not seen it before, the wall unpainted, dark in colour with even darker spots scattered over it. There are cracks in the walls that resemble the cracks on the surface of the earth. Hanging down from the ceiling is an electric wire with dead flies on it. The man is lying next to me on a large bed made of dark metal plates. His eyes are closed. Time does not move and the calendar on the wall still says 1956, to be exact July 23, 1956. I make an effort to open my eyes wide to penetrate through the mists of sleep, and discover that my eyes were already open. I had not closed them throughout the night. I kept thinking of escape, of how to escape, and where to go.

The night seemed infinitely long, endless. A white coat with spots of red blood near the collar hung from a nail in the wall. A small black leather bag lay on the floor in the middle of the room and around it were scattered medical accessories: a stethoscope with a long black rubber tube, a syringe with a large needle, gauze bandages and cotton pads. Next to them was an identity card, with a photograph partly torn off, and with my name on it.

He continues to lie on his left side, his face towards me, his right arm stretched out on the bed. I used to leave a big distance between us, a distance bigger than the length of his right arm. His hand was huge, his fingers thick. I had never seen fingers as thick as his. I keep turning round, throwing glances towards the door, but it is so dark I cannot see it, as though the room has no door, and there are just four high, dark walls with no opening from which to escape.

This summer night in the year 1956 keeps coming back to me and with it another night in the summer of 1941, to be precise the night of August 31, 1941. Forgotten moments of my life float up in my memory. Small black eyes shine in a sea of darkness like stars that appear in the night from behind a thick dark cloud. To escape from my father's house was less frightening than to escape from that of my husband. The word marriage in colloquial Arabic is *gawaza*, which means a 'permit'. My grandmother used to say, 'Daughter of my son, *gawaza* is "written",[1] and like all girls you are destined to be married. What is written on the forehead must be seen by the eye.[2] It is destiny. My *gawaza* was my *ganaza*,[3] daughter of my son. But we thank thee, Oh God, for all our travails, for thou alone are to be thanked for the trouble that befalls us.'

---

[1] Like a binding holy text.
[2] Must be lived and there is no escape from it.
[3] Funeral.

Ever since I was six years old I have continued to remember the three words: God, travails and marriage, as though they are linked together.

*   *   *   *

The word 'love' had little to do with the word 'marriage'. I used to sing in tune to the radio when songs of love were being broadcast on it. We girls never stopped singing about love; but I never heard a song being sung to marriage.

Love is the trap into which young girls walk blindly, unaware of what awaits them, only to open their eyes one day, shocked with the reality they have to face, at the fact that love has metamorphosed into four dark walls in a marital home ready to collapse at any moment.

I was ten years old when my heart beat with love for the first time. All I had seen in my loved one were his eyes but I would willingly have died for him. Fortunately he disappeared before I had time to run away from my father's house and catch up with him. He left nothing behind, nothing except a photograph which disappeared somewhere. It was as though he had never existed. I met him by chance thirty years later. What I saw was a strange face with a long sharp nose and lips so thin that it seemed as though he had no lips. I asked myself with what did he kiss a woman? His eyes were small and deep set, with not a ray of light in them. I wondered how his eyes had once drowned me with sunshine. I used to avoid looking into them for fear of being dazzled, and if his name rang in my ears I fell into a state of semi-consciousness.

I was twenty when my heart beat for love again. Like my first love, to me his eyes were like sunshine. This time I fled from the house where I lived with my father and my mother, left everything behind: my books, my pens, my paper, my clothes and my childhood photographs. I walked straight down the road which led to him, looking neither right nor left. Love led to marriage, but when I opened my eyes I found the four dark walls of a kitchen in an old house situated in the district of Giza, an old house that looked as though it would collapse at any moment.

Images of the past are dead, have turned to nothing. I try to bring them back in vain. Dark red stains cover their pure white surfaces when they come to me in my sleep, when consciousness slips away, and my subconscious creeps through and invades my consciousness.

Since I was a child my body has always trembled at the sight of blood. When I was a child there appeared on the white bed sheet a drop of red blood for the first time. I asked myself, where does the blood come from when one is a child? And why does it come back again and again? Since I was nine years old I kept seeing the red stain on the white bed sheet. I became used to seeing it month after month, and year after year until childhood abandoned me and it no longer made me tremble with fear. On the contrary I became frightened when it disappeared. I woke up every morning and searched for it in the bed sheets, in my underclothes, searched feverishly for a speck of blood in the intertwining threads of white tissue.

* * * *

When I was in secondary school, the girls were always searching for a red stain on their underclothes. It was a catastrophe if they did not find it, it could ruin their lives, for its absence was proof of an illegitimate pregnancy.

To wash away this 'shame' there was only one way. The girl had to shed her blood, to die. It was the men who undertook the task of removing the stain on their honour. The women paid for it with their blood but the murderer who had saved the honour of the family became a hero. The victim was buried under the ground in silence together with her name and that of her mother, but after that the name of the father became a shining example.

Ever since the Virgin Mary became pregnant with Jesus Christ girls have feared an illegitimate pregnancy. In their minds they always wonder: can what happened to her happen to me? God's Holy Books mention things which have occurred again and again. Did not the people of Israel repeatedly disobey His Commands? Did not God forgive them over and over again? How many were the times when he sent down his prophets and messengers to lead them back to the faith? We read of one prophet after the other threatening people with diresome woes if they did not return to the straight path of God. We read of one messenger after the other sent by God to our lords Abraham, Moses, Jesus and Muhammad. Why then would it seem so far-fetched that God would once again send his spirit to impregnate a girl just as he had done with the Virgin Mary?

The question often turned round in my mind as I lay in bed. I suppressed the thought as though it were a sinful dream. Then I discovered that the girls with me all had sinful dreams. My friend Safeya said that ever since she had read the story of the Virgin Mary she had started to dream of a messenger from God coming to her in the night. Samia told me that she did not believe in God and yet she still dreamt of a messenger from Him. And when I went to medical school Batta said to me that she had dreamt of the messenger and after that he had actually came to her while she was awake. Then she started to laugh in that characteristic gurgling way of hers, like water passing through the narrow neck of an earthenware jug.

* * * *

I was fast asleep that night when I felt rough fingers throttling my neck. I opened my mouth to scream, but my voice was unable to emerge. The fingers around my neck were stronger than mine, and I could not pull them away from my throat. I gasped for air, and was finally able to free my neck. I could have called out to wake up the neighbours but death seemed more bearable to me than the scandal I would face next morning.

Since childhood days the Virgin Mary had remained an example for me. She was the mother of Jesus Christ, the only woman whose name had been mentioned in the Qur'an. All the other women remained anonymous, even Eve the wife of Adam, even the wives of Muhammad the Prophet, peace be on him, including our lady Khadija his first wife with whom he lived for more than twenty years.

So it was natural for a young idealistic Muslim girl like me to consider the Virgin Mary as a role model, rather than any other woman. At the age of nine, when I reached puberty, I swore a secret oath to Allah that I would be like the Virgin Mary, that I would bear a child without having any sexual relations with a man and from that day onwards every month, I used to be waiting for God's messenger to come to me.

I waited for a long time.

The years went by, one year after the other and no messenger came. But one day a man came along and whispered in my ear that he had been sent by God. I was an idealistic young girl and when I heard the word 'Allah' my body trembled. I used to close my eyes and whisper to myself, 'Oh God, please mention my name in your Holy Book, like the Virgin Mary. For why should you choose to distinguish her from all other women? Can you not choose at least two women for this distinction? You chose more than twenty men to be your Holy prophets!

That was during the days of my childhood and early adolescence, when I was still very naive. But when I grew up and went to medical school I began to distinguish between dreams and reality, between illusion and truth. I found myself really in love, in a real marriage consummated according to the holy law of Allah and his Prophet and really pregnant. I had become a mother who was no longer virgin, no longer chaste. Something unholy, impure used to happen to me at night. Something that gave me pain, and a feeling of sin rather than pleasure.

My first husband was a complete man in every way, a courageous freedom fighter who risked his life for his country. But after he came back from the battlefield his feelings towards his country changed.

'We were betrayed, Nawal,' he kept saying.

'By our rulers,' I said.

'Our rulers are the country.'

'No, the government is not the country, not the nation.'

'That is no more than an illusion.'

'No, that's the truth, Ahmed,' I kept saying to him.

'No, it's an illusion. Everything is an illusion. Now I know the truth. When I believed in God, in country, and in love, I was living three illusions, Nawal!'

I trembled whenever I heard him whisper in the night, 'All three are nothing more than an illusion, Nawal.' He used to stay awake all night, inject himself with a double dose of Maxitone forte, then sit behind a desk and write one sentence: 'All three are just illusions,' cross it out and write it in the middle of the page, then cross it out again and write it further down at the beginning of a new line.

He used to write and cross out with the same pencil. If the pencil snapped under the pressure of his fingers, he pushed it into a sharpener and turned the handle again and again until it had a long, fine tip, crumpled up one sheet of paper after the other and threw it under the desk into the wastepaper basket. When the basket was full of crumpled sheets, he got up, went to the kitchen and tipped it over into the dustbin.

When the sharpener became full of pencilsharpenings he emptied it in the basket. He threw away the pencil only when it had become as short as the phalanx of his finger, went out of the house only when he needed to buy new pencils, or a ream of white paper, or a box of Maxitone forte ampoules from a drugstore in Manial Road.

I had graduated from the School of Medicine and was working in the new Kasr Al-Aini University Hospital in the district of Manial. It was half an hour's walk from where I lived. I used to leave our flat at half past eight in the morning, and return at three in the afternoon to find him sitting behind the desk in our bedroom. Our flat was small. It had one bedroom, a small hall in which we had our meals, a tiny kitchen and a narrow balcony which looked out on a small branch of the Nile. The building in which we lived consisted of four flours, with two flats on each floor. We were located on the third floor.

My monthly salary was ten-and-a-half pounds[4] and it served to cover food and house expenses. His mother gave him nine pounds a month which were his share of the income from property which his father had left behind when he died. He spent all the nine pounds buying pencils, paper and boxes of Maxitone forte. A short while before we separated, the nine pounds were no longer enough, since he kept injecting himself with doses of Maxitone forte which increased as the days went by. The human body has a capacity to absorb and withstand increasing amounts of any poison circulating in it, of stimulants or sedatives. Maxitone forte is a stimulant, and addicts need increasing amounts to experience the same effect and overcome the body's resistance to its chemical action.

He used to open my bag and take money out of it to buy the ampoules. So I started to hide my bag from him in places he would not think of. He retaliated by selling the little furniture we had in the house, and after a while all we had left were the bed, made of dark metal sheets, the desk and the chair on which he sat all night to write the same sentence over and over again: 'The three are an illusion,' after which he crumpled the sheet of paper in his hand and dropped it in the waste-paper basket.

Three days before we were divorced he unhooked the glass windows and the shutters in the flat, sold them and came back with his Maxitone forte. I spent the whole night shivering in the bed which was placed under the window. We had only one blanket left and, just before dawn, I opened my eyes to find him seated behind the desk writing, crossing out, and throwing balls of paper into the basket.

When he noticed me open my eyes he stared at me with an odd look. He looked strange to me and when he spoke it was no longer his voice.

---

[4] The equivalent of US$25 at that time.

'Have you woken up, Doctor?'

'Yes,' I said.

'Then tell me if the three of them are not just an illusion.'

'Which three?' I asked.

'God, country, and love.'

'Reality or illusion. It's not that which matters. What matters is that you stop taking the poison you keep injecting yourself with.'

'The only cure for poison is more poison. The proverb says: "Give me more of what is the cause of my pain".'[5]

'We cannot continue to live like this.'

'Naturally. Love is over isn't it, dear Doctor?'

'I really don't know, Ahmed.'

'I know. Love is nothing but a big illusion.'

'No, that's not true.'

'Then you still believe in love?'

'Yes, I do.'

'Who is the fortunate man?! It can't be me. I'm finished.'

'Everything depends on your will.'

'My will is finished. Everything is finished. There is nothing left, nothing other than death. We once said we will live or die together. So do you agree that the time has come for us to die together?'

* * * *

It was the night of July 23, 1956, just before dawn. The whole country was celebrating the fourth anniversary of the revolution. As I lay in bed his thick rough fingers encircled my neck, throttling me. I opened my mouth gasping for breath. I preferred to die rather than let the neighbours hear me screaming in our flat.

In the life of women death is often easier than calling out for help. The woman who lived next door often screamed for help. I used to hear her voice in the night and wake up. The neighbours would open their windows to listen. In the neighbouring building too there was another woman who often screamed at the top of her voice at night. It could be the father beating up his daughter for coming home late, or a husband hitting his wife because he found a small pebble in his rice, or stabbing her because he thought she had been unfaithful to

---

[5] An Egyptian and Arab proverb most commonly used when a lover is unable to stop pursuing the woman who is the cause of his suffering.

him. Things like that happened all the time and people would whisper, 'That's what she deserves'. Honour is more important than anything. A man must defend his honour. He's free to do what he likes in his home. He is responsible for the family, responsible for his women. God says, chastise your women if they do something wrong. The daughters of Eve are scheming creatures and can do much harm. Men have to be wary of their games.

The neighbours would listen for some time then shut their windows and go back to bed. But next morning the woman would wake up to face a scandal. Wagging tongues would keep spreading it around and after that she never called out for help again.

That night I did not scream. Since childhood I had never called out for help. Instead I thought of ways to resist, or to escape.

* * * *

For more than four years, from the summer of 1956 until the summer of 1960, I lost my memory, forgot the feel of those thick coarse fingers around my neck. They dropped away into dark space, as though nothing had happened that night. All that remained was the obscure image of dark shadows moving over a dark wall, then the image disappeared in turn as though it too had fallen away into space, into a dark void of nothingness.

But when I am asleep, and no longer conscious of the world or of myself, the shadows creep out again from the dark ocean like a mountain of ice showing its tip above water while its mass remains buried in the depths.

NINE

The Death Threat

The Beginning of Year 2000

I hold the pen in my hand, stare at the sheet of paper, at the empty white surface waiting for my words to be written on it. The window in front of me is open to the sky, to an empty neutral space, to a void that reaches into the distance. I search for what my father called 'the truth'. When I was still a child I used to argue with him. My mind refused to accept the things he said without sufficient proof. He used to get angry with me, insist that some truths needed no proof, those related to our faith. If I went on arguing he would give me one of his threatening looks to silence me, but my mind continued to question everything it could not accept.

My mind has always been a source of trouble in my life. From the time I was a child I kept trying to control it. By the time I reached the age of adolescence I had succeeded. I became an obedient, submissive girl who did not argue about anything. Questions no longer passed through my mind. Instead things began to go through my body, headlong, rushing desires that shook it to the core. At night and often during the day I dreamt of love, of something physical that I could touch, of a body embracing me as I lay in bed.

My mother used to give me threatening looks, silent warnings which meant that I should stop these dreams of love, but my body refused to give up the flushes of hot desire that went through it.

My body became the source of trouble in my life. When I reached adolescence I kept trying to rid myself of it. In my youth I became a girl without a body, an idealistic mature well-behaved young woman, then an obedient wife who obeyed her husband at home and her boss at work, sacrificed her personal life for the family, but was ready to sacrifice her family fighting in a war to defend her country.

There were days in my life when I walked through the streets like a shadow, like a phantom arisen from the dead, my face pale, my lips closed tightly in silence. Nothing moved either in my mind, or in my body. I had abandoned both of them. I swayed like a scarecrow in the wind as I walked through the city. Death was so close that I could almost touch it with my hand, death in the name of country, of God, of husband. God came first. He was above all others. Below him came my country, or the king, or the president. Last came my husband.

When I was still a child I used to scream at night, 'Down with the King!' 'Down with the British!' When I grew up and became a young woman, I heard young people shouting, 'Down with the President!' 'Down with America!' So I began to shout the same slogans but added to them a slogan of my own which was 'Down with husbands!'

My friend Safeya joined in when I shouted 'Down with husbands!' And it was not long before my other friends, Samia and Batta, were shouting the same slogan. These three obedient wives kept dreaming of divorce. They went on dreaming for forty-four long years, until the twentieth century had ended and the world had entered a new millennium.

Memory moves back and forth in time in a very strange way. Half a century can drop out of my life in less than a second or a moment stretches out in front of me to infinity. Past and present fuse into a single moment. A voice echoes in my ears as though I am hearing it now. 'Kill her! She is a heretic and the enemy of Allah.' I awaken to it suddenly rising up from the other side of Giza Street. Our bedroom has double glass windows and wooden shutters. Sherif is asleep in the other bed. We were in the habit of sleeping in the same room but in separate beds. The walls were a pure white and the bed sheets too. The floor was covered in tiles so clean and so smooth that I used to slip on them sometimes. The hands of the alarm clock pointed to one in the morning and the calendar on the wall said December 31, 1988. It was New Year's Eve. Terrible things always used to happen when people were celebrating nights like this. Ever since I was a child I had disliked festive occasions. When the world around was shining with happiness my heart would be very sad.

'Let her blood flow! She is a heretic and the enemy of Allah.'

My head is heavy with sleep. My eyes are closed as the voice continues to reach my ears. A faint light creeps through the shutters. I get up and tiptoe to the windows, stop for a moment and take a deep breath. I look out through a crack in the shutters. There is no one in the street, only a donkey-cart passing by with a man lying on his back in it, his body shaking with the movement of the cart. The lights of speeding cars flash, then vanish in the night. The crack is very narrow, but I am afraid to open the window. The voice continues to shout out names and again I hear my name loud and clear followed by that of my grandfather, Al Saadawi.

'Kill them! They are heretics and the enemies of Allah.'

From behind the shutters my ears pick up the names one after the other. My name Nawal El Saadawi rings out again loud and clear, goes through my head like a bullet. Sherif opens his eyes, sees me standing behind the window, immobile as a statue.

'What's wrong, Nawal?'

'Did you hear that voice?'

He opens the window and looks out trying to find out where the voice is coming from. Could it be from the microphone of the neighbouring mosque? Perhaps it was the mosque which had just been built in our back street, or the older mosque rising behind the church, or perhaps it was coming from that tall minaret showing at a distance between the buildings. It was difficult to tell. Sherif put his hand on my shoulder and said, 'Go back to bed, Nawal. Tomorrow we will try to find out what's happening.'

When I met Sherif for the first time in 1964 I remembered my encounter with Ahmed Helmi in 1951. His face suddenly came back to me as though emerging from the darkness, the wide forehead below his thick black hair, the dark eyebrows, the eyes, the nose, the walk and especially the way he spoke little and did things in silence. Ahmed Helmi died spiritually after facing defeat with his comrades at the front. His spirit died but his body lived on. I looked into Sherif's eyes and wondered. 'This time will I be wrong?'

TEN

Beyond Consciousness

I am fast asleep. I can see my father sitting in the hall, reading. He lifts his head and looks at me as though surprised to see me. 'Nawal,' he says, 'When did you get back? What was the party like?' 'Party? What party?' 'The party of the Medical Association to which you were invited,' he says. In the dream my memory has gone back more than forty years, and I say to myself, 'How does he still remember that night?' It was a Thursday, the night of February 19, 1959. I can see him talking to me as he sits in the hall, yet I know that he is dead. The twentieth century has ended and we are now in the twenty-first century, in what is called the third millennium. The figure 2000 after the day and the month looks strange. I did not think that I was going to live until the twenty-first century. I feel as though I managed to steal a whole century behind the back of time and am once more a seven-year-old girl. The older I become, the closer I come to my childhood and keep remembering it. When I was younger it seemed to be far away, to belong to a distant past. Yesterday seemed to be a year ago or ten years ago. But as I grow older time changes. The previous decade seems to me like yesterday. The face of my dead father is so close that I can almost touch it with my fingertips, yet it is more than forty years since I last saw him. I can almost hear the sound of his steps on the tiles of the hall, see his face in the mirror, the look in his eyes. It is as though he never went away, has always been with us.

Sherif says to me, 'You have never overcome your sadness at being separated from him.' Perhaps Sherif knows me better than I know myself. Perhaps my love for my father was the greatest love in my life, surpassed only by the love I had for my mother. My heart gave way under the weight of my love for her when death took her away from me, yet it seems that real feelings of love only came to me when time and distance separated us.

I woke up to the ring of the telephone. Samia's voice came over the line as she said, 'Demonstrations have broken out in Al-Azhar University, and they have been mentioning your name with other names on a death-list of writers.'

I was suddenly awake. The date on the calendar hanging from the wall said May 9, 2000 in bold black letters and numbers. Samia's voice continued to vibrate in my ears. 'The Sheikh who leads the prayer in the mosque next to my house gave a sermon in which he spoke about you. He said your books are nothing but heresy. The "Gama'at Islameya"[1] have incited the students in Al-Azhar to demonstrate against the publication of a book by the Ministry of Culture. They say that the book says things which are against Islam. They shouted slogans against the President and the Minister of Culture. It's not just a matter of a novel, it's developing into something against the whole system. The students aren't really aware of what's going on, and they're being used as pawns who will suffer the consequences, and you, Nawal, they can use you as a scapegoat, make you a victim. The Sheikh in the mosque kept inciting the congregation against you, but you know what happened? My brother told me that many of the people that were there went off to buy your books after the prayers were over!'

I said, 'Samia, my father often used to say to me, "Who knows, harmful things can lead to good,"' but she sighed deeply, 'Maybe they want to get hold of the books to burn them?'

'Let them burn them, Samia, it does not matter.'

'It would be a pity if they burnt them.'

'Fire devours paper but it does not destroy books.'

'Books are printed on paper, aren't they?'

'That was during the last century. Now we live in the twenty-first century and books can't be burnt any longer. They cross over through space and don't need paper or printing press.'

'But they can burn computers too.'

---

[1] A fanatical group that splintered off from the Muslim Brothers whom it considered too moderate.

'Books aren't stored in computers.'

'Where are they stored then?'

'On tablets made of material which does not burn.'

'And where are these tablets kept?'

'In heaven, Samia.'

'In God's keeping you mean.' I heard a short, stifled laugh suggesting that the non-believer in childhood had become a middle-aged believer.

'No, Samia.'

'Where are they kept then?'

'These tablets are kept on something called a disc made of very strong solid material, and thousands, millions of copies can spread out across space like viruses and be multiplied endlessly through the internet and web sites and other electronic forces known or unknown to us.'

'And what are the unknown forces?'

'Something new, smaller than the electron, known as a quark which possesses more stored energy in it than the electron, and carries with it other forces too inside the atom, or the brain cells. Our knowledge of the human brain is still limited, Samia. The human brain, the living cell, the genome, the atom, the planets, the sun, the moon, all these are still unknown. But what is most important is that books can no longer be burned.'

* * * *

When I was still a child of seven, my maternal grandmother Amna used to stare at me with anger. She said that unlike the other girls in Shoukry Bey's family I did not obey my elders. Every time she said something I found unconvincing I would question it. She would sting me with a cane and scream, 'I do not want to hear you pronounce the word "why"! Do you understand girl, or don't you?'

I did not cry like the other girls. Instead, I used to stamp the floor angrily and say, 'Why do you hit me?' When I stamped on the floor or asked 'why' Amna became even angrier. But what infuriated her most of all was that there were no tears in my eyes. She was my grandmother and, moreover, the wife of Shoukry Bey, the Director General of Army Recruitment responsible for the conscription of thousands of young men. She lived and died a humiliated and oppressed woman, imprisoned in a palatial house, then in a tomb of marble. The only way she could let out her frustration was by beating small children like me with a cane. At that time I did not know why she used to get angry at me until one day my mother whispered the sacred triad, God, father, husband, in my ear as an explanation. Then I remembered that she used to lift her eyes to the heavens and mutter angrily 'Oh God,' but then stop short. I asked my mother why she did not mention my grandfather's name after that of God. My mother clapped her hand over my mouth and said 'Hush'.

At night I used to wake up choking with suppressed tears. They seemed to collect in my throat and close it up. I could hear the snores of my grandmother as she lay in bed fast asleep. Her features looked submissive, peaceful, defenceless. During the day she seemed strong and even cruel, imbued with the power of evil, and I wished she would die. I hated her strength and her helplessness equally, hoped she would die in her sleep and never wake up. But when I fell asleep I would dream that my grandfather was the one who had died in his sleep. I hated my grandfather even more than my grandmother and prayed God that He take him away as soon as possible. In my dreams I could hear him snoring, and longed to put my hands around his neck and choke him, but then I would wake up in a panic, get out of bed, tiptoe to the verandah and sit on a chair. Awake, I would remember that my grandfather was dead, and that the person who slept beside me in the same bed was my Aunt Fahima, that it was she whom I had always heard snoring at night, she whom I really longed to throttle.

Under the light of a street lamp creeping through one of the windows I wrote in my secret diary: 'When a desire to kill seizes hold of me I pick up a pen and sit down in front of a sheet of paper. Were it not for my writing, I would have killed her or killed myself with a chopper'. (House of my late grandfather, District of Al-Zeitoun April 19, 1945)

Thirty-six years later I found myself in one of the cells of the Women's Prison in Al-Kanatir. I had a secret diary which I hid under the floor as I used to do in my grandfather's house when I was fourteen. In my prison diary I wrote: 'Writing needs as much courage as killing does. If my fingers had not learnt the use of a pen they might have learnt the use of an axe or a chopper. I wonder whether the hand of my prison mate, Fatheya the murderess, when it held up the hoe and brought it down on her husband's head, looked like mine when I hold the pen between my fingers? Nothing in my life is more precious to me than writing but I think that it requires even more courage than killing.' (The Women's Prison, Al-Kanatir November 14, 1981.)

*   *   *   *

That winter's night in the year 1960 I was sitting at my desk writing when my husband walked into my room. In front of me had accumulated sheets of paper covered in my handwriting. I had spent many a late night during the past years working on this novel. It had grown inside me like a child. I wrapped my arms around it, caressed it in the silence of the night. My head often dropped over it in sleep. My being escaped with it into the depths of the earth, where I was surrounded by silence.

It took me with it to another world where I forgot everything: myself, my daughter, my sisters and brothers, the people who were part of my flesh and blood. So what could this man who was not of my flesh and blood, to whom I was bound only by a piece of paper, mean to me?

When he charged into my room I lifted my head and looked at him. I felt as though I had never seen him before. He had a round face with pink cheeks, the kind of face that I disliked in men. His body was squat and fleshy, the kind of body which I found repugnant even in women. When I looked into his eyes I could not find what I was searching for. His nose was soft and flabby with nothing challenging or proud in it, and when he spoke there was no warmth, no ring in his voice. He had none of the things I found attractive in a man, and yet this man was my husband.

Some other woman must have slipped into my body, adopted my name and gone off with him to the office of a Ma'azoun[2] to get married! She was an irresponsible woman who did not believe in love, wore a doctor's coat but did not believe in the profession, a woman who hated sick people and the smell of hospitals and had gone to medical school only because she wanted to please her father and mother, both of whom were now dead. A woman who had hated the word 'marriage' even when she was still a child, and who had married a second time to forget what had happened the first time.

---

[2] A religious Sheikh licensed to marry people.

Every night when I went to sleep I felt that I would not wake up. In the morning my memory would return with the sunshine coming in through my window. I washed, slipped into my clothes and went out carrying a small black bag. It resembled a doctor's bag, and made me remember that I had graduated from medical school and become a doctor. The hands of my wrist-watch pointed to eight o'clock as I hastened on my way to the hospital. Suddenly I would stop for a short moment, take my breath and just as suddenly remember that I was married and had a child, that my child needed a bottle of milk, and my husband needed a roast chicken.

My memory was like a land buried under water. I did not remember the difference between my first and my second husbands. Both of them liked roast chicken. My friend Batta used to gurgle with laughter and say: 'When the lights go out all men are the same.' Safeya would protest and insist that the only difference between one man and another was love. Samia did not believe in love. She said it was childish, romantic nonsense. 'Love is a big illusion, Nawal,' she kept saying: 'Before marriage it is corrupting and after marriage it ends in divorce. Since you do not love him, Nawal, then you must marry him. A man is only good for marriage if your heart does not beat for him. At least if he is unfaithful you will not feel pain.'

When she said that her eyes looked as though she were holding back the tears. Then she started to shake with anger and gasped out in a faltering voice, 'Can you imagine, Nawal! Can you imagine?'

'What, Samia? Imagine what?'

'It's something I can hardly believe myself.'

'Tell me, Samia, what's wrong?' She seemed to choke with the words and her voice would break off. Then she would begin to sob and speak in panting, broken sentences: 'Can you imagine, Nawal ... I can't believe it to this moment ... Can you imagine that my husband Rifa'a, that model of a man who has such lofty principles, and who ended up in prison because he refused to give them up, can you imagine, can anyone imagine that he would do what he did? From the very first moment when they took him off to prison I kept going and coming and chasing around like a bee trying to get him released.'

'But what did Rifa'a do to you, Samia?'

'Can you imagine? He's been going around with another woman.'

'How did you find out?'

'I found a letter he had written to her. It seems they arrested him before he had time to send it.'

'That's all? A letter...!'

'A love letter, Nawal!'

'A letter that reflects no more than a romantic and chaste relationship.'

'Rifa'a is a Marxist, a dialectical materialist. He would never go for such nonsense.'

When Batta heard the story she burst out in a laugh full of irony and said, 'Samia, all men betray their wives, whether they belong to the left or the right or even the centre. And all women betray their husbands whether daughters of Eve, or of the Virgin Mary. The only difference is that men do not know how to hide, but a woman is as deep as the deepest of wells. The best thing you can do is to betray him with another man, to be unfaithful to him in the same way as he is unfaithful to you. God said "An eye for an eye and a tooth for a tooth and the one who begins is the greater sinner". It's your good fortune that they've put him behind bars.'

Safeya bent her head in thought. When she lifted her face it was deathly pale. 'Divorce,' she said 'is to me a much better solution than betrayal. Betrayal is above all a betrayal of one's self.' Her voice faltered as she spoke and her pallor struck me. Was she living the same tragedy? Safeya was not like Samia or Batta. She tended to keep silent. We were in the winter of 1960 and forty years had to go by before the day came when I heard her say, 'It's over, Nawal. I've decided to ask for a divorce from Mostafa.'

* * * *

I kept saying to myself, if I marry a man it must be because I love him. I cannot marry someone I do not love. How would I share the same bed with him if there were no love between us. Batta asked me, 'But why don't you love him, Nawal? He's a respectable man, a man of law in a good position. He has a car, a flat, and plenty of money, and he's head over heels in love with you, why reject him? What's wrong with him, Nawal?'

That question, 'What's wrong with him?' occupied my mind for over quarter of a century. I used to hear it all the time from my father, my mother, my grandmother, and my maternal and paternal aunts. And now here was Batta repeating the same phrase.

'Why don't you want to marry him?'

'I don't know.'

'What's wrong with him?'

'Maybe ...'

'Maybe what?'

'His eyes.'

'What's wrong with his eyes?'

'There's no light in them.'

'What use are his eyes when it comes to marriage?'

Batta's inimitable laughter erupts as she gasps with mirth, then breaks off only to start all over again. Her laughter is so infectious that I find myself joining in despite my heavy heart, for I have decided to marry him even though I do not love him, even though there is no light in his eyes and even though I do not like men of law. Law makes out of them people of a single, rigid mould, like plaster casts. But the question goes round and round in my head. Why, if I don't want to marry him, have I decided that is exactly what I am going to do? Is it some obscure force on earth or in the heavens that is forcing me to do it against my will? A mysterious force closer to an illusion than to anything else. A kind of atmospheric pressure exerting itself on me. A divine or satanic power pushing me towards him, against my will, and despite my full awareness of how I feel.

That winter night in the year 1960 I stayed late at the clinic. After finishing with the last patient I sat down at my desk. I held my head between my hands and dropped into a kind of lethargy, into a state oscillating between wakefulness and sleep, where the mind is no longer conscious, and the superego is buried deep under water. But the tip of the iceberg suddenly raised its head and something like a lidless eye suspended in the heavens stared down on me, wide open and unblinking. An eye that watched all night, that remained eternally vigilant. Was it the eye of God, or was it the eye of the Devil? For I feared both of them equally.

I picked up a pen and started to write. My words are halting, my sentences unfinished, my breathing irregular, gasping. A small source of light seems to move with the current of air coming in from an open window. It reveals what is hidden in the dark, what escapes the ritual of language, rebels against all that is familiar and accepted, creates disturbance and doubt and anxiety all around, upsets everything I ever believed in. It forces me to break away from the words we use in language, no longer to fear reward or retribution, to advance into the unknown, into the un-understood.

I came out of my torpor to the voice of Samia echoing in the waiting-room. She used to drop in on me at the clinic whenever she faced a crisis. Rifa'a her husband and the brother of Safeya were both still in prison. Since the events taking place in Iraq and the assumption of power by Abd Al-Kareem Kassem, a controversy had broken out between Egypt and Iraq over the issue of unity between the two countries. Gamal Abd Al-Nasser wanted to unify the two countries completely, under one president and one government. All those who opposed his views and declared that a federal union would work better because it would make the process more gradual and more democratic, suddenly found themselves in prison. Samia had taken upon herself the task of enlightening me on this issue, of explaining to me the differences between the two forms of union. She kept making speeches. Whether she raised her voice or lowered it, the rhetoric was always there, and I could not stand it. She had a thin, complaining voice and, even when she was happy or laughed, it did not change. A mournful tone threaded through everything she said, as though the world was dark and miserable and she was on the verge of breaking into tears.

She had remained my friend since we were in secondary school. The contrast between her and my other two friends Batta and Safeya, as well as my other colleagues, drew me to her. Her face was pale and devoid of any make-up, unlike the other girls. Her thin lips were pressed tight together with a kind of unfeminine determination. Her conversation, which kept mentioning Marx and the difference between dialectical materialism and idealistic dialectics, her descriptions of Abd Al-Nasser and Lenin, all this was new and different to me.

During the period of engagement to Rifa'a before their marriage, when she was still in a state of love, she had changed a little. She put kohl in her eyes, dabbed a faint pink colour on her cheeks, and painted her lips a pale red. Her voice, however, remained the same. Now it was even more high-pitched and complaining than before.

'Do you think that Abd Al-Nasser really cares about the country!' she exclaimed. 'The Union between Syria and Egypt has failed, and now Syria has seceded from it. Democracy is just a chimera. The opposition has been put in prison and democracy is no more than a word. His socialism has taken us nowhere. There is no economic development, no narrowing of the gap between classes. The money which Egypt repatriated by nationalizing the Suez Canal and other foreign companies has gone to fill the pockets of a new class mainly composed of army officers and their cronies. General Abd Al-Nasser cannot possibly be loyal to the interests of the country after all that has happened.'

Her voice became even more mournful when she switched from the subject of Abd Al-Nasser to that of Rifa'a, her husband.

'Do you think Rifa'a is faithful to me Nawal?'

My mind was preoccupied with another question which kept hammering in my head. Why was I marrying a man I did not love? But Samia went on: 'Do you think Abd Al-Nasser is loyal to the country, Nawal? And do you think Rifa'a is faithful to me? Can a man be loyal to his country and yet unfaithful to his wife. Don't you think the two are related?'

'What is there that can force me to marry a man I do not love, Samia?' I asked.

'The whole atmosphere in the country is bad and it steals into our personal life. It's really a pity, Nawal. Rifa'a and I had a beautiful relationship before we married. Do you think the problem is in the institution we call marriage?'

'The problem is with the whole system, Samia.'

I pressed my lips together, lapsed into a silent gloom. At one time I had told my first husband that he was the first love in my life, when in fact he was the second. Now I was going to tell my second husband that I loved him when I didn't love him at all. Something invisible to me was pushing me to lie. Maybe it had something to do with the year 1960, the year that my friend Raga'a said presaged a major defeat yet to come.

In one of the literary meetings I used to hold in my clinic he recited a poem, which went as follows:

Everything around us speaks of defeat, the clouds in the sky, the faces of our soldiers.

We have lost hope in the new class which rules us, in poetry and in everything else.

The graduates from the military academy know nothing.

But they become the Ministers and rule over our people.

We can expect nothing. Nothing awaits us, only prison or death.

Or maybe exile in a foreign country if we are fortunate enough.

Despair was driving me towards marriage as a way out. My future bridegroom was considered by everyone to be more than suitable. Even Um Ibrahim who had followed me from Kafr Tahla to Cairo kept insisting 'Marry him, Dr Nawal, marriage is a woman's refuge, you'll be able to give your blessed daughter a brother or a sister.'

During the small party we had on the day I got married, Safeya whispered in my ear, 'His eyesight is perfect, you can see. He's not wearing spectacles like my husband.' Batta gurgled with laughter and said to me on the side, 'It's a good thing he has no light in his eyes. That way be won't be able to see anything!' Samia listened in while they were talking to me, pouted her lips in disgust and commented, 'To tell you the truth there is no longer sincerity in this world.'

ELEVEN

The Photograph

He never gave me a chance to be alone when I was writing. He kept opening the door, walking in to my room to look over my shoulder, trying to read what I had written. No-one ever read what I wrote until it was published, and I always wrote in a room with the door closed on me. I did not like strong electric light, did not need more than the rays coming into my room from a street lamp, or falling on my desk from a small electric bulb which we kept burning throughout the night, or from a kerosene lamp when there was a power failure. All I needed was to see the letters dropping from the tip of my pen on to the white surface, shining ghost-like in the semi-darkness of my room. The novel would float in my imagination like shadows creeping out of dark corners. I sat there in the silence for two or three hours without a movement, knowing that my memory would wake up only when the whole universe was sound asleep, only when the remnants of the previous day had died away. I had to wrench off the upper layer of my brain, rid myself of my superego and the lies stored in it. It was like pulling out a lock of hair, or peeling off a part of my scalp. On my head would remain something like a furrow or an old wound which had not healed. But as time went by in the silence and in the darkness I could feel the wound closing, feel my memory awaken gradually, watch my pen move slowly over the paper, and gather speed as it wrote one line after the other.

A voice within me seemed to dictate the words, and the story would flow like a tranquil stream and then slowly become a rushing river. The pen trembled with excitement between my fingers, a warm current rose up through my arm to my head, then dropped down to my body and my feet pulsating with my blood. At one point my whole body would start to tremble, as though I was running a fever.

He never let me continue writing. It was as though my novel was an embryo impregnated in my belly by another man, so he insisted on aborting it. He would open the door and walk in. If the door was locked he banged on it with his fist, or he would put on the radio at its loudest, clatter with his wooden clogs on the bathroom floor, sit in the hall and carry on a telephone conversation in a voice that could be heard by the neighbours, or in the drawing-room with visitors talking and laughing at the top of his voice.

His mother used to visit us, and when she came their voices penetrated through the door of the room in which I sat reading or writing. I could hear him complain to her, 'Mother, I married a madwoman. She wakes up in the middle of the night and writes.'

His mother would suck her lips sorrowfully. 'Never mind, son, everything in life is what God has decided to bestow on us. Remember you chose her, and there is nothing wrong with writing. Isn't it better than her running the streets like other women and spending money on nonsense? What you needed, my son, was another kind of woman who wouldn't dare lift her eyes to you, who would sit at your feet and be like putty in your hands. But it's too late. She's your wife now and maybe God will guide her to the right path when she has a child. May God in His bounty reward you with a son who will call you "Baba"[1] and call me "Nena".[2] I yearn for the day when my eyes will see your son. May God in his bounty let it come true since she's now at least two months into her pregnancy.'

The last sentence echoed in my ears as I sat writing. I lifted my head from the desk and looked around me as though awakening from a dream. A voice had said 'at least two months into her pregnancy'. It was a strange voice that I had never heard before, and the woman it had mentioned was certainly not me, but some other woman unknown to me. Then I thought: but if it is me then the matter is really serious, then it is really a calamity. How could I possibly have become pregnant without having known love or sex or without even feeling that I was married? Maybe it was that childhood dream of a

---

[1] Papa.
[2] Granny.

messenger sent by God having visited me after which my belly filled up with a pregnancy. When I was seven years old I used to touch my belly under the covers, afraid that it might be swollen with a pregnancy. In school the girls used to whisper words I could not understand: 'A child born out of wedlock.' They tried in vain to explain to me what it meant. The Devil was behind all this, they said, so before I went to sleep I closed up the cracks in the windows with old newspapers so he could not get in. But my Coptic friend Isis did not bother about the cracks. She believed in a sacred pregnancy, not a sinful one, and told me what the difference was, told me that the Virgin Mary had been visited by a divine messenger from God and after that became pregnant with her son Jesus. So I stopped sealing up the cracks in the window and started to dream of a divine messenger coming to me in the night. My fingers would slip under the covers to see whether my belly had grown bigger than it was before. At the age of seven I was full of a naïve idealism, even where pregnancy was concerned.

'Two months into her pregnancy!'

The voice of that stranger pierced my ears like a knife. My body trembled and the pen dropped out of my fingers. I lifted my head, and there in the doorway was an old woman with a black **tarha** wound around her head. Her skin was white and her face round and fleshy. Her eyes were small, buried deep in the flesh of her face. She eyed me like a hawk. Her look slowly moved down, went through the wall of my belly as though probing for something behind it. In her mind she was imagining the child that lay inside, thrusting its legs open as she searched for a male organ, to make sure that it was an exact replica of his organ and that the boy had been born of her son's loins.

I started to suffer from nausea in the morning, used to rush to the bathroom, close the door and empty the contents of my stomach into the toilet bowl. I remembered my grandmother saying to me: 'Marriage makes a woman lose her appetite for food.' With my mother it had been pregnancy that did that, not marriage.

During my first marriage I went through the experience of pregnancy and gave birth to a beautiful girl. She was the product of love, not of marriage, for I believed in love but not in marriage. To me it seemed as though marriage could only lead to children with some deformity.

So now I began to touch my belly whenever I sat at my desk. I felt that my pregnancy had something unholy about it, that the embryo had been created by a relationship made up of falsehoods and lies. I had told the man I did not love that I loved him. He was sharing my bed because we were married, but that was all. His skin was white, his face round and fleshy like his mother's, but I liked dark, lean well-cut features. He had a short, squat body which was soft and flabby whereas I liked people who were tall and graceful. His hands were white, small and timid, his fingers short and always kept stuck together, reminding me of fishes. I liked big, open hands that spoke of courage.

Every morning as soon as I opened my eyes I looked for a red stain in my underclothes, or on the sheets, but they remained as white as snow. The white surface gave me a shock. It was the colour of sickness, of the coats worn by doctors, of hospital beds, of the shrouds wrapped around dead bodies. It was the colour of death.

When I was a girl I hated the sight of menstrual blood, had read that it was an 'offence' meted out to women by God. But now I began to dream of a blood-stained sheet, yearned for it night and day, willed for it with all my being, as though by force of will I could wrest it from the hands of destiny. I used to beat down on my belly with my fist, jump over the balustrade into the garden from the balcony on the first floor of our house, but the embryo clung savagely to the wall of my uterus like a louse digging into the scalp. I could see it sitting there inside me, see its round fleshy face, with small deep-set eyes just like the father, just like his mother.

I did everything I could to expel it from my body, swallowed pills to kill it, injected myself with drugs that could stimulate an abortion. One day as I was jumping from the balcony I fell and broke my right arm. Batta took me in her Buick car to Al Kasr Al-Aini Hospital. Her husband, Dr Hamdi, was in charge of a medical section there. I had an X-ray and it showed a fracture in the radius, a bone of the forearm. Hamdi bandaged my arm, put it in a sling and Batta took me off to one of the surgical sections to have it put in plaster.

Nothing in the hospital had changed since I worked there some years ago. The long wide corridor with huge broken glass windows looking out on to the Nile, the pale faces of the nurses and the even paler faces of the patients, the doctor walking along looking serious and important, everything was the same. One of the doctors recognized me and stopped short. It was Dr Rashad.

'Nawal! What a surprise. What's wrong with your arm?'

I was feeling sad, and exhausted from the continuous pain and nausea. Three years had gone by since the day when he had come to our house to ask for my hand. It had been a hot summer's day, heavy with dust, and my mother was lying sick in bed. He sat in the drawing-room talking to my father and I remembered everything about him was shining, his blue Chevrolet, his white sharkskin suit, his hair, his shoes, his necktie pin and the blue stone in his ring. Everything except his eyes. He stared at me with a searching look from beneath his spectacles as we stood there in the corridor, then shifted his look to my arm hanging in a sling from the neck, and returned to my face. It must have been very pale because he said:

'You look ill, Nawal. What's wrong?'

Batta volunteered an answer: 'She has a fracture of the radius, Dr Rashad.'

'And where are you heading, Batta? I'll take you to my section. You need to put your arm in plaster, Nawal.'

Forty years have passed since that meeting in the corridor of the hospital. After that I ran into him several times at the Medical Association, or in meetings at the Ministry of Health. He became an important official in the state administration, at the university, and at the Academy for Scientific Research. In all these he occupied very high posts. He was a fervent supporter first of Gamal Abd Al-Nasser then of Anwar Al-Sadat, despite the big difference between the policies of the two men. When I was imprisoned in 1981 he said to my friend Batta, 'Nawal deserves to be in prison. It will stop her from writing what she writes.' And in 1993 when I had to go into exile in the United States he said to her, 'She deserves what's happened to her for writing what she wrote against the Gulf War. I've never read such nonsense.'

A couple of years ago a journalist from an important daily paper asked him what he thought about the writings of different women.[3] He expressed his admiration for the women she mentioned and said they deserved the state prizes awarded to them. But when he was asked what his views were regarding the writings of Nawal El Saadawi, the answer was: 'She does not respect our Islamic values and the traditions of the East. In the East we attach great importance to spiritual matters in our lives. But people in the West care more for what is material. Besides, they are loose sexually and Nawal in her writings seeks to please the West.'

---

[3] Latifa Al-Zayat, Amina Sai'id and Soheir Al-Kalamawy.

I did not see the interview myself, but Batta read it to me over the telephone and when she had finished she said, 'He's never forgiven you for turning down his offer of marriage. A man never forgives a woman who rejects him. The wound never heals. Anyhow Dr Rashad is better than a lot of men. Do you remember Dr Zackareya, you know, the one who taught us physiology? He's been going around saying that I had a relationship with him because I put him off. You know, when a man starts spreading rumours of that kind about a woman, you can be sure that she's turned him down. And can you imagine, Nawal, all of a sudden he's become an important literary figure and has been chosen as a member of the Supreme Council for Culture, or something like that. I doubt if he's ever written anything except a few articles in the newspapers. Everything has become so messy, Nawal, so you must not be surprised if a man like Dr Rashad allows himself to express his views about literature and women when he knows nothing about either of them, and is probably impotent too.'

She gurgled with laughter but I could detect a hoarse note in her voice, a wheeze in her breath. She had begun to complain of age, of obscure pains in her body, and severe headaches at the back of her head. Her husband, Dr Hamdi, told me after examining her that she was as strong as a horse and there was nothing wrong with her, except in the head!

'Can you imagine, Nawal, your friend Batta going off to Mecca and coming back wearing a veil! Well, that's what she did,' he said to me.

*   *   *   *

Standing in front of the mirror I could see a long, thin, pale face, an arm enveloped in plaster hanging below it in a sling, and further down a loose gown rising slightly over a belly. I asked myself: 'This woman in the mirror, who is she?

'This woman has married a man she does not love, practises a profession that was not made for her, carries a child in her belly which is not hers, lives in a house belonging to someone else, leaving it every morning reluctantly to work in a smelly hospital she hates. This woman – how can she be me?'

My arm enveloped in plaster takes me back to the first day in the month of January 1955. I awoke feeling as radiant as the sunshine coming through my window. It was the New Year. I had just graduated with honours from medical school and had been appointed as a resident doctor in the University Hospital. So I put on a new dress to celebrate. It was white with small pink flowers. My eyes were black and shining, my heart beating with love. On my finger I wore the engagement ring with his name engraved on it. Through the open windows I could see him walking down the road towards our house with a bunch of flowers in his hand. The maid-servant led him into the drawing-room separated from the hall by a glass door on which my mother had hung a curtain embroidered with her designs. My father was sitting in the hall reading. He asked the maid-servant who it was and she said Dr Ahmed, since she had seen him when he visited us before and had been at the small celebration for our engagement more than two years previously.

My father took off his spectacles and stood up. I thought he intended to go into the drawing-room to welcome our visitor. Dr Ahmed was in fact still a student in the final year of medical school but students in the final year were in the habit of addressing one another as doctor. My father was angry because Ahmed's graduation had been delayed when he went to the Canal Zone to join the freedom fighters, and he told me to return his engagement ring and ask him not to come to our house again. He spoke in a quiet voice, for he rarely lost his temper or shouted, but he was very firm, said that his mind was made up, and that he was not prepared to see his daughter, the doctor, marry a failure and link her future to a man who was still a student, and had fallen behind his colleagues in medical school.

After that the situation started to evolve so quickly and strangely that I did not realize what was happening. I saw my mother come into the hall wearing a blue dress and fluffy blue woollen slippers. She walked quickly over to the glass door, turned the key to lock it, put the key in her pocket then went off to her room. After that the maid-servant came into the hall and told us that Dr Ahmed had put the bunch of flowers on the table and left through another door in the drawing-room which led into the garden and to a small outer gate.

I kept trying to figure out what had happened. Had he heard what my father had said? Had he heard the sound of the key being turned as my mother locked the door?

I stood in the hall petrified, unable to react. My father put on his clothes and left the house but I continued to stand there. My whole body was trembling as though icy cold water had been poured on me from above. I felt my heart beating violently, felt all the anger accumulated during the twenty-four years of my life rising within me like a storm, choking my throat, bringing the tears to my eyes.

Suddenly I rushed at the glass door and hit it with my fist, with all the force I could muster in my right arm. I was no longer a child who stamped her foot in frustration. This was the anger of a woman fully conscious, fully aware of what she was doing.

My fist went through the glass with a sound like an explosion, followed by the ring of splinters dropping on the floor, then by a deep silence. I felt no pain, so I slowly pulled back my arm through the jagged opening but something caught on an edge, and a broken pane dropped down on my wrist cutting through it like a knife. I saw my hand hanging down suspended, no longer a part of my body that I could move. My heart seemed as though it had stopped beating, but the blood pulsated out over my white dress, then down on to the white tiles and the freshly painted white door.

*   *   *   *

I came to from the effect of the anaesthetic to find Dr Abdel Al-Azeem, a professor in the surgical department, standing near my bed. He was just back from London after specializing in neurosurgery. Tall and lean, he smiled at me as he said: 'Congratulations, Nawal. The operation is ninety percent successful and the other ten percent depends on you.' I was still drowsy and could not follow what he was saying. But the following day he spent some time with me explaining that the operation had not been an easy one. The tendons of my wrist and some of the muscles had been cut or severally lacerated. 'I did the best I could,' he said. 'It took me almost five hours to repair the damage. I have done my job, and now the rest depends on you and God.'

The day I came home my father said to me: 'You could have lost your hand were it not for Dr Abdel Al-Azeem. It was the first operation of its kind he has done since he came back from London.' Mother hugged me and said: 'God loves you, Nawal, and your hand will be exactly as it was before and even better.'

My body was healthy and I regained my strength quickly. The fourth day after my operation I found Dr Sa'id Abdou standing next to my bed. He was the professor who taught Hygiene and Public

Health in medical school but at the same time he was a writer, and contributed a regular column to one of the big daily newspapers. His column appeared under the title 'They mislead you when they say ...'. He had read some of my short stories and articles in the magazine published by the students in the school, had heard me speak at the ceremony organized to mourn the death of Al-Menessi as well as on other occasions. He told me that the date had been fixed for the graduation ceremony and asked me whether I could make a speech on behalf of the students. 'The marquee will be erected in the courtyard of the hospital just a few steps away from here, and you seem to be in good shape. You can come across in a wheel-chair if you find it difficult to walk. You're the only graduate who has a real gift for writing and I'm sure your literary style will be reflected in your speech. You know it's an important occasion, Nawal, and I know that you'll make a great speech. The Dean of the Medical School, the Rector of the University, the professors and students will all be there, and this year we are expecting the Minister of Education to attend.'

I used to have a photograph of myself sitting behind the table on a platform in front of the microphone delivering my speech at the graduation ceremony, with my arm in plaster hanging from a sling around my neck. That was at the beginning of 1955, forty-five years ago. In the photograph the Minister of Education is sitting on my right, and the Rector of the University on my left. The photograph remained with me for over two years before it was torn up together with my identity card, my Medical Association card, and other photographs taken during my childhood and my youth. When I married and left my father's house I carried them with me among my papers. They were memories of my childhood, unforgettable moments of my life, and served to illustrate the memories jotted down in the diary that I kept carefully hidden from everyone else.

One day my husband pounced on them and started to tear them up. His big rough fingers were trembling, the dark of his eyes disappeared under his lids and all I could see were the whites with red swollen blood vessels running through them. He held up the photograph and screamed, 'This is the picture taken when you graduated, isn't it, and you're sitting with the Minister and the Rector? Of course, why not! Now you're an important doctor, aren't you, and I'm nothing but a failure and a drug addict? How can you go on living with a man like me? Didn't we swear to live together and die together? But now you want to go off and leave me to die alone, don't you?'

He tore up the photograph and threw it into the dustbin, then went on tearing up the rest. When he had finished he turned on me, took me by the throat and started to throttle me. He was craving for a dose of Maxitone forte but there was no money in my bag, no money in the house, nothing remaining that he could carry away and sell. He kept screaming at the top of his voice: 'Illusions, nothing but illusions, the three of them! Down with God, down with the nation, down with love and loyalty! There is no loyalty, there is no loyalty.' Then he wept.

His enemies had been the British, the King and those who ruled in the King's name. He shouldered his gun and went off, his heart full of faith in God, in his country, in the power of love. But he came back defeated, broken. All he had learned as a freedom fighter was how to kill. His beliefs had drained away step by step, had been shaken every time one of his comrades shed his blood, for there was treason in the air. So when he came back he took to drugs, injected himself with poison, let it rise up to his head, so that now he saw treason in everything, felt betrayed by the very things he had believed in and fought for: God, his country, and love. But he could not revenge himself on God, or his country. His hands could not reach out to strangle them. They had no body, no neck to throttle with his fingers. When he looked around all he could see now was the woman he loved. Her neck was there to strangle, even though she had given him love. So after he had torn up her photographs and papers and thrown them in the dustbin, he turned on her with all his pent-up fury, with all the madness of the drug. But the drug had made him weak and she was strong. She left him panting on the bed weeping like a child. Now she knew she had to go. She moved towards the door but before she left the room she put her coat on over her night-gown, and as she looked down at her bare feet, there on the floor was her Medical Association card with her photograph partly torn off. She bent down with trembling fingers, picked it up and put it in the pocket of her coat.

I heard him snore as I tiptoed to the room in which my daughter slept. My body was swaying slightly but my head was steady. I looked at her as she lay fast asleep in her cot, with a small angelic smile on her face. I carried her up in my arms, wrapped her in the pink woollen blanket, opened the door of the flat and went out closing it silently behind me.

It was shortly before dawn when I walked from Manial Road to my father's house in Giza. I stopped for a few moments on Abbas

Bridge to breathe in the fresh morning air. We used to walk on this bridge together before he went off to fight. I could see his eyes shining with pride and happiness, but now below me the Nile flowed slowly and sadly. Tears dropped from my eyes and fell into the water. It seemed to grow turgid, as though mud had risen from the depths and was suspended in particles stained red with blood. But I felt relieved as though the tears had washed away my sadness and let the Nile carry them away out of my life. I walked on with my daughter held close in my arms, with her face looking up at me and smiling, like a ray of sun. My father received me with open arms, and my mother got up from her sick bed and held me tight. For the first time since she had fallen ill I heard her laugh ring out.

In my coat pocket I found the photograph. It was torn into three pieces which were held to one another by threads. I stuck the pieces together with gum on a piece of cardboard, and kept it at the bottom of a drawer in my desk. I used to avoid opening the drawer, so as to avoided seeing it. I needed to forget, to overcome the pain and the sadness it brought back.

Ahmed Helmi and I remained friends until he died. I knew that he was a victim of those who had power, of the comrades who had betrayed the freedom fighters, but friends began to shun him. Even his mother closed the door in his face. With tears flowing from her eyes she once said to me, 'I began to be afraid of him. He used to threaten me if I didn't give him money to buy the poison with which he injected himself. I feel afraid that he might do harm to you also, my child. He's breaking our hearts.'

*   *   *   *

The torn photograph remained at the bottom of my drawer untouched. Five years went by, then one day during the year 1961 my door-bell rang and when I opened the door a woman walked in. Her name was Soraya Hamdan. She worked with government television where she held a responsible post, and she was also my neighbour.

After we had talked for a while, she asked me whether I had a story which could be filmed for television. I said to her, 'But I do not write for television, Ostaza⁺ Soraya.' She said, 'Why not, Dr Nawal?'

⁺ A term of respect used to address people of a certain standing, or older than the speaker.

'I don't know but the fact is I've never tried.' 'You are a talented writer and many people read you, both women and men. Our television is in need of good literary works and you have a remarkable style. Take the decision now. Start a story for television and let me know when you will deliver it to me.'

When night came I sat down and began to think about the story I could write. My hand strayed to the drawer where I kept my old papers. As I went through it I came upon the photograph. I spent the night awake, thinking. Every now and then I looked at the photograph. Before the sun came out I picked up a pen and wrote three words: 'The Torn Photograph'. They became the title of my story. I wrote it as a television series composed of forty-minute sequences.

When it was broadcast I used to follow it on the screen after coming home from my clinic. Om Ibrahim sat on the floor next to me, sobbing quietly and wiping her tears.

On one of my shelves I still keep a big folder with a label that says 'The Torn Photograph' and in the folder there are 220 typed pages. Often I think of publishing the story in a book to save it from being lost forever.

TWELVE

The Scalpel and
the Law

I stare at myself in the mirror, at the plaster cast around my arm. The calendar on the wall tells me that we are in the year 1960. My mind's eye goes back to the day when I stood in front of a mirror, thin and pale, with my arm hanging from my neck in a sling.

That time I had burst out in anger against my father and smashed my fist through a glass pane. My hand showed no signs of what I had done to myself apart from a deep scar reaching down my arm almost as far as the bones of my wrist.

This time I was angry at myself, at this woman inside the woman I was, who had married a man she did not love, had become pregnant with child without love, and jumped off the balcony to take away its life. However nothing had happened to it. Instead I had broken my arm, and now it was enveloped once again in a plaster cast.

I lifted my arm, struck the face of the woman in the mirror with the plaster cast. The mirror cracked. Now the woman's face was no longer one face, but two faces with a single eye in each.

I turned round. Behind me stood the old woman, her head enveloped in the black *tarha*. She stared at my arm with her hawk-like eyes. 'May God protect you from all evil. What's happened to you, Nawal?' 'Nothing, nothing at all,' I said. 'I just jumped off the balcony.' The way she laughed at my answer showed she did not believe me. She was like her son. Every time he asked me if I loved him and I answered 'no', he would laugh as though he did not believe what I said. Why do they not believe me when I tell the truth?

Next day she suggested I take a holiday from my hospital work. 'It will be good for your health and the health of the child in your belly,' she insisted, all the while eyeing my belly tenderly as though she could see her grandson, the son of her precious son curled up inside me, as though she were literally folding him tenderly under her lids. Then her eyes travelled upwards to my breasts, moved to my face and became hawk-like again.

Nothing linked me to this woman and her son other than the embryo inside me. It was a foreign body these strangers had implanted in me. I wanted to rid myself of my body, often thought of committing suicide. But then my eyes would wander to the pile of papers on my desk. My novel kept drawing me away from all this, telling me to finish it before I died. So I decided to postpone dying until I had finished it.

* * * *

I was no longer able to write. I held the pen in my left hand since the fingers of my right hand were still weak after months in plaster and I could not hold the pen in them. It slipped out from between them as though they had become lifeless but I brought them back to life gradually by doing the exercises the doctor had prescribed for the muscles and joints, by moving my wrist and arm, by repeating the exercises hourly for at least ten minutes.

I used to slip down to the small garden behind the house and hoe the ground for half an hour every day, then sit under the eucalyptus tree. From above, a small bird looked down at me with sad eyes.

I was twenty-nine years old at the time, yet I felt like an old woman nearing the end of her days. When I lay next to him in the wide bed in which we slept I wished that death would snatch me away and save me from my plight. I used to roam around the house looking for some poison I could swallow. In the white medicine cabinet I found a bottle of black sleeping pills, and began to swallow them one after the other. But suddenly I could see the face of my small girl with the tears of sadness running down her face, and the faces of my younger brothers and sisters, who were still dependent on me, as they sat like lost orphans in the flat where they had continued to live after my death.

The newspapers started to pile up on the small table in the hall. Every morning a newspaper would be left in front of our house. I used to kick it away with my foot but he would bring it in to read, and then leave it neatly folded on the table. Things were falling apart. The picture of Dr Hamdi, Batta's husband, kept appearing in the newspaper, together with what he had said about 'protecting, our guided democracy from the machinations of the enemies of the revolution'. He called on Allah to descend in wrath upon them, 'to send birds of prey to devour them so that they can be buried in the deepest of wells'.

Whoever opposed Abd Al-Nasser was labelled an enemy of the revolution. Whoever suggested that a federal union with Iraq was a more democratic and more durable way of uniting the two countries than a complete fusion under a single central authority was hunted down. My friend Raga'a the poet was forced to flee to Paris. Safeya's brother, Asa'ad, and Samia's husband, Rifa'a, were both sent to a concentration camp. Samia curled her lips in disdain and commented, 'The country has been taken over by a bunch of soldiers and they're imposing a regime of terror.'

*   *   *   *

The stage on which the events of our married life were enacted was composed of the big bed in our room, and the dining-table at which we sat to have our meals. Everything went on between four walls. At times noises reached the ears of the neighbours from behind them: solid bodies hitting against the partitions, china being smashed into pieces that flew out in all directions, or angry voices becoming louder and louder, then calming down until there was a complete silence and nothing further could be heard.

In the morning the husband and the wife would be engrossed in their work. At the end of the day they would come back and each of them would resume their place inside the four walls, then the drama would start all over again.

Every night she dreamt of running away but she felt unable to take this step. She kept asking herself why she was so hesitant. Was she afraid of failing in marriage for the second time? Of what people would say? Of solitude? Yet solitude beckoned to her like a shining planet she would never be able to reach. Was this yearning for solitude, and the need for company, the everlasting contradiction of that relationship called marriage?

I used to avoid going out with him so that people would not see us together. I was taller than he was. My hand was burnt brown by the sun and its fingers were thin and long. His hand was small, his fingers soft and pudgy, as though they had never known what work was. His feet were small too, their skin milky white, untouched by a ray of sun.

I walked with a powerful stride. His stride was short and hesitant and shaky. Whenever I watched him walk I felt ill. I did not know whether I should succumb to the state of anxiety that swept over me, or abandon myself to my dreams.

When we walked through the crowded streets of the city he used to move his arms as though one of them was shorter than the other, and his body advanced in a crawling way which was painful to watch. His muscles were flabby because he was always sitting either at home, or in his office, or in the car which took him from one to the other. He never played any sports, or exercised himself walking. If he rolled up his sleeves and bared his arms, under the white skin I could see long tortuous blue veins. This was normal, and yet whenever I saw them I felt their colour was strange although I knew that the red of blood in the veins seen through the skin looks a dark blue. It was as though I had forgotten my medicine, could no longer reason in a logical way. I used to be seized with a strange anxiety whenever he bared his arms, as though he was displaying some deformity.

One day a new friend of mine who was a writer came to visit me. When she rang the bell he opened the door and led her into the drawing-room, so she asked me, 'Was it your husband who opened the door for me?' I hesitated for a moment, then I said 'No, that's not my husband' but quickly retreated and said, 'Yes, it's him.'

People considered him a handsome man, a real male. But the writer in my friend could lay bare what was cancelled under the skin. I had always prided myself on seeing what others often failed to see, and wondered why for some time I had become blind.

I tried to massage the flabby impotent brain-matter in his head, to make warm red blood flow through it in place of his blood which was cold and blue. I tried to explain, to discuss, to have a dialogue with him but there was nothing doing. I realized that I was struggling against the natural order of things. Our arguments exhausted me, made me feel ill. He could not understand what was wrong with me, kept looking around the spacious flat and wondering why I did not show any signs of happiness at the sight of the luxurious furniture, the silk dresses, and the ornate golden high-heeled slippers he bought for me, at the roasted leg of lamb and rice with nuts and raisins lying on our dinner table, or the big car standing outside the door of our house. He kept asking: 'What more do you want?'

I would wipe away the tears in my eyes, feeling at a loss, unable to gather my senses together. Had I lost the ability to see straight? How could I be blind to all the comfort around me? But a moment later my real self would assert itself, and all the comfort surrounding me once more become no more than a calamity.

Writing novels was my only aim in life, the only thing that mattered. I postponed dying until I could finish the novel, and trained my left hand to write. Now I could use both hands. When one of them showed signs of fatigue I shifted to the other. I sat writing until the light of dawn crept in through the window, and I could hear the chirruping of a bird in the eucalyptus tree, see it spread its wings under the sun, cock its head at me with a smile and then fly away.

He used to share the same bed with me. Nothing spoiled our married life more than the fact that we shared the same bed, shared the same bathroom, than being exposed to these daily aggressions against privacy.

One day when I woke up I found him reading my papers. It was as though he were violating my body. Maybe if he had violated my body it would have been less painful. I said: 'Those are my papers and you have no right to read them.'

His answer was to pick up the pile of papers and throw them out of the window. I jumped out of the window thinking I would be able to save them from being lost. I could have killed myself, broken my head on the tarmac road. It was not a moment of madness. I was perfectly aware of what I was doing. I had worked on my novel day and night for months, and had covered three hundred pages with my handwriting. To me, rescuing the novel was like saving my life.

My imagination took over, I found myself walking on water, swaying from side to side but I continued until I reached a long corridor which branched out into underground passages. They looked like the corridors of a hospital. On either side, patients were bedding on the ground, and next to them there were huge baskets and children who waved their crippled legs in the air. With desperate eyes they looked up at the doctors who marched down the corridor striking their iron heels on the stone floor. The doctors wore snow-white coats, and behind their spectacles their eyes were dull, or hidden beneath lowered lids. Now and again one of them would stop to percuss the chest of a child who had been held up to him by the mother from a breast hanging down in ragged folds of skin.

Swaying from side to side I walked through the waiting lines, blood trickling down between my legs. The pale lips of the women lying on the floor kept opening to whisper, 'May God cure you of your illness, child.' They wiped their tired eyes with the hems of their dusty black *gallabeyas*. I cut my way through the throngs with difficulty, avoided looking into their eyes, but my heart was full of a feeling of warmth and I knew I would never forget their compassion.

I opened my lids to find myself lying on a table which resembled the marble tables in the morgue. Under me was a red rubber sheet, and my body was soaked in blood. Over my head was a powerful electric reflector. I lay on my back with my legs wide open, my hands and my feet tied by leather belts to iron bars which rose upwards from the table. I could hear the doctors exchanging words I could not understand, lifting their noses and pronouncing what sounded like 'evacuation'. My mind seemed paralysed, unable to think. The word 'evacuation' seemed to echo in my ears from a distance, from way back in time to 1946 when I was a student in secondary school marching out of the gates in a demonstration and shouting at the British soldiers, 'Evacuation by blood'.[1]

But now it meant something else. It meant that they were expelling the embryo from my womb with medical weapons. In other words I was going through an abortion as I lay on the table.

* * * *

He lay fast asleep on the bed by my side. His snores were like the chimes of an old, rusty clock. My eyes were open staring at the ceiling. Now I was free, rid of the chains that had bound me to him. The evacuation had freed me from the foreign occupation of my body. I had torn from my womb the foreign body that had become a part of myself. I could see the word 'divorce' creeping over the horizon like the light of dawn. My breath came and went quickly as I lay in bed, as though I were running to catch a train before it left the station.

---

[1] Meaning the need to wage an armed struggle in order to force the British troops to leave Egypt.

He was accustomed to cover himself with a sheet from top to bottom, but his small white feet, which resembled the feet of Chinese girls made to wear iron shoes, protruded from below. I could imagine his mother massaging them for him every night, wrapping them up in wool, and burning incense over them to protect them from the evil eye.

He opened his eyes, saw me gazing at the ceiling. I heard him ask, 'Why are you awake?'

'I'm thinking.'

'Of what?'

'Of divorce.'

He bounded out of bed, and stood over me angrily.

'Divorce is the prerogative of men only. It is the man who decides to divorce not the woman. According to the law it is an absolute right which he alone possesses.'

He was a man of law. So despite his small body he put his nose up in the air, and said, 'I am a man of law,' then he said something which made the blood rush to my head: 'It will be easier for you to see the stars at noon[2] than to have a divorce, dear doctor.'

*   *   *   *

Ever since I was a child I used to hear my father say: 'If the price we pay for freedom is high, we pay a much higher price if we accept to be slaves.'

A few months before he died he retired to live on his pension. He vibrated with happiness as though this was a rebirth for him. He stretched his arms out, took a deep breath and said, 'Free at last after thirty-three years in prison. At last I will be able to read and write what I want.' But, soon after, he died suddenly without writing anything, or leaving any legacy behind.

When I was nine years old I heard my father say to his sister Rokaya, 'Divorce is much better than continuing with an unhappy marriage. Divorce him, Rokaya. A woman has the right according to Islamic jurisprudence to repudiate[3] her husband if she returns the dowry he gave her when they married, and if she gives up her alimony.'

---

[2] An expression popularly used to indicate what is impossible to attain.
[3] In Arabic *khal'a*, which means literally 'to divest oneself of something'.

My father had studied Islamic jurisprudence at Al-Azhar University and Dar Al-Oulom. Were it not for him I would never have known that I could use this right drawn from Islamic jurisprudence to divorce my husband.

When I divorced my first husband my father accompanied me to the Ma'azoun.[4] I remember him walking into the Sheikhs' office, tall and imposing and saying, 'My daughter, Dr Nawal, wants to divorce her husband, and she is prepared to return his dowry and forgo her alimony.'

The dowry my first husband had paid was only a nominal twenty-five piastres, since I had been against the idea of receiving a dowry. Marriage for me was not a business affair in which I was selling myself on the marriage market. But there were legal formalities which could not be avoided.

My father was not present this time. He had died a year and a half before my second marriage. I had to face this man of law alone with no support or help from anyone. I knew almost nothing about legal matters, but his voice kept echoing in my ears: 'Repudiate him, Nawal. It is your right. Do not be afraid. Save yourself before it is too late.'

That day my husband and I were standing in the hall facing one another. He was shouting at the top of his voice, 'The stars in heaven are more within your reach than the divorce you want.' He was wearing white silk pyjamas which stuck to his short squat body, and his small white feet protruded from the trouser legs. He glared up at me with his deep-set eyes as I stood over him from my height.

'A woman cannot ask for a divorce. She does not have the right. Divorce is the sole prerogative of the husband!' he shouted.

'A woman has the right to repudiate her husband if she agrees to return the dowry to him, and forgo her right to an alimony,' I said.

'That right does not exist in Shariah.'[5]

'Do you want to live with me against my will?'

'It's my legal right.'

'But I don't want to live with you.'

'Then go to court.'

'Court.' The word went through my head like an electric shock. Throughout my life I had never stood in court. Courts in Egypt do

---

[4] The religious Sheikh who presides over marriage and divorce.
[5] Religious jurisprudence.

not give women their rights. They are male-oriented. The result is that women are exploited by lawyers, are the victims of unjust law, and spend years of their lives running from one court to the other without obtaining a divorce. Anger rose within me in hot floods. I took a step towards him. I felt like strangling him with my bare hands. Suddenly I remembered that I was a doctor, that I had a small surgical kit in my bag lying on the desk and was accustomed to use a knife to cut through an abdominal wall, or open a chest. I walked towards the desk, opened the bag, took out the kit and extracted a scalpel. As I lifted my head and half turned to walk back I glimpsed myself in the mirror. My face was as white as a sheet, my eyes black and staring. The knife shone in the morning light as I stood there barefoot on the white tiled floor wearing an old crumpled nightgown.

I stepped towards him slowly. I felt calm, could see everything clearly: the wall behind him, a chair in the corner with a red cushion, his white face. As I moved closer I saw him retreat step by step until his back was to the wall. My eyes stared into his. I read terror in them, in the sudden pallor of his lips, and the twitching of a muscle in his neck.

There was no need for the knife. I just said, 'I repudiate you.'

*   *   *   *

Twenty years later in the autumn of 1981 I was arrested and put in prison. There I met a woman who was known as 'Fatheya the Killer'. I had never met a woman who had committed murder before, and when I saw her I could not imagine that she was capable of killing anyone. She was soft-spoken and docile. The other inmates were often angry and vicious but she was always calm. But one day I saw her angry and realized that she could kill. She had eyes that were blue and limpid. Now they were dark and muddy and her face had turned white and steely. I remembered the day I had held a scalpel to my husband, and realized that in a moment of justified anger a woman or a man can kill. Fatheya the Killer had cut her husband to pieces when she caught him raping her eight-year-old daughter.

My divorce papers were sent to the new home where I had settled with my daughter. I did not need to go to the Ma'azoun's office, or the court. My scalpel had set me free from the shackles of the 'law of obedience' which rules over women in marriage.

I had a small party at home to celebrate my divorce. My friends Safeya, Batta and Samia were present. Om Ibrahim let out a long trilling 'yooyoo' and said, 'What a blessing, doctor, to have you back in our midst, unharmed.' Batta gurgled with laughter, lifted her hands to the heavens and exclaimed, 'May Allah bestow the same blessing on us soon.' Safeya looked at me with admiration and commented in her calm voice, 'You have more courage than we have, Nawal.' Samia lifted her fist in the air as though she were walking in a demonstration and shouted, 'Down with the institution of marriage!'

THIRTEEN

The Defeat

I met Sherif at the Ministry of Health in 1964, one year after he came out of prison where he had spent fourteen years. When Batta heard that I intended to marry him she gasped, 'You must be mad, Nawal. An ex-prisoner, and a Communist too.' Safeya in turn warned me. 'Communism has ruined the life of my brother Asa'ad. Besides, it has no future in our country.' Samia pouted as usual before proclaiming her stand on the matter. 'The problem is not with Communism. There's nothing wrong with that. The real problem is marriage. It's an institution that has failed miserably. It has no future and, God willing, it will disappear one day.'

Batta laughed. 'You've never said anything more right. But that's not the issue now. The real problem is Nawal and not anything else. She believes the marriage institution was born with the slave society and has gone on since then without any real change, and yet she's going into it for the third time. A believer should not allow himself to be bitten from the same hole twice, let alone three times.'[1]

I was now over thirty-three years old. Many of my illusions had evaporated, and my heart no longer beat for love as it had when I was much younger. My life was full even though there was no man in it. I had my work as a doctor, my writing, my daughter, my brothers,

---

[1] A popular saying advising that you should not stick your hand in the same snake hole more than once, so as to avoid being bitten again, i.e. one should learn from experience.

sisters and friends. So why should I marry? Why should I put myself at the mercy of a law which took me back twenty years, to the time where I had not yet come of age, when neither my body nor my mind belonged to me? Why should I once more need a husband's permission to travel, or to go to work? Why should I put my daughter at the mercy of what might happen if I shared my life with a man?

I asked Sherif, 'Do we need a marriage licence governed by the marriage law? Why not live together without it and be free to continue or to separate without any legal constraints? People talk a lot about faith in God, so why don't they marry with just God as their witness?'

He laughed and answered in his usual quiet voice, 'Nawal. Do you want to marry, or do you want to change the world?'

I said, 'Both.'

'But changing our world may take a century or a century and a half and we want to live together now. You know how difficult it is for an unmarried couple to be together without meeting all sorts of problems every day. Both of us are public figures and that makes it even more difficult. Then if we have children they will be considered illegitimate, and we won't be allowed to send them to school.'

Today things are changing. But that was thirty-six years ago. So on December 10, 1964 we went off to the office of a Ma'azoun and signed a marriage contract. The Ma'azoun looked at us and asked, 'What about the dowry?' The fees of the Ma'azoun depend on the size of the dowry, but I said, 'Twenty-five piastres is enough for me. I don't need more for what is a symbol of slavery.' The Ma'azoun wanted to be paid a fat fee, so he was angry and tried to complicate matters, but Sherif gave him a generous sum and said, 'Go ahead. We have appointments after this, and have no time to argue with you, my Sheikh.'

Our appointment was with my daughter Mona. She was seven years old and her honey-coloured eyes lit up when she opened the box we had brought her and found her new dress in it. It was pink with a white lace collar and after she had put it on we sat around the table in our flat and celebrated our marriage with our little girl, a bouquet of white and red flowers, a bottle of wine and laughter.

In my very first meeting with Sherif I felt I could trust him. I looked into his eyes. They were like windows wide open onto what was inside. There is a proverb that says, 'Talk so that I may know who you are '. But I say, 'Show me your eyes and I will know who you are.'

I was at ease with him. One of my first questions was, 'Sherif. What do you think of writing and literature?' In the days when I still believed in a life after death, I used to wonder whether, when I went to Paradise, I would find pen and paper there. In secondary school my teacher expelled me from class because I asked him whether there would be pens and papers in Paradise. That was in 1946 and I remember it was spring because the flowers on the school fence were blooming: morning glory, honeysuckle, and Indian jasmine. In 1981 when I was imprisoned the jailer used to search our cell every day and the officer in charge would threaten the jailers saying, 'If I find pen and paper, that is more dangerous than finding a gun.' But I succeeded in hiding a pen and paper under the floor. When I slept, there was always a pen and paper near my bed, but when I was a child I kept them concealed under my pillow. It was pen and paper that made me divorce two husbands. So my question to Sherif was important because later he was to become my third husband. At the time when we met he wrote only political articles, or studies. But from the very first meeting I sensed the artist in him. I said: 'You are more of an artist than a politician or a medical doctor.' 'Maybe,' he said. 'Ever since I was a child I have always loved music and I have always read novels and literature. My mother used to hold my hand and say, "You have the fingers of a musician."' He had long, sensitive fingers, strong and yet gentle.

Before we married we used to sit up on the Mokattam Hills, or near the Nile and he would tell me about his life, his childhood, his political activities, his years in prison. He was born in London in 1923. His father belonged to a feudal family, descendants of a land aristocracy that went back as far as the Mamelukes and sultans, who were followed by a succession of Khedives that ruled Egypt until it became a kingdom and a British colony. Eighty percent of the land of Egypt was owned by this feudal class headed by the royal family, by King Fouad and after 1936 by his son King Farouk, but a substantial portion of this land ownership was also in the hands of foreigners: British, French, Belgians, Greeks, Italians. The feudal landowners invested in banks, industrial and trading companies and other activities, and became partners with the foreign capitalists. They were great admirers of the royal family, of King Fouad and King Farouk, and of the courtiers who gathered around them. They said they were proud of their origins, of their roots in Egyptian soil, but married foreign women who were preferably blondes if they went abroad as tourists or as students to pursue higher studies and obtain a degree from universities in Paris or in London.

The city of Cairo in the thirties was a city where the aristocracy indulged freely in its pleasures. The men married women who were either foreigners or belonged to rich feudal families. But at night they would sneak out to their Egyptian mistresses, to women who came from the lower classes. At home they spoke English or French, but in the nests of love and debauchery they spoke colloquial Arabic or street language. They wore red roses in their buttonholes and red fezzes on their heads, occupied the higher ranks of political parties, carried the title of Pasha or Bey, conversed over glasses of whisky and small plates of caviar about how bad the situation was, especially for the poor who lived in the villages or thronged to the big cities and towns. During the day they competed for seats in parliament and at night for dancers and prostitutes who distributed their favours to men in the night clubs, or in the houseboats floating near the banks of the Nile.

In the 'big family house' they kept the first wife, the ageing mother of their children who had remained as chaste and pure as the Virgin Mother. In the other house, the secret or shadow house, lived the second wife, young and plump who was there to restore their youth, through love and passion. Loyal and obedient to the precepts of their religion, to their God and His Prophet, they had two, three or four marital homes according to the number of wives. In addition there was the *garconnière*, a French word meaning the flat where a man behaves like a *garçon*, that is a young bachelor, and receives his mistresses.

From these different love nests the man would return at the end of the night to his first wife, smelling of alcohol and women's perfume. Once home he took off his fez, his coat and trousers, the red flower in his buttonhole, got into bed, turned his back on the mother of his children, and snored through the night until noon the following day.

Sherif grew up differently. From his mother he inherited determination. From his paternal grandmother, who was the daughter of a feudal family and the niece of Saad Zaghloul, the leader of the Egyptian revolution which broke out against the British colonialists in 1919, he inherited his straightforward character and inward pride. Despite his grandmother's feudal background she remained illiterate, a peasant woman linked to the land, handling and overseeing a huge household. She had not read God's book. Like my grandmother she used to say, 'God is justice and we know of him through reason.' She had a severe, uncompromising sense of justice which she imposed on her family, and at the same time she embraced them all, and in particular Sherif who remained her favourite grandchild, with a warm tenderness. She instilled in his depths her sense of justice, this consciousness of the need to defend what is right and he grew up with it; that is why in his memory and his memoirs entitled *Open Windows* she occupies a special place.

As a child Sherif was sensitive to the fate of the numerous servants in the household and of the numerous peasants who worked the land. He remained a sad and lonely child in a household that was huge and full of people, dreamt of becoming a prophet or a priest, and of working for the poor. His father was almost never there, too busy with himself and his fancies, so in his loneliness he grew up to love books and music, and later medicine, and his ideal was that of the village doctor, caring for those in need. His mother dreamt of his becoming a famous pianist or a skilled surgeon because, according to her, he had the fingers necessary to become either one or the other. Nowadays he laughs and says, 'Instead of that I became a prisoner.'

We used to take long walks along the Nile in Giza. He spoke to me about his days in medical school, how he came to dislike surgery – and surgeons because they were conceited and rough –, of the meetings of the National Committee of Students and Workers in which he participated, and the demonstration of February 9, 1946 in which the police raised Abbas Bridge as the students were crossing over it, and then charged from both ends – some students drowned in the Nile, while others were shot in the back or the chest, so that their blood spattered the black tarmac of the road and the iron barricades of the bridge.

He graduated with honours from medical college in 1946 believing in his vocation as a healer of the sick. In the wards of Kasr Al-Aini Hospital where he received his training as a resident doctor, he lived and worked with poor patients who had come from the villages, cities and towns to be treated free of charge in this university teaching hospital. There he was brought face to face with reality, with the smell of sweat, pus and blood, with the dark gaunt, half-starving faces, with the emaciated bodies bleeding from their lungs, or with blood in their urine, with all the ugliness and suffering of extreme poverty, sickness and death, but more important he found out that disease was not only a matter of germs invading these bodies but mainly the lack of food, of knowledge, of clothing or housing, of poverty in the midst of unending toil.

The naïve idealistic, young doctor became a revolutionary dreaming of abolishing class differences, of social and economic justice. But words like 'class' or 'justice' were forbidden, even sacrilegious. To pronounce them meant that you were a Communist, even worse an atheist who did not believe that it was God who in his wisdom had created the rich and the poor. Everything belonged to God, including money and riches, and it was He who decided how it should be distributed. If He had given it to the King, or the feudal landlords, or the British colonialists, and deprived tens of millions from it, whose business was that?

Sherif's tranquil voice reaches me with the night breeze. It is the spring of 1965. His eyes are misty as though covered with a film of dreamy sadness. His features remind me of my father, of my first husband. The features of freedom fighters, of saints, of believers in a sacred cause. Love is part dream, part reality. My heart beats with love despite death, despite war or suffering, or sacrifice. Perhaps it beats because of them. Things are never clear in love.

He had spent fourteen years in prison. When he tells people that, they gasp, 'Fourteen years!' and he smiles. 'It must have been difficult,' they say. 'Sometimes it was,' he replies. He went into prison in 1948 at the age of twenty-five and came out in 1963 at the age of forty. Ten of those years were under Nasser with three years in chains cutting stones from a quarry.

I walk by his side listening, silent, glimpse the faces of people under the lamplight. The men look listless, their faces seem to sag, and here he is after fourteen years in prison by my side, slim, taut, thoughtful, perhaps still a little sad but there's a light in his eyes, and a dream in his words, and I know he will go on in his own quiet determined way.

Now it is June 10, 1967. It is four o'clock in the morning just before dawn. The streets are thronged with people. They came down from their houses, poured into the lanes and streets in an unending flow. Their shouts resound in the night like rumbles of rising thunder: 'We want arms! We shall fight back until death! Long live freedom!' I am walking by his side in Giza Street. Sixteen years ago,

I walked by the side of Ahmed Helmi in a silent procession which stretched for miles and miles through the city of Cairo. In Sherif's eyes I can see the same mist, the same light. He walks with the same steady stride, and his voice is tranquil when he speaks.

Since the age of ten my voice has continued to ring out with thousands of other voices in one demonstration after another: in Menouf when I was in primary school, in Helwan with the girls in secondary school, in medical school when the students walked out into Kasr Al-Aini Street, in the Medical Syndicate amidst thousands of medical doctors, in the Ministry of Health when we marched down Majlis Al-Umma Street,[2] in the streets of Cairo, Alexandria, Ismaileya, Port Said, Giza, Beni Soueif.

I heard Sherif's voice ring out loud and clear: 'No surrender!' He was there amongst the millions of people filling the streets, the misty light still in his eyes, a dream still floating in his head after fourteen long years in prison, still lean and taut, his head held high, his step steady, his determination, obstinate and unbent, after twenty years of police harassment, after experiences of solitary confinement, of being hunted down after an escape from prison.

I used to see him sitting in a room full of men. They smoked and talked, never stopped smoking and talking, never stopped interrupting one another, never stopped talking all at the same time, never stopped pronouncing phrases about socialism, or justice or freedom. And there he would sit, saying nothing, with a dreamy look on his face that made me wonder sometimes what he was thinking, and more often made me rage.

Then sometimes he would come out of his reverie and start to talk and the room would suddenly go quiet, because no matter how hard they tried they could not forget that he had spent fourteen long years in prison for the things that they were talking about.

In July 1961 Gamal Abd Al-Nasser promulgated what were called the 'Socialist Decrees' and established a one-party system with the Socialist Union, the only political party allowed. Administrative directives obliged everyone in institutions, state organizations, industrial and commercial establishments, social services, and universities, villages and towns to become a member. Not a single man or woman working in any of these could refrain from joining for fear of the consequences.

---

[2] Parliament Street.

The Egyptian state apparatus is the earliest highly centralized administration in history, and people have submitted to it and obeyed it for thousands of years. This bureaucratic system has maintained itself until today. Names, faces, governments, rulers, forms of exploitation have changed, but this pharaonic oppression has remained and been reinforced by foreign invasion and occupation.

The word 'socialism' was first pronounced by Gamal Abd Al-Nasser on July 26, 1961. After that it became an integral part of his language. Once pronounced and repeated by the head of state it was picked up by ministers, civil servants, intellectuals, writers, newspapermen and columnists. The head of state would appear on television surrounded by high-level state officials, literary figures, journalists, thinkers and responsible people in the Socialist Union, in short what came to be known as the intellectual elite. Gamal Abd Al-Nasser had only to pronounce the word 'socialism' and everyone was talking socialism. He had only to say: 'We must dissolve class differences' for the elite to repeat the same phrase in everything its members read or wrote. They pronounced it in a voice which resembled that of Gamal Abd Al-Nasser, in a way which had the same inflections, the same emphasis on the 'd' in the word 'dissolve'. Their tongues curled up or protruded in exactly the same way as his.

I noticed that the word rarely appeared in Sherif's vocabulary. On the other hand, my friend Batta suddenly discovered that she had come from a poor family in the village of Sinbilawain. Her husband Dr Hamdi in turn discovered something he had never known before, namely that his father had been a textile worker in a factory based in Mahalla. He started to wear a blue linen uniform like that of Mao Tse-Tung, made of material from Mahalla. It was very smart and had a collar like that of a similar jacket worn by the Minister of Interior. He then presented himself for elections and won a seat as a workers' representative. Fifty percent of parliamentary seats were reserved for workers and peasants in the new electoral law, which also defined who was to be considered a worker and who could be considered a peasant.

Dr Mostafa, the husband of my friend Safeya, donned a *gallabeya*, put on a skullcap and decided to run for election in parliament as a representative of the peasants. He toured the villages, sometimes on a donkey, and made sure that a long rosary made of rough wooden beads moved piously between his fingers as he muttered verses from the Qu'ran. But he was not successful despite these efforts. To compensate for this failure he published a book in which he analysed the difference between a socialism that had its roots in Islamic religion and the socialism defended by Communists. He explained in detail how the former was very different to the latter kind of socialism, which had an atheistic, materialistic conception of the world. In this book he maintained that socialism in Islam had started with Abou Zar Al-Ghafari and Muhammad the Prophet. Muhammad, God's peace be on him, had been a socialist since he had fought against the rich tribal leaders of Quraish with the aim of dissolving class differences in the Arabian Peninsula. He hastened to add that 'dissolving the differences' did not mean 'abolishing' them since God had created people unequal. This, he said, was one of the essential differences between Islamic socialism and Communist socialism. Communism aimed at establishing a world without classes. This was in contradiction with Allah's words in the divine texts. In the Qu'ran there was a statement that left no room for ambiguity in this matter: 'And we have created thee of different degrees' (that is of different classes, one class above the other, so that there is an upper class and a lower class). God created us male and female from a single breath, but he placed the male above the female when he said 'and men are a degree above them' (i.e. women). Women who want to be equal to men do not follow the words of Allah and of the divine texts.

Dr Mostafa Al-Zohairi (that was his full name) came to be considered one of the foremost thinkers in Egypt. My friend Safeya, who was married to him, agreed with him on the issue of class, but objected when he said that men were superior to women. Samia disagreed with his views on both these issues. She would pout and say: 'People are like the teeth of a comb, all equal. Arabs and Persians, men or women, differ only in piousness and good deeds.'[3]

Batta no longer gurgled with laughter. She took a dignified stance, sat with one leg crossed over the other, her big fleshy knees showing from under the short, tight silk skirts that she had taken to wearing. She had now been given an important responsibility in the Socialist Union and was also a prominent member of the Syndicate of Journalists. I wondered how she could have been transformed

---

[3] Sayings of the Prophet Muhammad.

suddenly from a medical doctor into a journalist. But high-standing members of the Socialist Union had invaded the newly founded Ministry of Culture and Information and from there spread out to occupy high-level positions in radio and television broadcasting, in newspapers and publishing houses, in the Supreme Council for Culture and in a number of other institutions and so-called permanent committees.

Om Ibrahim's only comment was that nothing was permanent except God, since he alone was eternal.

After a while Batta became head of one of the permanent committees in television. She began to appear quite often in television programmes, wearing a wig of hair that rose in one abundant layer above the other like a pyramid, protruding her fleshy carmined lips into a pout which reminded me of my friend Samia, pronouncing words with a slow arrogance, and cocking her head with a new-found importance as she said: 'Workers and peasants are half the population and therefore they should occupy half the seats in parliament.'

We watched, sitting in the small hall of our flat in Giza, and Sherif would smile half-amusedly. Batta was carrying on a dialogue with Dr Rashad on the subject of democracy. He too had given up his medical profession and his teaching at the university to devote himself to a political career. He was a close advisor to the Minister of Health, headed a number of permanent committees, and appeared often on television. I sometimes met him in the Medical Syndicate or in the courtyard of the Ministry of Health on his way to one of his committees. He would stop short to exclaim, 'You, Nawal. Impossible. Your hair has turned completely white. But it makes you even more charming' (pronounced in English).

In 1962 I was elected by the Medical Syndicate to represent the medical profession in the National Congress of Popular Forces convened by Gamal Abd Al-Nasser to discuss the National Charter after the promulgation of the Socialist Decrees in July 1961. Dr Rashad sat in the front row. I was perched up somewhere at the top of the big auditorium where the congress was being held. Gamal Abd Al-Nasser sat on the platform and I could see his bronzed face and his dark shining eyes. Next to him sat the Minister of Interior.

One of the points under discussion was to define who was a worker and who was a peasant, since they were being given 50 percent representation in elections to parliament, and to all levels of the Socialist Union. At one point I raised my hand and said, 'A peasant is a man or a woman whose urine is red.' The faces of the men on the platform froze. But I had simply expressed what was common knowledge, namely that 99 percent of the peasants in rural areas suffered from bilharziasis and bled into their urinary passages. My grandmother used to say to me: 'There's not a single peasant who does not piss blood, daughter of my son, so don't go swimming in the stream again, you little devil'. Then later, when I worked as a rural doctor, all the peasants who came to the outpatients' clinic had blood in their urine.

That day the Minister of Interior noted down my name on a sheet of paper in front of him. After the meeting Dr Rashad stopped me at the main entrance of the university in Giza where the congress was being held and said: 'How could you say something like that, that a peasant is someone whose urine is red? You were being sarcastic about what was going on, making fun of socialism and of the President personally.'

From 1962, the year in which the congress was held, my name was put on a black list. It was kept in a secret file somewhere in the Ministry of Interior with a label on which was written 'Nawal El Sayed El Saadawi' and a code number. Then, after I married Sherif in December 1964, the disreputable word 'Communist' was added to my name, so that sometimes I was described as a 'Red'. By marrying Sherif I had added another crime related to the colour red to my phrase about the red colour in the urine of poor Egyptian peasants. To boot I was a woman, and to be a 'Red woman' is much worse than to be a 'Red man'. When I was a young woman of about twenty there was a man called the 'Red Pasha'. He belonged to the feudal aristocracy and had been appointed as Egypt's ambassador in Moscow. After spending a few years in the Soviet Union he expressed his admiration for some of the changes he had seen there and was labelled the Red Pasha, meaning the Communist Pasha.

A man can be a Red without necessarily being attacked on grounds related to his 'moral behaviour'. For a man it is used as a description of his political stance. But when a woman is described as a Red, then it follows that her personal life is licentious, that she runs around with men, freely indulging in 'Red nights' with them. In our language, a man of the street means an ordinary normal citizen, but a woman of the streets is a prostitute. To be a free man means to be a proud, courageous person who believes in freedom and defends it.

A free woman is, however, a woman who is licentious, immoral, and sleeps around.

After we married, Sherif left the family house in which he had lived with his mother and moved into my small flat in Giza. Throughout the thirty years of our life in this flat the political police kept us under careful supervision. This supervision varied in its nature and continuity with changes in the political atmosphere. The system would sometimes swing a little to the left, then go back to the extreme right or settle somewhere to the right of centre. There was no stability and the swings could take place almost overnight. One day the government would be cursing imperialism as though it were Satan and the next extolling its virtues and kneeling to it as though it were God. And with every change in position friends could become enemies, and enemies friends.

A system which functions this way carries defeat within it, even if at times some progress in made. Since I came into the world right at the beginning of the thirties, the periods of hope and change for the better have always been cut short before we have had time to take our breath, and I have continued to witness one defeat after the other. The Americans have replaced the British and Israel, the nuclear power, which has the blessings of the United States, rules over the region. Since Sadat inaugurated the open-door policy in 1974 the word 'socialism' has become a dirty word, which the intellectual elite and the politicians of the presidential court carefully refrain from pronouncing. Egypt has once more become a land ruled by a shrinking minority, after Nasser had followed a policy which consolidated and broadened the ranks of the middle class and reduced the differences between the very poor and the very rich. Now the gap is widening rapidly, the rich becoming richer and the poor poorer. The stock market is functioning once again, words like 'liberalism', 'democracy', 'free enterprise' are the stock language of the day, and a multi-party system has come into being by presidential decree. Sadat one day gathered the political leaders who represented the different tendencies within the Socialist Union in a meeting and ordered them to form parties. The government party formed at that time was by far the biggest, and therefore capable of exercising an almost undisputed hegemony over the political scene, of swallowing up the other much smaller parties in the same way as the staff carried by Moses turned into a snake and swallowed up all the smaller snakes.

I have never joined any political party. But one day I wrote an article in the newspaper *Al-Shaab*[4] which was published by the so-called Workers Socialist Party, a populist party in opposition which later swung to the right and allied itself with the Muslim Brothers. The title of my article was 'Who creates political parties in Egypt? The people or the ruler?'

On September 6, 1981 the police broke down the door of my apartment in Giza and took me off to the Women's Prison in Al-Kanatir. The accusation levelled against me was that I had conspired with a foreign country to overthrow the regime. The foreign country was Bulgaria! Why my accusers had chosen Bulgaria in particular, I do not know! I had never travelled to Bulgaria, I did not know a single Bulgarian woman or man, I knew nothing about Bulgaria and sometimes I even forgot where it was situated on the map.

Trumping up charges against people is something practised by all governments, and in all countries. But this charge was more of a joke than anything else.

Sherif said to me: 'Nawal, how could you do such a thing? How could you conspire with Bulgaria to overthrow the regime without telling me!' and his laughter rang out in the air.

---

[4] The people.

FOURTEEN

Searching for Love

In the summer of 1963 I started to write a novel entitled *Al-Bahitha an Al-Hob.*[1] In my heart there was a yearning for something obscure. I was thirty-two years old, a promising physician and a successful writer with many friends, both women and men, whom I received at home after clinic hours, or chatted with as we sat near the Nile, or up in a casino close to the Pyramids while we sipped our wine and ate stuffed pigeon, or as we vagabonded through the streets of Cairo after everybody else was fast asleep in bed. My mind was clear as crystal as I gazed at the stars in the night, and remembered how, as a small girl of seven, I used to point to them and ask my father. 'Who made all these stars?' Yet in that same mind there remained an obscure yearning for something undefinable.

* * * *

At the age of twenty I stopped asking all the questions I used to ask when I was a child. My mind was preoccupied with my studies in medical school, and with the need to succeed in the examinations at the end of the year. A few days before the exams I prayed regularly. I had not seen my mother pray except in times of crisis, but the radio had said that women were lacking in reason and in faith. After hearing that I began to imitate my father and to do my prayers

---

[1] Literally *The Woman Who was Searching for Love*, published by Zed Books in English under the title *Searching*, London (1991).

regularly not only just before the examinations. I reached the peak of piety at the age of twenty-one when I became a full-fledged citizen eligible for all human rights except those that God had bestowed on men but not on women.

The Egyptian constitution stipulated that all citizens were equal before the law, but the Shariah of God said men were 'a degree' above women. The contradiction between the constitution and the Shariah was glaring but I did not notice it when I was twenty-one. Absolute faith had made me blind, unable to see contradictions which were easy for all to see.

I used to walk at a fast pace from home to medical school, advance like an arrow looking neither left nor right, then walk back home from school at the end of the day. I went back and forth like a blindfolded cow turning a water wheel, until one day I ran into Ahmed Helmi. I was walking across the courtyard of the medical school when I heard him call out my name, 'Nawal!' When I heard his voice I stopped short in my tracks as though I had never heard anyone call out my name before, as though Nawal was not my name but that of another woman who had come to life at that very moment.

Perhaps it was his eyes not his voice, his eyes looking at me as he stood in the courtyard in front of me. I could see nothing but his eyes as though they had taken a hold on me. Or maybe it was something else, something I was unable to define as though I lost my courage the moment we met and could not really look at him.

He was standing near the small door leading out of the courtyard to the entrance of the old Kasr Al-Aini Hospital, wearing a white shirt and carrying a magazine in his hand. He stretched out his arm, gave the magazine to me and said, 'Nawal, this is the latest issue of our magazine, *The Spark of Liberation*.' He pronounced my name as though he was familiar with it, had pronounced it many times before. I took the magazine and busied myself with trying to shove it between the books, the lecture notes, and the dissecting instruments in a leather pouch crammed inside my bag. I wanted to avoid having to look him in the face. The magazine shone bright and new. Its title *The Spark of Liberation* printed in red ink flamed in the sunlight, and the contents of my bag looked old and colourless.

'I would like you to read the short story and tell me your opinion,' he said.

I was on my way to the Ali Ibrahim Auditorium, in a hurry lest I miss the beginning of the lecture. The professor was called Anrep. He was head of the Physiology Department and he gave his lectures in English, a language which he pronounced with a thick Russian accent. He had arrived in Egypt from Russia at the end of the forties to head the Department of Physiology. I remember him as a short squat man with a white square face looking like a white bear in his short white coat. He had a bushy beard that made me think of Chekhov and Dostoevsky and he expounded at length about Pavlov and his work on conditioned reflexes, which he said had led to a leap in our theory of knowledge.

My writer's imagination used to wander with Professor Anrep, with the dogs salivating when the bell rang even when no food was put in front of them. Pavlov's experiment had led to a new understanding of the reflex relationship between the material and the imagined, and its role in the training and education of dogs, and also of human beings. I had started to wonder about the relationship between the material and the spiritual, and these lectures helped me to realize that body and mind were inseparable, that imagination was a part of reality.

I used to feel that my whole being, body and mind, was absorbed in what Professor Anrep was saying to us. He was not in the habit of reading from a written paper like many of the other professors. He often told us stories about himself or others, and I was able to understand the science of physiology, and the new theories of knowledge, to follow the link between imagination and reality, between the material and the spiritual through his stories.

The questions I used to ask as a child started to come back to me. My faith, my blind belief in the existence of a body and a spirit separated from one another started to be shaken.

After the lecture I walked over to the students' room, opened my bag and took out the magazine. Batta's experienced eye spotted the sparkle in my eyes and she said, 'What is it Nawal, a new love story?' Love stories between the girls and boys in medical school were a never-ending topic of conversation. I was one of those adolescent girls who believed in a 'spiritual love' which had nothing to do with the body, just as I believed in a divine spirit high up in the heavens separated from our bodies down below.

Ahmed Helmi was engaged in literary activities with a group of students independent of the political parties. They published *The Spark of Liberation* and covered its expenses from their own pockets. He was the editor-in-chief and some of the medical students who had literary leanings wrote short stories that appeared in the magazine.

I read the short story he had published in the issue he gave me. It was entitled 'The Boy and the Dog'. Fifty years have gone by since then, but I still carry a vivid picture in my memory, that of a small crippled boy and a small crippled dog sitting side by side as they eat out of a dustbin.

Ahmed Helmi also used to organize seminars. In these seminars he was often able to show the connection between the different areas of knowledge, between areas we had been educated to deal with as separate, between poverty and ill-health, medicine and literature.

At that time the well-known short story writer and playwright Yusif Idris, a graduate of medical school, had not become involved in literary activities and wrote only political articles. He was editor-in-chief of a magazine called *Al-Gami'i*.[2]

During a seminar on literature and short story writing, Yusif Idris said to Ahmed Helmi, 'You know I read your short story "The Boy and the Dog". When I go to sleep at night I see the crippled dog and the crippled boy eating together out of the dustbin. I felt it was more effective than a hundred political articles dealing with poverty.'

'The Boy and the Dog' is the only short story Ahmed Helmi ever wrote. After that he went off to the Canal Zone as a freedom fighter. My father had taught me to have faith in God and in the country where I was born. My belief in them was very firm at the time. One day Ahmed Helmi and I were sitting in the tea-garden of the zoo near the big duck pond. It was a quiet place, especially on weekdays and we often went there and sat talking, while the ducks paddled around and the birds flew from tree to tree.

I was wearing a new blouse, felt the warm blood flushing in my cheeks, and every now and then glimpsed my face reflected in the water. My heart was beating strongly and my breath was coming fast, but I pretended to be engrossed in the ducks as they flapped their wings and spattered drops of water that shone like pearls in the sunlight. Suddenly he asked me.

'Nawal, do you believe in God?'

I was taken aback by his question. Instead of answering I said, 'You believe in God, Ahmed, don't you?'

He was silent for a moment before replying in a quiet voice, 'No, I don't,' he said.

---

[2] All of us.

It was the first shock in our love relationship. My heart stopped, and my breathing too. I was struck silent. I could no longer see the pond or the ducks. A cloud covered the sun and everything went dark. It seemed to me that God had heard him say no and had decided to destroy the earth, the sky, and the whole universe.

I opened my eyes and looked at him sitting in front of me. He looked like a dead body. I shifted my eyes away from him, heard him say: 'Sorry, Nawal, if I have given you a shock. It's something I have been thinking about for a long time. I find it difficult to accept the way the Holy Books describe the creation of the world, how God created it in six days and rested on the seventh. I have dissected the human body and I have read Darwin's book *The Origin of Species* and I think it refutes everything that was written in the Holy Books about how the universe and man were created.'

My throat felt dry. There was a pain in my chest and my heart beat slowly. I felt the blood coursing in a cold stream through my body.

'Have you read *The Origin of Species*?, Nawal?' he asked. 'It's a book you must read. You should also read something of Karl Marx. Darwin died in 1882, the year in which Egypt was occupied by the British. They buried him in a magnificent tomb in Westminster Abbey. Karl Marx died one year later but before he died he dedicated his book *Capital* to Darwin. But Darwin was a devout Christian and believed firmly in the civilizing role of the British empire, so he refused to accept Marx's dedication of this book to him. When the book was sent to him he sent it back. He was afraid the church and the government would react unfavourably if he accepted Marx's gesture. I'm not a Marxist, Nawal, but I think you should read at least some of what Marx wrote.'

After our conversation in the Zoological Gardens I walked home. My feet seemed to advance alone as though they had nothing to do with my body. My mind wandered chaotically, and I was nearly run over by a car as I crossed over the road to pass under a railway bridge. I felt I was traversing a dark tunnel, and was unable to see clearly, to distinguish between reality and dream. Everything seemed all mixed up in my mind, unreal: love, faith in God, the Holy Books, the creation of the world and of life. I looked up at the heavens seeking an answer to my questions from someone above.

When I reached home I kept looking at my father, but my voice remained stuck in my throat. I felt as though I was carrying a charge of dynamite, that if I so much as touched on the subject which preoccupied me everything would explode and I would let out what had been suppressed inside me since my childhood, that my belief in God had been nothing else than fear of my father, of God and of hellfire.

Ahmed left for the front. After he left the world seemed empty, without a God, or a Satan, or anything at all. The School of Medicine became devoid of any meaning for me. Students were like phantoms hurrying to the hospital, moving in a world of make-believe. Spirits and genies, everything in the Qur'an had become chimera, had no real existence. When I saw my father prostrate himself in prayer I felt sorry for him, for the illusions he was living. There was no Paradise after death, no use in kneeling to God, or in prayer, or in anything else. I kept ready to clap my hands over my mouth at any moment, lest the words burst out of me, had to make an effort to bottle up what was inside of me.

I felt I had to do something so I volunteered for training as a nurse. I had a friend called Wadeeda who was a nurse. Her fiancée was a freedom fighter and she was thinking of travelling to the Canal Zone to spend a few hours with him. I wanted to see Ahmed too, so after I had picked up a few things about first aid I packed a small bag and we got ready to leave. Ismaileya was less than two hours away from Cairo and we had arranged to take some medical supplies with us.

We sat near the driver, and a first-aid male nurse rode behind us with bottles of plasma, transfusion equipment, antiseptics, bandages, sterile gauze, cotton, plaster of Paris, splints and other things.

I was jerked out of my wandering thoughts when the driver said, 'Another kilometre and we'll be in Ismaileya.' My heart beat like a drum. In a short while I would be with Ahmed. Wadeeda whispered in my ear, 'I must introduce you to Captain Ragab. We intend to get married as soon as he gets back from the front. It's going to be a big surprise for him. He doesn't know I volunteered to become a nurse. I miss him very much, Nawal.'

As we got nearer we heard noises like explosions and the sound of the motor rose higher. He shouted so that we could hear: 'We have to get there before the sun comes out.' It was very dark and I couldn't see anything, except a thin red line on the horizon. I do not know why I remembered Copernicus at that moment, how he had maintained that the sun was the centre of the world, not the earth, and insisted that the earth circled round it.

I heard the sound of explosions again. The lorry kept swaying and leaping over lumps, and the bottles of plasma knocked against one another at the back. From behind me I heard the male nurse shout loudly: 'It must be an air raid or something'.

I was twenty years old at the time and we were nearing the end of 1951. I had no idea what war was like, had only heard of such things as bombs and machine-guns. The nearest I had come to a weapon was the fly spray which I used in our home to kill flies. And when Ahmed went off to fight I used to dream that I was holding a fly spray and pointing it at enemy soldiers, that with every spray they were coming down like flies.

When I was a child the sound of air-raid sirens used to fill me with joy. Everybody rushed out of the house to go to the air-raid shelter, the women in their nightgowns, the men without shoes or ties. Under the ground, in these shelters, everybody became equal and mixed freely with one another, rich and poor, men and women, grown ups and children. In the semi-darkness the children used to play *siga*,[3] draw small squares and look for stones or pebbles with which to play. When the all-clear signal went off I used to feel sad. We went back to our house to be once again closed in between four walls. Boys and girls were separated, the girls like me sent off to the kitchen, or to clean the bathroom, whereas the boys went out into the street to play. My grandmother in answer to my protests would say: 'God in his wisdom created families, boys and girls, and walls and you're not to argue, even if you don't like what He did.'

The lorry stopped when it came to the camp. I glimpsed dark tents hiding under the trees, jeeps, a few armoured cars on the side of the road covered with tree branches, carts drawn by horses or donkeys, with food utensils and leather water bags piled upon them, young men walking about in parachutists' uniforms, and desert Bedouins standing near their camels, who carried guns concealed under camel hair or rough woollen cloaks.

The young men started to unload the medical supplies we had brought with us in the lorry. I glimpsed the commandant of the camp standing near the open door of his tent. He was watching the young men as they erected tents, or dug trenches and the air was heavy with dust and sand.

---

[3] A popular game played with stones placed in small squares – something like drafts or chequers.

I asked one of the young men whether he knew where Ahmed Helmi was. But no-one there was known by his real name, for reasons of security.

At a distance I could see what looked like a huge dark mass lying on the sands. This was the military base of the British occupation forces situated on either side of the Suez Canal. In my mind the name Suez Canal remained linked to the Khedive Abbas, to De Lesseps, to the peasants who had dug the waterway to serve Allah and their country, just as the slaves had built the Pyramids to serve the Pharaohs and their gods.

We were unable to find Ahmed Helmi or Captain Ragab anywhere. At night as we lay in the darkness of the tent Wadeeda whispered in my ear: 'Nobody has been able to give me a clue. They all use false names. I can't sleep. I'm afraid that I'm going to go back without seeing him'.

I said: 'You know, Wadeeda, I can't stay here any longer. I told my parents that I was going to be on duty at the Kasr Al-Aini Hospital. I must be back tomorrow.'

It was the first time I had slept out and lied to my parents about it. So I arranged with the lorry driver to take me back next day. I had lost hope of seeing Ahmed and was very worried. The previous day I had seen the nurses bandaging the wounds of freedom fighters who had been injured, seen blood spattered over the sand, watched them as they made sure plasma was dripping regularly from a bottle hanging over the head of a young man to flow into his veins as he lay on the floor. I saw dark harassed eyes look up at me from haggard faces.

In those days, we were never able to know how many freedom fighters lost their lives in the struggle against the British occupation forces. Thirty years later in 1981 I was living in a cell, in Kanatir Prison. One morning Zouba the prostitute who used to bring my ration of bread to me every day had wrapped the three loaves in a page torn from a newspaper. The date on the page said October 27, 1981. This was her way of smuggling newspapers to us since we were not allowed to have them. I remember the date very well because it was my birthday. The page contained short commentaries and a few items of news. At the bottom was a small item which said that the number of freedom fighters killed in the guerrilla war of 1951 was two hundred. These were the youth who had paved the way for the 1952 revolution, but no-one remembered them any longer.

I used to follow the freedom fighters with envy as they marched up and down in their training camps, their heads held high, their eyes shining. They could die fighting for their land, killed by a bullet, or a bomb, but a woman like me was only good to be a nurse, to die in her bed, to die an ordinary death like millions of other people!

I returned to Ismaileya fourteen years later during the six-day war of 1967. Over the camps on the opposite bank of the Suez Canal a different flag was flying. It did not have red, blue, and black patterns and bands crossing over it. Now it carried the blue star of David on a white background.

That night in 1951 I remained wide awake until a red streak showed over the horizon. Wadeeda fell fast asleep, perhaps dreaming of the day when her betrothed would return from the front and they could get married. I was scared that I might not wake up in time to get back home in the morning, or that a bomb would fall on me. If I did, father and mother would discover that I had lied to them, and to me this was worse than death.

I left the tent to take a walk in the open spaces of the desert. The red streak showing on the horizon seemed to flow into my body with the fresh morning air. In my heart I felt a deep yearning for love. I walked towards a spring of water flowing up from a well. Maybe Ahmed had awakened and would come here to drink. Maybe he would sense that I was here in Ismaileya, and would come to meet me at the well. I could see two small dots in the huge universe moving towards one another, like stars in the firmament, like two eyes wide awake when everything else in the world was plunged in deep slumber.

But there was no-one there. I felt sad, disappointed as though he had made a promise and not kept it. I washed my face and arms, filled my hands with cold water. It had a taste of minerals, different from that of the Nile. Had it been poisoned by the Bedouins? I had heard stories about Bedouins who worked with the enemies and betrayed their countrymen. But the Bedouins I had seen here had come with their camels, erected their tents and were part of the camp, just like the peasants who had come from neighbouring villages to join the freedom fighters. Some of the peasants were women and I spoke to one of them. She was tall and strong wearing a long black *gallabeya* tied at the waist with a raw linen rope and carried a rifle on her shoulder.

Mingling with the peasants were brigands and thieves who were in the habit of raiding British camps at night to steal from them, or of striking deals with some of the soldiers and officers who sold arms and other things kept in store. They had been drawn into the struggle. In their eyes the British were an occupying force, and they helped the freedom fighters by stealing arms and providing them with detailed information about the military base and its camps.

When the lorry driver came to the tent to tell me that he was ready to leave, Wadeeda was still lying on her bed looking up at the roof of the tent. She kept turning her hand over and over again, examining her thin pale fingers which cast shadows on the canvas walls of the tent. Her eyes were wide open and staring, and for a moment I thought something had happened to her. I whispered 'Wadeeda' but she did not answer. I could see her small hand now lying quietly on her breast, see her five childlike fingers, and the engagement ring around one of them, giving out a pale golden glimmer in the dark.

More than a year later as I was walking down the long wide corridor of Kasr Al-Aini Hospital I saw Wadeeda moving slowly in the same direction. Her shoulders were lowered and she wore black. For a moment, I thought her fiancée must have been killed, but when I asked her about him she burst into tears and said, 'No, he came back.' Then she wiped her tears and was silent. We talked for a short while then parted. As I walked on I thought of Ahmed Helmi and said to myself, 'What is it that war does to people?'

Later when we met again she said to me, 'When a man's conscience dies it's worse than physical death. And a man who is unfaithful to his love can easily be disloyal to his country.' Then she went on to tell me that her fiancée was an officer in the secret police and had disguised himself as a freedom fighter to spy on them. Before the burning of Cairo on January 26, 1952[4] he left the Canal Zone secretly. She did not hear of him for over a year, but meanwhile the 'revolution' of July 1952 had taken place. She opened the newspaper one morning and saw his photograph. Under the photograph there was an item of news about his marriage to the daughter of one of the prominent figures in the revolution. The wedding celebration was scheduled to take place on the first night of the year 1954.

---

[4] On this day Cairo was set on fire by incendiary bombs. The King, the British and the secret police planned the burning of Cairo in order to proclaim martial law and suppress the national movement.

She put on black clothes and next day swallowed a bottle of black pills, then lay down on her bed in the nurses' home to die. But one of her colleagues rushed her off to the hospital and they gave her a stomach pump. A few weeks after I had spoken to her in the corridor of Kasr Al-Aini Hospital she tried to commit suicide again. This time she was saved by a young resident doctor. She fell in love with him and stopped trying to commit suicide.

Ten years later while I was taking a walk in the Zoological Gardens, I ran into Ahmed Helmi. The summer of 1963 had been hot and I was in the habit of going down to the gardens early in the morning. I just had to cross over the road from my building in Mourad Street and walk for a minute to find myself in front of the small side entrance reserved for employees. The veterinary doctor in charge of the zoo had given me permission to enter free several hours before opening time, after I told him that I was writing a new novel and that the best ideas came to me when I was walking over the winding paths that went through the zoo. An entrance ticket at that time cost only five piasters but thirty-seven years ago it seemed enormous, and my friend the vet used to read the short stories and articles I published in the newspapers and magazines.

'What is the title of your novel, Dr Nawal?' he asked me.

'The Woman Who was Searching for Love', I said.

His face seemed to light up for a moment as though a distant memory had flashed through his mind. He was standing next to me in front of a rocky space in which the monkeys were enclosed. Short and fat, about fifty years old, he resembled the chimpanzee which was squatting in front of us and examining him with a gleam in its eyes. I left them looking at one other, went off to the tea-garden and sat down at the table in the corner where I settled every morning to write. There I felt relaxed, far away from the world, with the ducks paddling through the pond, or spreading their wings under the warm sunshine, shaking the water off them in drops that shone in the golden light, like a shower of rain falling from the sun.

I was approaching the end of my novel, writing a final chapter in which the woman tells the man she was in love with that everything between them is over. He is taken aback, hardly able to believe that she is serious, asks her:

'How can our love end? It's not possible.' She says, 'Like a flower when it dies, or a butterfly crushed between the fingers of a child.' 'Is their another man in your life?' He asks, 'No, I have no other man in my life. But I am escaping from the prison of love to go out into the wide world where I have many men and women friends'.

The sun had started to drop down towards the West. I lifted my head. Standing nearby was a man who wore a white shirt and dark sunglasses. He smiled at me. It was Ahmed Helmi.

'How are you, Nawal?' he said.

'I'm fine, Ahmed. And you?'

The way he pronounced the name 'Nawal' no longer shook me. My heart no longer jumped when I saw him. Time had done away with pain and sadness, with joy and love. His white shirt was like any other white shirt. His sunglasses were like all the other sunglasses I saw when I walked on the streets. When I pronounced his name it sounded ordinary, like any other name.

He sat with me for a while then left. I bought him a glass of tea. He said, 'Do you remember how we sat here the first time almost twelve years ago?'

I remembered, but the memory no longer hurt. I sat there drinking tea with him just as I would have done with any other friend. We talked with ease. I felt that our relationship was now more natural, more human. It was no longer a relationship between a man and a woman, it had freed itself from the heritage of oppressive sexual relations. Our conversation, the tea we drank, had a different flavour now that he was no longer my husband.

FIFTEEN

An Aborted Revolution

Saturday 15 July 2000

I am seated at my desk trying to write. I want to finish the last part of my memoirs but I am not making any progress. Sherif reads the newspapers every morning then sits at his desk and begins to work on his novel. I do not know how he is able to move so easily from reading the newspapers to writing a novel. If I read the newspapers I have to wait one or two days before the tension disappears, before my anger subsides so that I can resume my writing. I have to the forget the wars that are going on, the children who are being killed, the declarations of peace made by the leaders who send tanks against them, and their faces looking out at me from the front page, their hands behind their backs, as though concealing a weapon.

This morning they were there on the front page, the president of the United States, the president of Israel, and the president of Egypt. The three of them were meeting at Camp David for the second time. The first time was twenty-one years ago. The faces were different, but the smiles were saying the same thing: 'We are here to make peace'. But what does peace mean for them? It means surrender to the tyranny of those who possess the arms, the money, and the media.

After the first Camp David negotiations the Egyptian president came out of the meeting with a broad smile and announced that he had achieved a great victory that heralded an era of peace. On October 6, 1981 as he watched the parade on Victory Day, more than a hundred bullets were fired into his body while balloons and coloured rockets continued to rise up in the air. The funeral procession was attended by the American and Israeli presidents and high dignitaries of state. But the people of Egypt did not walk behind the cannon which accompanied his body to its burial ground.

That day I was sitting in one of the cells in Al-Kanatir Women's Prison. The president had ordered my incarceration with hundreds of others who had opposed the Camp David treaty, described by him as the Treaty of Peace and Victory. But today people have discovered the reality hidden behind these words. What happens in negotiations, the secrets that are hidden in treaties, come to light only twenty or thirty years after they have been signed. The people of the countries concerned never know what goes on behind the scenes. The media publish trumped up news and distort facts. People are made to live in the illusion that a great victory has been achieved. They are made to die, or made to see their sons die for country or God with smiles on their faces and the vision of a Paradise awaiting them somewhere above.

After the negotiations of Camp David Two the picture of the Palestinian leader Yasser Arafat appeared on the front page. His face exhibited a broad smile as he stood there, his hands behind his back to hide the fact that they were empty, that he held nothing in them, neither arms, nor money, nor the media needed to defend his people's rights.

That day my mind went back to the 1967 war. I had volunteered with a group of doctors to go to the Canal Zone and help in providing the medical services that might be required for people living in the rear lines of the Egyptian army. The group I joined was composed of six doctors, and we divided the three cites of the Canal Zone between us: two went to Port Said, two to Ismaileya, and two to Suez. I went to Ismaileya with a colleague of mine, Dr Talaat Hammouda.

It was a windy, dusty morning when I got into the lorry next to the driver who was taking us to Ismaileya. Talaat Hammouda who was slight of figure got into the van of the lorry and sat on a wooden bench surrounded by boxes containing medical equipment, drugs, bottles of plasma, plaster, bandages and other things. The driver was a man aged about fifty, but to me he seemed older. He had big dark, rough hands which he held tight on the wheel, and deep-set eyes which he kept fixed on the road looking ahead anxiously for whatever might come. He wore a threadbare yellow suit, and a faded yellow cap from under which showed his thick unruly hair threaded with grey, and addressed me as 'Doctora'.[1] I called him 'Am[2] Muhammad' but we hardly spoke. He kept his silence, as though plunged in his thoughts and his short squat body swayed with the movement of the lorry as it advanced with a rattling noise and the heavy thud of its wheels on the tarmac road. I heard Talaat Hammouda's voice emerge from behind us as he asked, 'How far have we still got to go Am Muhammad?'

'Four kilometres, doctor.'

'I can hear something like the sound of explosions.'

'Yes, doctor.'

'Where are they coming from?'

'The Israelis are firing at Ismaileya from the other side of the Canal.'

I followed their conversation distractedly. I had had nothing to do with war, had never heard explosions, or seen people blown to pieces by bombs except in the cinema, but suddenly I heard a strange, long drawn-out, sharp, whistling noise which seemed to go through my ear. The driver turned off abruptly away from the water and started to drive through side streets at a rapid pace, and within a few minutes we reached the hospital. My mind ceased to function and Talaat Hammouda seemed to have disappeared somewhere amidst the boxes.

I heard the driver say, 'God saved us just in time. That was a **dana**[3] that passed behind us.'

It was the first time I had heard the word **dana**, but I had no time to reflect on it. Once more I heard a sharp long drawn-out piercing noise followed by an explosion, then the explosions seemed to multiply. The wall of the hospital crumbled and flames shot up. I closed my eyes as though by shutting everything out I would escape, felt myself carried away, by something like a vision of fire in which I could hear my mother's voice saying, 'Throw Nawal into the fire and she will come back unhurt.'

I opened my eyes to find myself standing at the entrance to the hospital. I looked dazedly around. The lorry was still standing near the pavement and the boxes were there inside the van. But the driver's seat was empty. All I could see was his right arm and his five

---

[1] The feminine for doctor in Arabic.
[2] Uncle.
[3] A big shell.

dark rough fingers holding on to the driving-wheel. I wondered where his body had gone. I could see faces around me and heard myself ask in a voice which was not mine, 'Where is Am Muhammad? Where is Talaat Hammouda?'

They extricated Talaat Hammounda from under the boxes where he lay flat on the floor of the van, then helped him to get out of the back door. He emerged pale-faced and trembling, whispered in a hoarse voice:

'What happened?'

'I don't know,' I replied.

A number of male nurses in white aprons were standing around. They shouted at us, 'Come with us quickly' and led us to a shelter beneath the hospital. There we found the director of the hospital, the doctors, the nurses, and a number of patients all gathered together. I heard someone say, 'Poor Am Muhammed. The shell blast hit him.' A moment later the shelter shook as though a volcano had erupted nearby. Dust and pieces of plaster fell on my head and for a moment I thought the whole ceiling was going to cave in and crush me under its weight.

Shells and rockets continued to fall in the area around us, and the people in the shelter cringed up near the walls, or lay flat on their faces with their heads buried in their arms. At moments it seemed to me as though I was the only person in the shelter still alive, and that it was my turn to die next. I saw the director stand up and heard him say: 'The bombs this time are falling very thick. It's as though they want to destroy the hospital.' One of the doctors responded in a shaky voice: 'It's because they're now very close, just opposite us on the other side of the Canal. I think they can even see us.'

The Israelis in fact had overrun the whole of Sinai and reached the Suez Canal in five days. The shelling, and rocket firing went on and it seemed as though we were cornered, that it would not stop until they had finished us off. I was covered in dust and pieces of brick as I lay on the floor. A short distance away there was a table with a television set on it which continued to broadcast, and every time there was a lull we watched it. I do not know exactly what was being broadcast but every now and then I could glimpse a woman who resembled Samia Gamal belly dancing, or a man singing soulful love songs. It was amazing, like a dream or a nightmare. Here we were in this shelter with the rockets and shells falling all around us, and enemy soldiers a few hundred metres across the water and Cairo was dancing and singing.

I felt like an actor in some kind of absurd play, that I could die at any moment for a country making merry while enemy troops were getting ready to strike right at its heart.

*   *   *   *

When hostilities ceased I went back to Cairo. Two weeks later my colleague Talaat Hammouda died of a heart attack while driving his car. Sherif came back home from Port Said, and that evening we sat up all night talking of our experiences. I said to him, 'Can you imagine, Sherif, there I was almost buried in rubble with bombs falling all around, watching the belly dancer doing her contortions to the beat of drums. I felt as though I were living in quite a different country from the one in which our rulers live.'

Months after that night I wrote a short story entitled 'Another Country?' But before that I went through another strange experience. One morning the bell rang and when I opened the door there was a man standing outside. He handed me a small slip of paper which said: 'You are requested to present yourself at the headquarters of the General Intelligence Agency in Saray Al-Kobba.'

Next day Sherif drove me there in our small Fiat car. When I went into the building a man wearing a beret and plain clothes led me through a long corridor into a room with bare walls covered in cement, and left me there. They made me wait in this room for four hours. Then an officer came in and questioned me for two hours. His first question was really strange: 'What made you volunteer to go to Ismaileya while the war was on?' My answer was: 'There would have been no sense in volunteering to go after it was over. Or what do you think'? But I realized that nothing much had changed since the days when Ahmed Helmi and the freedom fighters had been hunted down by the police.

Talaat Hammouda left behind a young wife and two small girls. The Ministry of Health organized a mourning ceremony for him which reminded me of the ceremony organized to mourn Ahmed Al-Menessi many years ago when I was still a student in the School of Medicine.

Nevertheless in the summer of 1968 the Syndicate of Medical Doctors decided to send a volunteer medical team to the Palestinian camps in Jordan. After all the experiences I had lived through I do not know what made me volunteer once again. Maybe I needed to

distance myself from many things in my daily life, from the city of
Cairo with its newspapers and its television screens, from the faces
which appeared on them every day. I was tired of lies, of words which
concealed the truth. So I signed up with the group of doctors and
travelled with them to Jordan, maybe hoping that amongst the
Palestinians fighting for a homeland from which they had been
driven away I would find a genuineness of spirit to which my heart
could respond, and beat again.

When I arrived I was put up in a tent. The area where we were
camped was called Al-Aghwar, near the town of Al-Salt. I used to
move around in an ambulance car accompanied by a woman who was
called Om Al-Fida'iyeen.[4] She was tall, burnt by the sun and covered
her head with the scarf worn by the Palestinians with its black and
white, green and red colours. The ambulance car was an armoured
jeep driven by a young woman freedom fighter, who kept her eyes
fixed on the sand tracks leading to the Jordan River. Next to her she
always had an automatic rifle. I could see the big strong fingers of her
hand tight around the thick metal steering-wheel. I used to steal
glances at my long slender fingers. They looked so fragile compared
with hers, so I held my hands locked together on my lap and when I
looked up I noticed that she always drove with her right hand. Then
I realized that she had no left hand, that her arm had been amputated
below the elbow because now and again she would use the stump to
steady the steering-wheel. She hardly ever spoke, just drove in
silence, her face set in an unchanging expression as though carved in
some bronze-coloured precious stone, her eyes fixed on the track
ahead of her, whereas I could not take my eyes off her.

Om Al-Fida'iyeen sat behind us on the back seat, her eyes misty
and shining in the night. She resembled Om Ibrahim, resembled my
grandmother in the village with her prominent forehead jutting out
above deep-set eyes. The freedom fighters called her 'our mother' and
she called them 'my children'. She had no home, no father, no
mother, no man. All the homes here were her home. All the men here
were her men, her brothers, and all the women were her sisters. In
her memory there was a love story lived thirty years ago, and a child
never born, or lost somewhere in the caves of Al-Aghwar.

The night is dark with no moon, no stars. The jeep moves
through the darkness as though feeling its way. Israeli soldiers look

---

[4] Mother of the *fida'iyeen*, those ready to sacrifice their lives as freedom fighters.

out into the night from the turrets they have built, but the darkness is a protection. In a few moments we will reach the ruins of the town of Karameh. Two months ago on March 21, 1968 savage fighting broke out in this area. Most of the inhabitants in the town were killed. Only a few were able to escape.

The jeep came to a stop in front of a charred wall. There were holes scattered all over it where it had been pierced by shells or bullets. In the middle was the coloured drawing of a child with a smile on his face and a bullet hole in the place of his right eye. Under the drawing was a sentence grafted into the stone in crooked letters: 'We will fight until death.'

The houses were all in ruins, the streets and lanes deserted. My foot hit into something on the ground. The young woman who had driven us bent over with her taut, graceful body and picked it up. It was the shoe of a child. She held it close to her chest and walked on, her eyes trying to pierce the darkness as she searched for the old house in which she had been born. She was ten years old when the Israeli soldiers surrounded their home. They shot her father in front of her eyes, violated her mother, then cut off one of her breasts and took away her brother to a prison called Al-Ansar where he was tortured for weeks because he refused to divulge the names of his comrades. One day he was found dead inside a solitary confinement cell.

We returned to the jeep. She was still carrying the shoe. She put it on the seat next to her automatic rifle, then we got in and drove off winding our way between the hills of rock until we reached the river. Lying in the tall grass was a badly wounded guerrilla fighter. Om Al-Fida'iyeen and the young woman driver carried him to the jeep on a stretcher. He kept saying, 'Mother, go slowly, slowly, it hurts. Give me an injection for the pain.'

We took him back to the camp. Three months later I saw him moving around in a wheelchair. He had lost both legs and one arm, was just a trunk. He had deep blue eyes which burnt like a flame, and beautiful white teeth which flashed in his face whenever he smiled.

When I used to attend primary school in Menouf I had a schoolmate called Hameeda who had lost both legs under the wheel of a loaded horse-drawn cart on the day when people were celebrating the Eid.[5] I remember how I could not bear to look at her truncated body, how I used to tremble all over if I looked at her.

---

[5] The religious festival after Ramadan, the month of fasting for Muslims.

In the camp I slept on blankets laid on the ground with a smooth stone under my head as a pillow. By my side slept Om Al-Fida'iyeen, her eyes half open. Her breathing, deep and regular, was the only thing that broke the silence except the occasional clink of a rifle, or the whisper of guards being changed. But as the days went by I began to hear a voice whisper in the night, and slowly the whispering grew louder until it became almost like a shout repeating the same word: 'My son.'

I had left my two-and-a-half year old son in Cairo together with my ten-year-old daughter Mona, in the care of my husband Sherif. I had been away from them for more than three-and-a-half months. I was yearning to see them, longing to go back and yet at the same time wanting to stay on. I had started to think of a new novel. The title was already floating in my mind, 'Ain Al-Hayat'.[6] The heroine was a strong tall woman like Om Al-Fida'iyeen. My shared experiences with this unusual woman brought me very close to her, and we talked together about many things, so I was eager to get back to Cairo and start writing again.

When I did get home I followed news of her as closely as I could. She continued to occupy my mind, and sometimes I saw her in my dreams. Then I heard that she was killed during the days of fighting known as Black September. That was in 1970, one month before Gamal Abd Al-Nasser died.

I brought her back to life in my novel *Ain Al-Hayat*. Thousands of people in the Arab world read about her in my novel, and in other countries after the English translation was published.

I can still see her walking along the bank of the river searching for something. It was not an ordinary search. She was not a woman who knows what she is looking for, knows that she might find it, or might not. There was something strange about the way she searched, like a woman looking for a child to which she never gave birth, or like a woman looking for a child to which she gave birth yet is never able to find when and where it got lost.

* * * *

It was my last night in the camp of Al-Salt. I went out of my tent to take a walk. I was wearing the uniform of the *fida'iyeen* with my

---

[6] Later translated into English under the title 'The Well of Life'.

doctor's coat on top. The night was silent except for the rustle of trees, or the sound of wind in the caves of rock. A soft summer breeze flew across from the river. I could hear the thud of my boots on the rocky ground, red in colour like blood with a covering of green grass.

He was lying in the wheelchair outside his tent. When I saw him I stopped. I said, 'Good evening, Ghassan,' for that was his name. He beckoned to me so I went up to him and sat on a stool by his side. I remember what he said, word by word. I never forgot.

'Every night I watch you walking alone wearing your white coat, picking your way through the tents. I see you with an eye in me which is not like the eyes in my head. Do you have the time to listen to me? I want to tell you about that eye, reveal it to you? I want to tell you why I have the courage to confront death once more, just as I confronted it on that day when I lost my arm and legs. Across the river I have enemies who think that I am finished, that I am dead. I am not dead. I am just a man who has been injured, but the injury has not affected my sight. I can see you at this very moment, in this very place in the light of the moon which has not come out. I can see beyond death. Why are you silent? Are you suffering from a wound like me? Don't be afraid of me. Don't be afraid if you lose your arms and your legs as long as you are able to listen to me. You have defeated the enemy within you and that is more important than being victorious over the enemy that lies on the other side of the river. Only people like us can come closer to one another, and allow their bodies to touch. Give me your hand, let it rest on my chest. Do not go away. Do not be afraid of me if I am different. If I have lost my limbs, I have not lost my heart. I am not one of those men who violate women in the dark. I no longer have a body, the body of a man or a woman. I have desires but my desire is other than that of the flesh. Do you know that other desire?'

He was lying there on his back, a truncated body with only one arm, a bandage over one of his eyes. He was not a figment of my imagination. He was a real human being, a freedom fighter living his last moments. He opened his mouth to speak, closed it again, as though trying to reveal something before he passed away. I brought my ear close to his mouth and said, 'Ghassan, go ahead I am listening.'

'Dr Nawal, have you known what I call that other desire? All those bodies lying in the tents were young poor boys like me. They owned nothing except their bodies. In fact they did not even possess their bodies. Their bodies were owned by the leaders, and the leaders stink. They have a smell which you can recognize from a distance. Do you know that smell? It resembles the stifling smell of heavy air rising from a cesspool. At one time I did not know that leaders had a smell, that they emitted a noise like that of steel hitting against steel, a noise that is like the sound you can hear now carried by the wind. Listen, can you hear it?'

I strained my ears, turned my head in different directions but could hear nothing other than the thousands of minute sounds which make up the silence of dark space.

'I can hear nothing, Ghassan,' I said.

'You lost your sense of hearing a long time ago, Dr Nawal, from the moment you were born on this land and decided to protect yourself from insulting words like 'mara'.[7] The first insulting word you heard in your life was *mara*, wasn't it? When they want to insult a man they say, "You son of a *mara*". My enemies cut my body to pieces but for me it was less painful than this insult. One day our leader called me "Son of a *mara*", because I forgot that he took very little sugar in his coffee, that he drank it with just a smell of sugar as you say in Egypt. He used to get into a bad mood if he did not drink a cup of coffee with just a smell of sugar first thing in the morning. He would behave like a mad dog, snap at everyone around him, mouth insults beginning with "Son of a *mara*", following it up with the whole range of insults he possessed. I learnt to dull my sense of hearing. I lost my right arm during an attack on an army camp inside territory occupied by Israel, inside what was once our motherland. The operation I carried out succeeded, but as I was crawling back on my belly the smell of the earth filled my nostrils. It reminded me of the smell of my mother and I stopped to breathe it in. The bullets were flying around me like white pigeons in the dark of night, but I gave myself up to the wonderful feeling of being a child once more, buried my nose in my mother's breast and filled my lungs with her sweet smell. Do you remember the smell of your mother, Dr Nawal?'

I was taken aback by his question. My mother had died more than nine years ago, and I had forgotten what she smelt like. But when he

---

[7] *Mara* in colloquial Arabic means woman and is used in a derogatory and humiliating sense, unlike the classical *mara'a*.

asked me the question, I began to remember. It was as though the breeze had stirred in the night and was carrying the smell of her body to me. I tried to hold on to it, but it escaped me like a small fish slipping through my fingers into the sea.

I moved to a flat stone closer to where he was lying. My body was aching but I could not tear myself away from him as he lay there, staring at me with one eye that gleamed like a star in the dark night.

'I ran away from this camp, on a plank of wood with four wheels, pushing it over the ground on one side then the other with my remaining arm. I did not know what to do with this stunted body of mine. It was no more than a length of meat on a plank of wood. Yet beneath my ribs, my heart continued to beat with a yearning for love. I could see the eyes of the children as they stood at a distance, staring at me with fear, touching their arms and legs as though afraid to lose them, as though in me they could see their future. The older people too kept their distance, shot quick glances at my body, and sometimes threw a coin at me which fell on my belly, or on the ground near me. They seemed to feel that if they came closer they would become bodies without arms, or legs or eyes, so they threw the coins and walked quickly away.

'The leadership decided one day to open a file on me. I was now considered a handicapped veteran, or a beggar – I don't know which, since I had to pick up what others threw away to feed myself. If an important personality came to visit our leader, they would round up people like me and put them together in one place, sweep everything clean, hoist flags and banners everywhere. Instead of being the pride of our nation, a guerrilla fighter who had sacrificed everything for the cause, sacrificed his very flesh, his limbs and eyes, I became a source of shame, a spot on our reputation that had to be concealed, hidden away.'

'But what brought you back to this guerrilla camp?' I asked him.

'The leadership sent someone to ask me whether I wouldn't prefer to join in some of the guerrilla operations than to live the way I was living. So I agreed, because if I did not kill an enemy with the weapons they would give me, I would have turned whatever weapon I could lay my hands on against myself. But you, Dr Nawal what brought you here to our camp? Are you looking for a hero, for a man on whose shoulder you can rest your head? Our leaders, despite everything, have a certain attraction for women, and the higher up they move in the ranks the greater the attraction they are able to exercise on women looking for some excitement in their lives, and the more they can pick and choose.'

'No Ghassan, I'm not looking for a shoulder on which to rest my head. But after the defeat we suffered in the 1967 war the atmosphere in Cairo became suffocating, and I could not stand it any more. It became a sad, dreary city. Everybody seemed to be carrying a heavy load, even Abd Al-Nasser. His face went old, the look in his eyes was no longer defiant, it was defeated, like a badly wounded lion that feels its death is approaching.'

'I heard from my comrades that you are a writer. Have you come here looking for a story? When I was young I used to write poetry. Across the narrow street from our house there was a girl. She was only thirteen and used to stand at her window and listen to me reading my poems. I remember she had black eyes in which I could see sunlight. Your eyes resemble hers, Dr Nawal, and your voice resembles that of my mother. Sometimes at night I dream that I have gone back home to our land, that my mother is holding me in her arms. I dream of a woman whose breast feels like that of my mother when I lay my head on it, whose body is voluptuous, feminine. But it's difficult for a woman to combine the two. You are a doctor and a writer and it's not easy for a man to come close to you unless he is badly wounded, or is going to be the subject of your novel. I dream of dying now, of going to the Garden of Eden. Do you dream of going to Paradise, Dr Nawal, or is there no place in Paradise for women? How I wish I could have had a child from a woman like you.'

He clenched his teeth as though suffering from a deep pain. He kept moving his body on the wooden plank. I realized he wanted to urinate and was ashamed to do it in front of me. I lifted his shirt. Above the dark pubic hair I could see the swelling of his bladder. His body no longer repelled me. It no longer seemed ugly or deformed. I held him up in my arms like a child and embraced him.

He died that night just before dawn. They dug a pit and dropped his body in it, then covered it over with red earth.

When I got back Sherif was waiting for me in the airport. He looked at my pale, haggard face and asked, 'What happened in Jordan, Nawal?' 'Ghassan is dead,' I said. 'Who is Ghassan?' he asked. 'An unknown poet and guerrilla fighter. Maybe he will give birth to a wonderful child in the Garden of Eden, a child that will never stop throwing stones at the Devil.' 'That sounds like a new novel,' he said.

It was the end of 1968. Ten years later the Intifada broke out.

Thousands of children thronged the streets and lanes of Gaza, and of what remained of occupied Palestine, built barricades, burnt tyres and threw stones at the Israeli occupation forces. The whole world watched and it looked as though the balance of forces would be tipped in favour of Palestinian rights. But American, Israeli and Arab circles dismayed by this mounting popular uprising decided to recognize the Palestinian leadership for the first time and engage in 'peace negotiations' to halt the uprising. Negotiations would then be used to impose the solution favoured by the ruling circles in the USA, Israel and Europe.

Since then we have witnessed negotiations at Camp David, Madrid, Oslo, Sharm Al-Sheikh, Camp David again and many other places kept secret.

But the Palestinians are still struggling to retrieve the remaining 22 percent of their land, much of it arid, all of it surrounded by Israeli armed colonies and military bases. Palestinian children, like the child that was once Ghassan, are still throwing stones, and are still being shot in the head, or the belly, or the heart by Israeli bullets.

SIXTEEN

The Dream of Flying

From the window of the plane, I peer at Duke Forest as it moves slowly backwards. The winds from the Atlantic Ocean, a hurricane and the cold of winter have laid bare the trees, derobed the elms of their green. They stand in rows, their heads shaven, like soldiers in a military parade. The conifers rise between them in triangular shapes, their leaves shining under the small circles of sunlight that shimmer over them as though celebrating Christmas.

It is the last day of the last month in 1996 and I am on my way home after years of exile. The pine trees sway their slender trunks in farewell like ballet dancers on a huge open-air stage. I wave my hand at them from behind the small oval-shaped window, at the six students, four girls and two boys, who have come with me to the airport to say goodbye from my class. Their eyes were shining with tears and smiles as we embraced. Chris, the youngest student in my class, the one who had always been the most responsive to what I said on 'Dissidence and Creativity', the slender, twenty-year-old boy with the deep blue of the ocean in his eyes, Chris had composed a song for me and played it on his guitar.

Take me with you to the African shore, Daughter of the Nile
Let me ride with your magic eyes
At night I am imprisoned in my internet
By day I gallop through the forest trees like a horse
My ears blocked with ear phones

232

My head held straight by wires
My eyes looking ahead but not seeing
You teach me dissidence and creativity
So I want to fly with you
To where I can find
The self that I have lost
On the wayside.

Sitting next to Chris was Caroline. Sometimes we used to walk in Duke Forest together. She preferred painting to writing. Like me, when she was a child, she was always dreaming of flying, but her sister never had these dreams. She asked me why it was that some people never dreamt of flying. She was born in New York, in the district of Harlem, had blue eyes and a dark brown skin. Her mother was a white American and her father was black. He was sent to Vietnam during the war and never came back. She had to work and study at the same time, but she did very well in college and was given a scholarship for a doctorate degree in the arts, and that is how she came to Duke to continue her studies. 'I work in a restaurant in Durham,' she said, 'and send money to my mother because her pay in the plastics factory where she works is not enough to cover the expenses of my three young sisters.'

At the airport, when we embraced, she whispered in my ear: 'I'm going to save up money to pay for a ticket to Cairo, Nawal'. She had got into the habit of calling me by my first name and we used to behave like friends despite the age difference between us. When still a small girl, she used to go to church regularly with her mother and was in great awe of the priest who to her was like God or Jesus Christ. One day she stole a box of coloured pencils from her schoolmate. She loved drawing but there was not enough money for her to buy the pencils. It made her feel very guilty, so she decided to confess to the priest. After she told him the story, he patted her on the shoulder and said, 'God will forgive you, Caroline.' His hand slid down to her breast then her belly as he whispered, 'Don't be afraid. God loves you, Caroline.' She told her mother, and her mother kept it a secret, but after that she stopped going to church and ceased to believe in God and the Bible.

On the first day in class I used to ask the students, 'Why did you choose this course?' Chris said, 'I was always rebelling against the rules I had to follow in my parental home, and at school. At the same time at an early age I was enamoured of music, so I came to this course to find out whether there is a relationship between dissidence and music, and if it exists, what that relationship is.' Another student called Maya whose family had immigrated from India told me that she had read my novel *Woman at Point Zero* and it had changed her life. Then to her astonishment she found my name inscribed with the list of courses. 'So I came,' she said. She never missed a class, sat always on the right-hand side of the large U-shaped table near to me, her large black eyes shining, her silky hair flowing down her back. Before the year was over, she had started to write a novel.

Sherif had taken a plane to Cairo sometime before me. We had decided to return now that the situation in Egypt had calmed down and there seemed to be no immediate danger. So he left to see what prospects there were, and I stayed for another three months until the end of the academic year.

So here I was sitting in the plane looking down at the blue of the ocean as we headed North to New York. The first time I travelled by plane was thirty-seven years ago on a trip from Cairo to Algeria. But the dream of flying never left me. Asleep, I continued to see myself up in the air, my arms going round and round like propellers. I could feel my body moving away from the earth as though carried on a horse with wings, piercing the clouds higher and higher, shooting off towards other worlds, towards lands unknown to me. I would look around me in fear, could see the earth below me, a distant mass stretched out in the dark, glimpse a small lamp in a window and a little girl awake in the night, looking up at an airplane shining like a star in black space.

When I told this dream to my grandmother she would gasp: 'That's not a dream for small girls'.

'What do small girls dream of grandmother?' I would ask.

'They dream of a bridegroom and a beautiful wedding dress.'

I never dreamt of wedding dresses. Every *Eid*[1] my father bought me a new dress, but he bought my brother an aeroplane which was wound up and made to fly. My brother used to turn the screw violently and then throw the airplane up in the air to make it fly, but instead it used to drop down and land on the ground where it lay forlornly on one side. I used to sit next to it with a heavy heart. But

[1] The festival celebrated after the Muslim fasting month of Ramadan. There is also the Big **Eid** or Festival of the Sacrifice two months later.

then I would pick up the fallen parts, fit them together and replace the screw in its hole under the belly of the airplane, wind it carefully just two or three times and suddenly it would take off and do a turn or more in the room with me following behind, clapping my hands with joy. Sometimes my grandmother or one of my aunts would hear the noise, charge into the room with an angry face, wrest the aerpolane out of my hands, throw it on the ground and scream, 'Come with me to the kitchen. There's no time for these games.'

Since I first travelled by plane in 1963 I have never ceased flying across the globe, East and West, North and South. During the thirty-seven years of travelling I visited many countries and wrote about my experiences in them in a book entitled *My Travels Around the World.* . This book was published fifteen years ago but there is a second volume which I have not yet completed.

Out of the corner of my eye I glimpsed a cart with bottles on it and awoke from my reverie. I had changed planes at Kennedy Airport, and now it was dark. The flight attendant bent over me to make sure I was awake, then asked:

'What would you like to drink, madam?'

'Gin and tonic, please,' I said and I saw Batta's face floating in front of me, plump and dark, with that mischievous gleam in her eyes. She was the first person who had offered me a gin and tonic. It was just after my father's death in 1959 and since then it had become my favourite drink, because it gives me a feeling of exhilaration. My body comes alive but at the same time I feel relaxed, my mind is no longer occupied with small, irksome worries, as though a layer in the cortex of my brain has ceased to function, at least for a while, and the fears that hovered somewhere in it have disappeared. They are fears I have carried with me since I was a child. I am unable to rid myself of them except rarely. One of them is the fear of flying, for although I love travelling, love the feeling of being suspended in the air far from the earth, of being free from the obligations of everyday life, yet deep down inside me is this fear that the plane might drop down from the sky and fall to the ground, that this might be the last time I will ride in a plane.

As I held out my hand to pick up the glass from the small table on which the flight attendant had put it the plane was lifted up suddenly, then dropped down and started to quiver. I heard a voice say over the microphone, 'Please fasten your seat belts. We are passing through a slightly stormy area.' It was a sentence that I had heard tens of times, hundreds of times. Each time nothing happened, each time the plane continued on its way, and yet each time I hear it I am seized with the feeling that this time the plane is certain to fall down and crash on the earth.

I drank my glass of gin tonic, followed it up with a second, and then went on to empty a small bottle of Bordeaux wine. I felt warmth flow through me, felt a slight mist around my mind as though everything was separated from me by a distance yet pulsing in me with life. The fear of death was no more. The flight attendant came back with her cart and gave me a smile, like a ray of sunlight. I felt she was the most beautiful woman I had ever seen. I heard her ask in a gentle voice, 'What would you like to drink before dinner, my beautiful lady?' The word beautiful echoed in my ears like music. No one in my father's or my mother's family had ever described me as beautiful. Sometimes they said I was intelligent. The word beautiful was often used when speaking about one of my sisters. They had white skins, soft rounded fleshy curves, and tender brown or honey-coloured eyes. They were the accepted models of female beauty. But I had inherited my father's brown skin, his tall stature, his bold black eyes that looked straight at people without blinking, 'Eyes that called for a bullet to go through them,' to use the expression used by my grandmother.

Sitting on the seat next to me was a man sipping his wine slowly as he read *The Guardian*. I only noticed him after I had drunk the two gin and tonics and the bottle of wine. His features in a way seemed familiar. The nose slightly raised, the thick eyebrows, the broad obstinate forehead which resembled that of Sherif. His complexion was a ruddy brown and he had snow-white hair, like the hair I was accustomed to combing every day in the mirror. Despite deep lines around the nose and mouth his face showed no wrinkles and his skin was taut. There was a natural handsomeness about him that was not overtly masculine, a handsomeness which seemed to embrace childhood, youth and maturity all in one, and was made more visible by his upright tall body, the snow-white hair and the calm repose in his features. But what attracted my attention to him most were his eyes. There was a quiet gleam in them, something between the glitter of madness and the light of wisdom and thought. Or perhaps what I saw was less the reality of his features than my imagination unleashed by this flight between heaven and earth, the gin and tonics, and the bottle of Bordeaux.

I noticed him glancing at me out of the corner of his eye. I pretended not to notice. Maybe his attention had been attracted to me by the thick snow-white hair and the brown complexion which we shared, or by the gleam in my eyes when I asked for another bottle of wine and pistachio nuts.

The flight attendant gave me an encouraging smile as though pleased to see that I was enjoying myself, put the bottle of wine on my table and three packets of mixed nuts. I opened one of them and began to bite into them with a loud crunching noise like a child. I was very hungry, savouring the smell of the food as they brought out the trays and laid them on the cart. I heard him ask me in clear quiet tones which cut through the hum of the plane, 'Where are you going?'

'To Cairo. And you?'

'To London,' he said.

'Are you a cinema star? Your features seem very familiar to me as though I've seen you on the screen. Maybe a film by Fellini, or Kubrick.'

I laughed. It was a laugh that I had not heard for many long years, for thirty-nine years to be exact. In the summer of 1959 Salah Abou Seif, a well-known Egyptian cinema director, visited me at home after reading my novel *Memoirs of a Woman Doctor*. He wanted to make a film out of the novel and as we talked, he asked me whether I would agree to playing the role of the heroine.

I laughed when he asked me that. It was the same laugh I had heard emerge from me a moment ago, the same joy, the same thrill. I said, 'That's impossible. I can't do it.' 'Why,' he said, 'you have a face that is photogenic and you have artistic talent? So why not?' 'I have a talent for writing but not for acting,' I said. 'Artistic talent is artistic talent irrespective of the mode of expression. It can flow into many areas at the same time, into music, writing, acting, painting. Think it over and I'll call you back in a week's time.'

Exactly one week later Salah Abou Seif's voice came to me over the telephone.

'Have you decided anything about my proposal?'

'I think the censors will reject the film.'

'Perhaps, but we can make some changes when we write the script. This is something we do very often with novels.'

'But if you make changes it will no longer be my novel.'

'Maybe I can get the censors' approval for the novel. But you haven't told me what you think about taking the role of the heroine.'

During the week which had gone by after his visit I had asked my friends what they thought of the idea. Batta gurgled with laughter as she said, 'Why not? But take me in the film with you. I've always dreamt of being a film star.' Samia pouted at me and remarked, 'Acting in a film. What nonsense are you up to, Nawal? In our country that's not something respectable to do.' Safeya shied clear of giving an opinion as she often did: 'I'm sure the censors will refuse to approve your novel, so there won't be any problem to worry about.'

In that year the country kept swaying between left- and right-wing tendencies. Gamal Abd Al-Nasser's administrative machinery suppressed everything and everybody who did not exhibit total obedience to his system. Censorship was imposed on books, films and newspapers, on almost everything.

The censors rejected my novel. Salah Abou Seif made another attempt two years later, a third in 1966 and a fourth in 1972, but all were in vain. His voice came to me over the telephone full of disappointment. 'The problem is not the novel. It's with the name of Nawal El Saadawi.'

'What's wrong with the name?' I asked.

'They say you're a Communist.'

The flight attendant arrived by my side with the food cart and I forgot my travails. 'What would you like: chicken, fish, or beef?' I hesitated for a moment before saying, 'What do you think?' 'They're all very tasty,' she said. 'Then I'll have all of them,' I said.

The man next to me laughed. 'Have the beef. It's the best.'

'Why?' I asked.

'Because there's madness in it,' he said.

The flight attendant squirmed with laughter, then putting on a straight face she put a small steaming earthernware pot in front of him. I smelt roast meat, glimpsed the green of peas. But despite the gin and tonic and the wine a pulsating, vigilant cell in my brain told me not to take the risk, to opt for the chicken or fish. But my friend, who I now felt looked a little like Gregory Peck, was already busy devouring the meat and peas like a wolf, his eyes shining, their irises hovering somewhere between the blue of the ocean and the green of clover in the fields around my village house.

'Has any one told you that you resemble Sophia Loren?' he asked between two mouthfuls.

'And has any one told you that you look like Gregory Peck?' I replied before turning to my chicken breast.

He almost choked with laughter, and before our meal was through, the words had started to fly back and forth, so that the flight attendant had to call out several times before she could remove the trays with the empty plates.

After that we settled down to talk undisturbed, he with a small bottle of cognac 'Remy Martin' and I with my favorite orange liqueur which I learnt is called 'Cointreau'.

We spent most of the distance form New York to London talking. The other passengers dropped off to sleep one by one, but we went on in this seemingly endless dialogue, I myself fired by an ineffable and yet powerful joy which flowed through my whole body, from the top of my head to the tip of my toe, a joy which I had hardly known since I was ten years old. Through the window I could glimpse the dark steel wing of the plane cutting through the white clouds, as they floated in space like a scene from a film I was watching and living at the same time. I was the woman in it living this chance encounter suspended between heaven and earth.

We talked for six or may be seven hours as though flood-gates had opened to let the river of words flow through without a stop. I did not ask him his name or his nationality, or his religion, or his family, or anything else of this nature. And he in turn did not ask me who I was. None of these things seemed to matter. None of the things written in passports had any sense for us – the things people call their identity, or consider as a way of defining who they are, and their worth. They seemed to us no more than a cover that hides the truth of who we are, rather than revealing it.

'It seems to me that you have travelled to many countries,' he said. 'What about you? I feel that you also have travelled a lot.'

'Yes I have. But I've never visited your part of the world. I've never been to an Arab country or to Israel.'

'Why not?'

'Because I do not like what is going on in your region at all. I had a responsible post in the United Nations and had to deal with problems related to the Middle East. The policies followed by both the Israeli and the Arab governments made me very angry. So I resigned.'

'You resigned from the United Nations?'

'Yes, three days ago during a meeting in New York.'

He stretched his arms above his head, took a deep breath then let it out slowly and said, 'At last I am free, after thirty years as a bureaucrat in the United Nations, no longer a prisoner of a system controlled by the powers which rule over the world today and of those who serve their interests. I felt I couldn't close my eyes any more to what is going on, so I ran away. But I don't want to talk about that now. What about you? What do you do?'

'I'm a writer, a novelist mainly.'

'Good for you. That's wonderful. Then you're a free woman. Are you married?'

'Yes.'

'With children?'

'Yes, a boy and a girl. And you?'

'Yes, I'm married too. But I have three daughters and no sons. The eldest graduated from the School of Pharmacology, but she did not like the smell of drugs and loved music, so she is now studying music in Switzerland. The middle one specialized in comparative literature and she's now living in Paris. The youngest has settled in Los Angeles for the time being, and is busying herself with a new feminist movement which she describes as "post-feminist".'

He let out a childish gurgling laugh as though much amused by what was going on in his family and added, 'She lives with an American girl friend, and is very proud of being a lesbian. I am not against the emancipation of women, but I don't like homosexuality either for women or for men. But these days being gay or lesbian has become the fashion, especially among young people. Maybe when we are able to solve the problems between the sexes, things will move in a different direction. But what about your children?'

'My daughter graduated from the School of Political Economy and has a doctor's degree in environmental problems, but she abandoned all that and devotes herself to writing short stories, songs and newspaper articles. My son graduated from the School of Engineering and immediately after plunged into making films and is a cinema director.'

'Wonderful. That's really great. I sometimes wish I could be infected by the madness of children like mine and yours.'

I laughed.

'But you know, I and my husband are also a bit crazy. I graduated as a medical doctor, but gave up medicine to write novels. My husband too is a doctor but has left the profession to write novels.'

'What an interesting family. And do you all live in Cairo?'.

'Yes.'

We were silent for a moment, then he said 'Excuse me' and got up to go to the toilet. I noticed *The Guardian* sticking out from the pocket in front of his seat, pulled it out and started to turn the pages, and there was his picture with a few lines underneath announcing his resignation from the United Nations Organization. I slipped the newspaper back into the pocket, and closed my eyes for a moment.

When he came back he was carrying a small parcel tied with a green ribbon.

'A little present for my wife to compensate for my numerous sins,' he said smiling.

'I read what was written in *The Guardian* about your resignation while you were buying the present. And I was happy to see that there are still people like you who are prepared to sacrifice a high post in the United Nations for a just cause. But why did you decide to resign instead of fighting on inside the organization? They'll find someone else to do what you didn't agree to.'

'Maybe you're right. I hesitated for a long time but to tell you the truth I felt tired, very tired.' He passed his hand over his forehead, and I saw the strong fingers tremble before he continued. 'I've been living in the middle of what's going on for thirty years. Meeting after meeting, declaration after declaration, decision after decision, but the same political game goes on in the name of the United Nations, the same crimes are covered up in the name of the United Nations. Let's take your region as an example. Israel supported by the United States has never applied any of the decisions taken in international meetings. The Arab countries including Iraq and Egypt have been obliged to conform to the agreements on nuclear disarmament. Yet Israel, supported by the United States, maintains its nuclear arsenal and refuses to accept international inspection. It possesses over 250 rockets with nuclear warheads. Who are these rockets going to be used against? They have made out of Israel a formidable military base that can threaten any country that does not comply with the interests of the ruling powers in the world. How can there be real peace when the Palestinian people, Palestinian women and children, are being killed in order to reach an agreement which will deprive them in fact of any control over the remaining 22 percent of Palestinian land now supposed to be under negotiation? Or when the people of Iraq are being starved to death?' He was cut short by a voice on the microphone saying, 'Please fasten your seat belts, close your tables and put your seats in the upright position. We will be landing at Heathrow Airport within a few minutes.'

'I will be living in London, so this is the end of our journey together. My wife is English, and she has found a job at the university. She's a professor of physics, but at the moment she's attending a conference in Geneva. She's a bit of a feminist too, but not like my daughter. She likes women, but not in the same way. Are you a feminist?'

'Well, you know, you're using an English word. In our country we use different words which mean the liberation or the emancipation of women. Of course I believe in the emancipation of women. It will change a lot of things in society for the better. But, you know, the class patriarchal system under which we live oppresses men too and the discrimination from which women suffer is not good for the life of men. Don't you think so?'

I had no time to hear his answer. People were standing up. We descended from the plane and walked through the tunnel into the carpeted corridors. I took out my small watch from my bag. I had not adjusted the time since I left Durham and there was a seven hours difference. I turned the hands round. Every time I adjust my watch in an airport I feel dizzy. Time seems to me like a game, like an illusion, a universal illusion like the United Nations we had just been talking about, like many things in my life that make my feet unsteady as I walk down the corridor next to this man. Maybe it is the long hours spent in the plane which make me sway somewhat. But after a little while I felt my head clearing, my tread firm on the stone floor over which we were now moving with long rapid strides. I can feel him close, hear his breathing, glimpse his tall upright figure topped by a mane of white hair moving easily, hear him laugh at something I said with a childlike gurgle, before he looks around with a kind of astonishment as though he were seeing Heathrow Airport for the first time. I heard him say: 'I'd like to buy you a small present from London.'

'Thank you for the thought but I really don't have the time.'

'When does your plane leave for Cairo?'

'At four in the afternoon.'

'Ah. It's still seven in the morning and you've got nine hours in front of you. I hate waiting in airports.'

'So do I. But I have a novel with me which I intended to read in the plane.'

'Oh! I'm sorry to have wasted your time talking in the plane.'

'No, no, I really enjoyed talking with you.'

'The seven hours went by like seven minutes. I did not feel time passing.'

'Time is a universal illusion. Like the Security Council.'

He emitted his childlike laugh. I stretched out my hand but he took a step back. And said, 'Why say good-bye now. We still have eight hours in front of us. What do you think of a cup of coffee and a croissant? There's nobody waiting for me at home, and now that I've left my job I have no work. I'm a free man. I can stay with you for a while. Say you agree.'

We walked over to a coffee shop. The smell of coffee always lifts me up. But this time perhaps it was not only the coffee, which I always drank scalding hot. It would burn my tongue and my throat but each time I did the same thing, never learnt my lesson. It had always been like that since I was a child. Every morning I poured out the hot tea into my cup, added the boiling milk, let the steam rise up to my face, fill my nostrils and go through my pores, then gulp it all down scalding hot.

I bit into the flaky croissant, the way I used to do into my mother's pastry, felt his gleaming eyes on my face as he watched me with a kind of delight. It was as though his eyes had looked at me like that in some other place, at some other time – where and when I could not remember, I had seen light in them before, had been sitting in this cafeteria in Heathrow Airport ever since I began to realize what life was all about. I felt that I would remain sitting here until that realization would be no more and death would take its place.

'You look as though you're far away. What's on your mind?' he said.

'You know, life is very strange, can you imagine...?'

'No, I could never have imagined that we would meet like this. Fortune has its ways.'

'We have an Arabic proverb which says: "A chance meeting can be better than a thousand encounters arranged beforehand".'

'It looks like chance but I don't think it's really that. I've travelled in hundreds of planes. Hundreds of people, men and women, have sat beside me and yet I do not remember having exchanged two words with them. No, it's not chance.' He stopped short and his eyes seemed to open wide in surprise. 'Can you imagine, I still don't even

know your name. You must have found out mine from *The Guardian*.
Anyhow, my friends call me Bill.'

'My name is Nawal, Bill.'

'Na'aval.'

'Nawal with a 'w' and the first 'a' is not prolonged in the way that
you pronounced it.'

'Nawal,' he said.

'Yes, that's right.'

'What a wonderful name. Nawal!'

'Do you know a few words of Arabic, Bill?'

'Very few. I know *shoohran*[2] for example.'

'It's pronounced *shukran*.'

'*Shukran*,' he said.

'Yes, like that.'

'*Shukran*, Nawal.'

'My name comes first. You should say Nawal, *shukran*.'

His laugh rang out in the air. I joined in his laughter, pronounced
other words and he repeated them carefully as through he really
intended to learn the language.

'I'm going to tell you a secret,' he said, 'but promise not to tell
anyone else. I'm going to buy a ticket and travel with you to Cairo. I
know you're going to be wise and say "No", I shouldn't do that. But
wisdom made me a prisoner, a part of the United Nations
bureaucracy, for thirty long years. My mind, my reasonable thinking
destroyed any happiness in my life. I had a few opportunities to
escape from my prison but each time I was too scared to seize them.
Ten years ago I met a woman who resembled you in many ways. It
was in 1986 during a conference in Geneva. I was on the verge of
giving up everything, but I retreated at the last moment and went
back to my prison. Every now and again I encounter people like you,
encounter that rare kind of friendship which refuses all forms of
discrimination created by race, or class, or religion, or colour, or sex,
or by the name of the family. There remains only Nawal the human
being,'

The cafeteria had not stopped emptying and filling up with
travellers from all over the world as the hours went by. Suddenly the
smell of grilled meat floated over to my nostrils. He said, 'You must
be hungry. It's lunch-time and I'm dying of hunger. Let's have

---

[2] Thank you.

something to eat, but before that would you like a gin and tonic?' he asked with a smile.

I told him about Batta, how she had been the one who offered me my first gin and tonic in the Giza clinic.

'But why did you give up the clinic?' He asked. 'Medicine can be a good profession.'

'I couldn't stand the sight of illness, of poor people who paid me the last piastre in their pockets to be examined. So I gave it up and concentrated on writing.'

'Crazy but wonderful. I'm attracted to people like you because they have that madness which makes them ready to risk everything. I've always been too cautious, so I opted for a career in international politics, which I hated, although I loved music. So the result is that I jailed myself for thirty years. Now I am free, but it's too late.'

'It's never too late, Bill,' I said.

'When I look in the mirror I see an old man.'

'Mirrors are deceptive, like international politics,' I said and we laughed.

We sipped our gin and tonics, ordered grilled fish and steamed rice served in small earthenware pots and drank a bottle of wine.

Then it was time to leave. I embraced him and said, 'We'll meet again, Bill.'

'Yes Nawal, we will. Don't be surprised if you find me in Cairo, one day.'

*   *   *   *

I turned round before going into the departure lounge. I saw him wave to me from behind a glass door. There was sadness in his eyes, a sadness I could see as the plane lifted high into the sky. Next to me was a man. His face was white, rounded, full of soft flesh. He sat in his seat filling it up with a paunchy body. Before sitting down he took off his jacket and handed it to the flight assistant with a gesture of authority. Sitting next to me I could see his globular eyes, his gold watch, his coloured silk tie. Soon he was fast asleep.

*   *   *   *

In Cairo Airport they were there waiting for me, Sherif, Mona and Atef. I saw the faces I loved looking at me through the crowd as I emerged from the arrival hall pushing my baggage in front of me. We embraced. I filled myself with the feel of their bodies and their warmth, with the smell of dry desert air. Bill was there at the back of my mind but when I looked into their eyes I knew this was where I was loved, this was home.

Index

247